CONTENTS

FROMMER'S

COMPREHENSIVE TRAVEL GUIDE

LOS ANGELES
'91-'92

by Mary Rakauskas

PRENTICE
HALL
PRESS

NEW YORK • LONDON • TORONTO • SYDNEY • TOKYO • SINGAPORE

FROMMER BOOKS

Published by Prentice Hall Press
A division of Simon & Schuster Inc.
15 Columbus Circle
New York, NY 10023

Copyright © 1977, 1979, 1981, 1983, 1985, 1987, 1989, 1991 by Simon
& Schuster Inc.

ISBN 0-13-326893-4
ISSN 0899-3238

Manufactured in the United States of America

MAPS

Inflation Alert

I don't have to tell you that costs will rise regardless of the level of inflation. For that reason it is quite possible that prices may be slightly higher at a given establishment when you read this book than they were at the time this information was collected. Be that as it may, I feel sure these selections will still represent the best travel bargains in Los Angeles and environs.

A Disclaimer

Readers are advised that prices fluctuate in the course of time and travel information changes under the impact of the varied and volatile factors that affect the travel industry. The author and publisher cannot be held responsible for the experiences of the reader while traveling. Readers are invited to write the publisher with ideas, comments, and suggestions for future editions.

LOS ANGELES

1. HISTORICAL BACKGROUND
2. WHY GO TO LOS ANGELES

A New York friend once said that the expression "flying to the coast" was the most romantic phrase in our language.

Unless you are actually from the "The Coast," Los Angeles remains the "Getaway" incarnate—a fantasyland of dreams and ambition, a sunny pleasure ground of movie and TV studios and Disneyland extravaganzas, a place where inhibitions are released and imagination given full rein—an entranceway to the real-life magic of Southern California.

There's no city in America where you're so likely to see movie and television stars in your everyday rambles; if you don't see them, you're just not paying attention. Los Angeles is, and always has been, a haven for the offbeat and eccentric, somehow coexisting with what has been called "the most seriously dedicated conservative constituency in America." It's also one of the most fashion-conscious cities in the world, trailing only New York, Paris, and Milan. But it leads the country in lifestyle—from shopping malls and sprawling suburbs to jogging, nude beaches, holistic medicine, hot-tubbing, and roller skating. Apart from this frivolity, Los Angeles has become the cultural center of California.

A visit to this changing and dynamic metropolis is more compelling than ever. Each year there are more things to see and do. Moreover, each year increasing numbers of visitors come to realize that Los Angeles is just the beginning. What lies beyond is an extraordinary stretch of land that is too simply termed "Southern California." For those two words describe one of the greatest tourist attractions in the entire world. Your only problem may be that you didn't budget enough time to take it all in. "It," in the context of this guide, includes everything from the palm-fringed beaches of Santa Barbara to the border of Mexico.

1. Historical Background

Wherever I've traveled, I've sought to bring you the best of Southern California—in all price ranges, and for most tastes. But before I get to specifics, first a bit of history.

FROM PUEBLO TO METROPOLIS

The odds that Los Angeles would become one of the world's important cities appeared slim when it was founded in the 18th century. Los Angeles was founded on August 1, 1769, when a Spanish expedition party—led by Gaspar de Portolá, with Father Crespi taking notes—discovered an Indian village on the spot and named it "Pueblo del Rio de Nuestra Señora la Reina de los Angeles." The name was too much work for the ordinary tongue and, eventually, it was shortened.

In those days Spain was the power in Mexico. The Iberians looked with increasing apprehension at the establishment of Russian trading posts on the North Pacific coast, and also at the growing power and potential of the American colonies in the East. Hence, Spain ordered a colonizing party of fewer than 50 souls to trek upward through the desert from Mexico to found a settlement on the site of the present city of Los Angeles. What must have been a rather unprepossessing and haggard group arrived on August 18, 1781, to begin what must have seemed like a fruitless venture.

By 1822 Mexico was free of Spain, and new rulers were in control in California. In the following decade, Los Angeles was made the capital of California (an unpopular choice with many San Franciscans). Following the annexation of Texas into the Union in December 1845, open conflict with Mexico seemed inevitable, though it was delayed temporarily by efforts of conciliation. War was declared the following spring. On August 13, 1846, Union troops—led by Commodore Stockton and Captain Fremont—moved into Los Angeles, and routed its south-of-the-border government. But the new ruling garrison met with such disfavor that it, too, was booted out. In January of the following year the city was reclaimed for the United States by Commodore Stockton and Gen. Stephen Kearny.

AN EPIDEMIC OF GOLD FEVER

California was ceded to the United States by Mexico in 1848, and on September 9, 1850, it was admitted to the Union as a free state. Its admission was greatly accelerated by a discovery on January 24, 1848: gold at Sutter's mill! The rush westward—one of the great sagas in the history of human migration—was on.

It seemed that few were spared from the gold fever sweeping the nation. What army could keep its soldiers? What ship its sailors? Even midwestern Babbitts were transformed into daring forty-niners, and set out to strike it rich.

Washington, D.C., bureaucrat J. Goldsborough Bruff typified many of the pioneers lured by the yellow dust. In his *Gold Rush,* written in 1849–1851, he evoked the drama of the mining camps, the boom towns that sprang up in the wake of the discovery. Across the wide Missouri, through the Sierra Nevadas, he traveled with the fortune seekers. Disease, hostile Indians, and eventual starvation were the lot of many. As it turned out, Mr. Bruff got not one nugget, and eventually returned east—except this time by an easier route, via the Isthmus of Panama!

Of course, San Francisco was the queen of the Gold Rush But all those miners and exploiters flocking north had to be fed. Los Angeles ranchers never had it so good. In the lawless decade preceding the Civil War—perhaps the most turbulent and violent in the city's history—it was not unusual for a "rancho" master to sell cattle at $435 a head, even more if he were a shrewd bargainer.

TO LOS ANGELES FOR $1

When the final tracks of the cross-country railroad were laid on May 10, 1869, by the Central Pacific and the Union Pacific, a new era opened up for California, and the railroad was a major step in turning America into one nation. In 1885 the Southern Pacific and the Santa Fe rail companies—fierce competitors—dropped fares to only $1 from Mississippi junctions to Los Angeles. Another "rush" was on.

Of course, not everybody rode out on the rails. It is said that Charles F. Lummis (1859–1928), later to become a well-known writer, editor, and historian of the Southwest, walked from Cincinnati! Obviously, he was a man to take his own advice: He originated the slogan "See America First."

Long after the gold fever waned, California drew thousands of homesteaders in the post–Civil War era. Many men came seeking not gold—but orange. In Los Angeles and Southern California, citrus belts were planted to satisfy the ever-growing demand from such "back east" port cities as New York and Boston.

Actually, it was "black gold," or petroleum, that proved the most financially profitable in California, and in Los Angeles in particular. Production began in the closing years of the 19th century, and it soared in the boom days of the 1920s, when derricks, such as those on Signal Hill, were silhouetted against the bright western sky.

PIGTAILS, VAMPS, AND SHEIKS

The 20th century provided yet another lure, except that this time the gold was flowing into the state instead of out.

The "flickers" were to spread the fame of Hollywood around the world, eventually making legends, or at least household words, out of a host of its star-kissed actors and actresses. In rebellion against Thomas Edison and his eight partners in the Motion Picture Patents Co., and their monopolistic stranglehold on the fledgling eastern industry, independent filmmakers headed west. Many found the character, and especially the sunny climate, of Hollywood more suited for their camera work. By 1911, 16 motion picture companies were operating out of Hollywood. Films such as *Birth of a Nation* in 1915 established Hollywood in the eyes of the world and earned for its director, D. W. Griffith, a reputation as "the father of American cinema."

By World War I the star system was established, and a triumvirate was formed by "Charlie, Doug, and Mary" (the young Charles Chaplin, Douglas Fairbanks, Sr., and Mary Pickford). William S. Hart rode into the hearts of Saturday-afternoon moviegoers as the first prototype of the American western hero. Theodosia Goodman, the daughter of an Ohio haberdasher, vamped across the screen as Theda Bara.

In the '20s, salaries and box office receipts multiplied fantastically. An opulent spending spree was launched as each star or producer tried to outdo the other. Newly rich stars created an aura of luxury and glamour. His nostrils flaring, Valentino as *The Sheik* electrified women around the world. Mae Murray, the eternal *Merry Widow* with the patented "bee-stung" lips, was "self-enchanted." Clara Bow, with her red chow dogs to match her flaming hair, was the "It" girl. And Cecil B. DeMille saw to it that Gloria Swanson took a lot of on-screen baths!

HOLLYWOOD TALKS

On August 6, 1926, the Manhattan Opera House in New York screened Vitaphone's *Don Juan*, with John Barrymore. The great actor didn't talk, but there was background music. Warners released *The Jazz Singer*, with Al Jolson, in October of the following year. The Talkie Revolution was on. Garbo could talk, albeit with a Swedish accent, but her romantic leading man, John Gilbert, couldn't—at least not very well. The invasion of voice-trained Broadway stage stars began, including the likes of Tallulah Bankhead, who made a number of films of which she said later, "I'd rather forget about them."

Perhaps no invader was as formidable as the author of *Goodness Had Nothing to Do With It*. Mae West herself wondered if she could "show my stuff" in a "land of palm trees, restaurants shaped like derby hats, goose-fleshed bathing beauties, and far-flung custard pies." She could and did! Her invitation to "Come up 'n' see me sometime" was accepted around the world, and she became a phenomenal success at the box office. Or to use her own modest summation: "More people had seen me than saw Napoleon, Lincoln, and Cleopatra. I was better known than Einstein, Shaw, or Picasso."

The '30s marked the rise of some of Hollywood's greatest stars: Bette Davis, Joan Crawford, Humphrey Bogart, Cary Grant, Jean Harlow, Clark Gable, James Cagney, Marlene Dietrich, Gary Cooper, Shirley Temple, James Stewart, Katherine Hepburn, Spencer Tracy, and Claudette Colbert. The decade was climaxed by the release of the money-making classic *Gone With the Wind*.

Even during the lowest slump of the Depression, the magnetism of California continued—persuading poverty-stricken inhabitants of near-starvation areas to turn in the direction of the land of plenty. "Okies" from the Dust Bowl abandoned their grubby existence, packed their possessions—including the rocking chair and sewing machine—into broken-down cars, many of which would never make it west. This moving drama was compellingly portrayed in Steinbeck's *Grapes of Wrath*.

AIRPLANES, PINUPS, AND TV

In 1940 Dudley C. Gordon wrote: "Having survived a long, leisurely pioneering infancy, and an uncouth adolescence characterized by intensive exploitation, Los Angeles has now blossomed into one of the major cities of the nation." It was at the dawn of great change.

World War II brought even greater prosperity and growth. Pinups of Grable and Lamour were plastered in dugouts around the world. Hope and Crosby went on the road. West Coast defense plants, centered in Southern California, attracted workers in industry, marking the rise of Los Angeles as a leading manufacturer of aircraft, both military and civilian. The postwar era brought an even greater influx of residents.

After the war, the threat of television loomed over Hollywood. Though the movie colony valiantly hung on with 3-D movies and earphones with stereophonic sound, the die was cast. The demands of television brought a fresh wave of life into Hollywood, as studios converted to make way for television serials and commercials. By the 1960s the great day of the Hollywood cinema industry had passed. Studios now opened their doors to show visitors film sets, such as Ashley Wilkes's Twelve Oaks in *Gone With the Wind,* and Lana Turner's dressing room.

Indeed, as Los Angeles entered the 1970s, it appeared to some that the dream factory had become a near nightmare. One large studio reported a loss of $67 million; another, whose stars had once included Gary Cooper, Gloria Swanson, Frederic March, Betty Grable, Jean Arthur, Richard Arlen, Rudolph Valentino, and Mae West, announced that its 52-acre main lot was for sale. In the months to follow, MGM, which once boasted that it had "more stars than there are in heaven," was auctioning off Clark Gable's trench coat. The days of film glory were over, but few doubted that a more stable cinema would emerge and remain as one of Los Angeles' chief attractions and employers.

2. Why Go to Los Angeles

Millions who have moved here have answered this question satisfactorily for themselves. But for the tourist who has only a few days or weeks at most to spend in L.A., the reasons are different, of course. The most compelling reason to go to Southern California is to have a good time. No place in America, perhaps the world, offers such a unique blend of man-made attractions and natural sights compressed into such a small area. In one hour you're out at Calico Ghost Town, then you're calling on Roy and Dale (and a stuffed and mounted Trigger!) in Apple Valley, or you're being serenaded by Mexicans in the Padua Hills. Or you're watching the swallows return to San Juan Capistrano . . . thrilling to the attractions of Disneyland . . . seeing the surfers at Laguna, the bikinis (or bare skin) at Malibu . . . following in the footsteps of the stars along Hollywood Boulevard . . . enjoying a concert at the Music Center . . . driving around to see where the stars live in Beverly Hills . . . touring Universal Studios . . . watching Johnny Carson tape the "Tonight Show." You're being served tea in a simulated Japanese garden, before going on to enjoy boysenberry pie at Knott's Berry Farm; then it's on to relive *The Loved One* as you tour Forest Lawn. Or you may even run down to Tijuana to watch a bullfight.

Finally, Greater Los Angeles has some of the finest hotels and restaurants in America.

There seemingly is no end to Los Angeles. And although the events I've cited may sound frivolous, the city is increasingly taking itself more seriously. Los Angeles is perhaps the personification of American fulfillment, revealing both the country's shadow and its strength. If you come away from it with an increased understanding of the people who created and are creating Southern California, your trip will not have been wasted. At least you should give Los Angeles a chance to shake up your preconceptions.

Other Prentice Hall Travel Guides to California

In addition to the guide you are now reading, Prentice Hall publishes four other guides that cover California. Each provides information for travelers with particular needs.

Frommer's California and Las Vegas discusses accommodations, restaurants, and sights in all price ranges, with an emphasis on the medium-priced.

Frommer's California with Kids is a must for parents traveling in California. It provides key information on selecting the best accommodations, restaurants, and sightseeing for the particular needs of the family, whether the kids are toddlers, school-age, preteens, or teens.

Frommer's San Francisco is a pocket-sized guide to hotels, restaurants, nightspots, and sightseeing attractions covering all price ranges.

Gault Millau Los Angeles and **Gault Millau San Francisco** are irreverent, savvy, and comprehensive guides with candid reviews of over 1,000 restaurants, hotels, shops, nightspots, museums, and sights.

For order forms with which to order these and all the Prentice Hall travel guides, turn to the last two pages of this book.

II

SETTLING INTO LOS ANGELES

1. GETTING THERE
2. GETTING AROUND

Los Angeles is an incongruous collection of communities, joined like a crazy patchwork quilt. Each town or district has been sewn onto the ever-expanding blanket, none more notably than **Hollywood,** eight miles northwest of "downtown L.A.," which was annexed in 1910. New areas in suburbia, as they emerged, were continuously tacked on.

However, there were holdouts, such as monied **Beverly Hills**—a separate municipality that is a virtual island inside Los Angeles. Similarly, the mile-long **Sunset Strip,** between Hollywood and Beverly Hills—long the refuge of nightclub operators and other businesses wanting to escape the restraining hand of the City of Los Angeles—is under the jurisdiction of the county.

Though some towns or cities are independently incorporated, their destiny is linked with Los Angeles. Examples include the sheep ranch that became "Beautiful Downtown **Burbank**" (NBC-TV, major aircraft industries, Warner Brothers), **Pasadena** (setting of the New Year's Tournament of Roses and the Rose Bowl Classic football game, and home of the Pasadena Playhouse), **Culver City** (original home of MGM), and **Santa Monica** (known for its beaches).

Sprawled between sea and mountains, Los Angeles meets the Pacific at settlements such as **Venice,** while in the east it encompasses treeless foothills leading toward the **Mojave Desert** and **Palm Springs.** There are those who live in the hills, such as **Laurel Canyon,** and there are the "flatlanders." Generally, with notable exceptions, of course, the better homes are in the hills—built on shelves scooped out of granite, shrub-covered mountains. These are usually low and rambling houses—many occupied by movie stars of yesterday and today.

On the crest of the Santa Monica mountain chain from the north—forming part of Beverly Hills and Hollywood—is the "sky-high" **Mulholland Drive,** where tourists go for a bird's-eye view, and young natives park at night beneath the California stars. From here one can see a flatland called the **San Fernando Valley,** between the Hollywood Hills and the Mojave Desert mountains. Once all orange groves, it is now both residential and commercial. There are those who say that it—not Hollywood—is the movie and TV capital of the world, because of the location of such studios as **Universal City.**

The more commercial areas of Los Angeles have remained in the flatlands, including **Wilshire Boulevard ("Miracle Mile"),** running from downtown to the sea. The highest point in Los Angeles is Mount Hollywood. **Sunset** and **Hollywood Boulevards**—the main thoroughfares—run along the foot of the mountains.

Because of earthquake scares, no skyscrapers were allowed until recent times—which partially explains why the city is so spread out, encompassing more than 450 square miles.

WEATHER

Los Angeles enjoys a mild climate, or one of "little variability," as one expert put it. The rainy season usually begins in January and lasts sometimes until May. From then until October there is little, if any, rainfall. The winter days are likely to be mild and mostly sunny, although the temperature drops dramatically at night.

It's possible to sunbathe throughout the year, although only die-hard enthusiasts and the more adventurous surfers in wet suits venture into the water in winter. In spring, summer, and fall, however, you can swim though the Pacific is still quite chilly.

LOS ANGELES AVERAGE MONTHLY TEMPERATURES
(in degrees Fahrenheit)

Month	Temp	Month	Temp
January	55.8	July	73.0
February	57.1	August	73.1
March	59.4	September	71.9
April	61.8	October	67.4
May	64.8	November	62.7
June	68.0	December	58.2

1. Getting There

Many people drive to Los Angeles, especially those coming from San Francisco or San Diego who want to enjoy the scenic route along the Pacific Coast Highway. A good map is their best source of information. For those planning to fly or come by bus or train, I've provided information below.

BY AIR

Airlines

Some 36 international carriers, and every major domestic carrier, serve the Los Angeles International Airport (LAX)—third largest in the world in terms of traffic. Domestic carriers include **Alaska Airlines** (tel. 213/628-2100, or toll free 800/426-0333), **American Airlines** (tel. 213/935-6045, or toll free 800/433-7300), **Delta Air Lines** tel. 213/386-5510, or toll free 800/221-1212), **Northwest Airlines,** (tel. 213/380-1511, or toll free 800/225-2525, 800/252-2168 in California), **Piedmont Airlines** (tel. 213/977-4937, or toll free 800/251-5720), **Southwest Airlines** (tel. 213/485-1221, or toll free 800/531-5601), **Trans World Airlines** (tel. 213/484-2244, or toll free 800/221-2000), **United Airlines** (tel. 213/772-2121, or toll free 800/241-6522), and **US Air** (tel. 213/410-1732, or toll free 800/428-4322).

Airports

The **Los Angeles International Airport (LAX)** is situated at the far western end of the city. If you're driving, two main roads will get you there—Century Boulevard, which runs east-west, and Sepulveda Boulevard, running north-south. The San Diego Freeway (#5)—it's called that even in Los Angeles—and Hwy. 405 have exits to West Century Boulevard leading to the airport. Going north on Sepulveda Boulevard will take you directly to the airport; going south, you should turn right on 96th Street to get to the airport entrance. The city's RTD bus lines go to and from LAX. For the schedule and running times, call RTD airport information (tel. 213/646-8021). Free Blue, Green, and White shuttle buses ("Airline Connections") stop in front of each ticket building. Others, also free, will take you to parking lots (a distance you definitely do not want to walk). For information about thrifty alternatives to airport lots, see "Alternative Airport Parking" below. Special handicapped-accessible minibuses are available. If you need more information call 213/646-8021.

Unless you plan to stay at one of the hotels near the airport, a taxi is *not* the preferred mode of transportation to your hotel or motel. Just about everything is miles away from the airport and the cost of taking a taxi can be more like a down payment on one. If you must take a taxi, confirm the price to your destination *before* getting in.

Airport shuttles and commercial commuter vans provide direct airport service to most major hotels (see "Airport Buses" below). Some hotels have private shuttles for their patrons. When in doubt, ask about transportation at the time you make your hotel or motel reservations.

Los Angeles is surrounded by airports; however, the largest by far, in terms of size, service, and air traffic, is LAX. To the north is

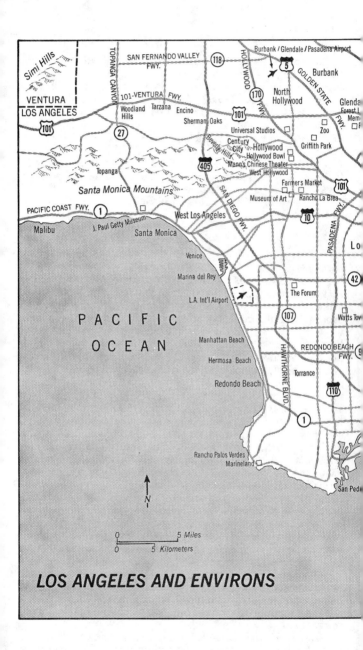

LOS ANGELES AND ENVIRONS

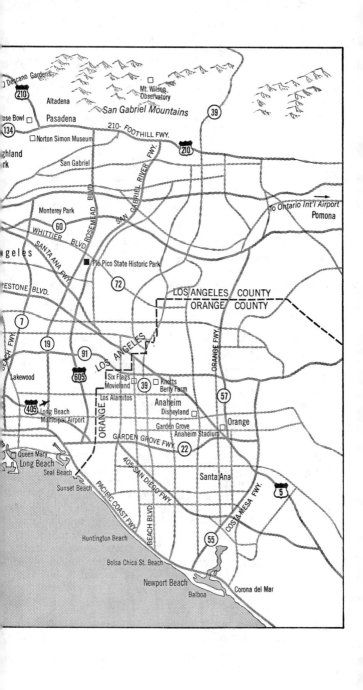

the **Burbank-Glendale-Pasadena Airport,** at 2627 North Holly-wood Way, Burbank (tel. 818/840-8847); to the south are the **Long Beach Municipal Airport,** 4100 Donald Douglas Dr., Long Beach (tel. 213/421-8293), and the **John Wayne Airport,** 19051 Airport Way North, Anaheim (tel. 714/834-2400); and to the east, the **Ontario International Airport,** Terminal Way, Ontario (tel. 714/983-8282). Most of the smaller airports are for charters, some commuter lines, or private planes.

Airport Buses

When you arrive at the airport, your best bet is to pick up a rental car and drive to your hotel. However, if you aren't planning to rent a car, don't blithely hop a cab as you might in other cities. Los Angeles is so big that cab fares tend to mount at alarming rates.

Super Shuttle (tel. 213/338-1111) has minivans that will take you from LAX to hotels or private residences within the L.A. area, Beverly Hills, West L.A., etc. To hotels, the fare ranges from about $10 to $16; to private residences it averages about $17 to $27. Give them the location and they'll give you a more specific price. If you go to LAX on the Super Shuttle, you'll need a reservation at least one day in advance.

Airport Transportation serves Orange County (tel. 714/558-1411, or toll free 800/854-8171, 800/422-4267 in California). The fare to the Anaheim area, the home of Disneyland, is $12 per person from the airport. The fare to the Newport Beach area is $17.

Logo Express (tel. 213/641-0044) serves Pasadena and nearby areas. The door-to-door rate is $15 per person or $10 to a hotel.

Alternative Airport Parking

Parking at LAX can be trying at best, and utterly maddening on holidays with the added traffic and crowded lots. Parking in the terminal lot is $10 a day, which in a week or two adds up to a notable sum. A thrifty alternative is **Auto Air Porter** at 2222 E. Imperial Highway, between Douglas and Nash (tel. 213/640-1111, or toll free 800/752-3339 for about 50 miles around the airport). Rates are $5.50 per day for the first 10 days, $4.50 for each additional day. A van takes you from the facility to the terminal at LAX and picks you up when you call on return. It's a 24-hour service. Auto Air Porter suggests that you arrive at their facility at least one hour before your departure time.

BUSES

Greyhound/Trailways Bus Lines serves most cities in California. In Los Angeles, Greyhound/Trailways's main terminal is at 208 E. 6th St. (tel. 213/620-1200).

TRAINS

Amtrak service south to San Diego, and north to Oakland, Seattle, and points in between, operates out of the station at 800 N. Alameda (tel. 213/624-0171).

---

2. Getting Around

You need a car in Los Angeles as much as you need your liver! The analogy is apt for many Angelenos, who view their trusted automobile virtually as an organic part of their bodies. In Los Angeles, to which automobile-manufacturing Detroit pays homage, the two-car family is already passé. The three- and even four-vehicle household is common.

Although there is bus service, it is almost imperative that you drive your own car—particularly if you have a sightseeing agenda that includes more than just a trip down to Disneyland in Anaheim.

DRIVING TIPS

To aid you in your auto touring, you'll first need a good map. Some think Los Angeles has the world's most brilliantly designed freeway system—though there are others who suggest it is the work of a madman. At its best, it allows experienced motorists to reach long distances in a relatively reasonable amount of time. For example, from a motel in Hollywood, you can arrive at a restaurant in Chinatown in about 15 minutes during the nonrush hours. At its worst, the freeway system evokes a futuristic, soul-less city of tomorrow, with streams of pollution-making traffic barely moving into vague nothingness.

One word of advice on travel time—always allow more time than you've been told your trip will take.

Here are just a few pointers that may help you to avoid some frequently encountered problems in driving throughout the state as well as in Los Angeles.

For a start, California law requires buckling up seatbelts. This applies to both driver and passengers.

Be sure to pay attention to signs and arrows on the freeways and streets, or you may find that you're in a lane that requires exiting or turning when you wanted to go straight on.

You'll be pleased to know that you can turn right at a red light, unless otherwise indicated—but be sure to come to a stop first.

CAR RENTALS

Your adventure in Southern California can be enhanced tremendously with a car—in fact, having or renting one is almost a necessity. The sights and restaurants are so numerous and so spread out that it's very difficult to make the rounds without a car.

If you do a minimum of traveling, then you might consider the

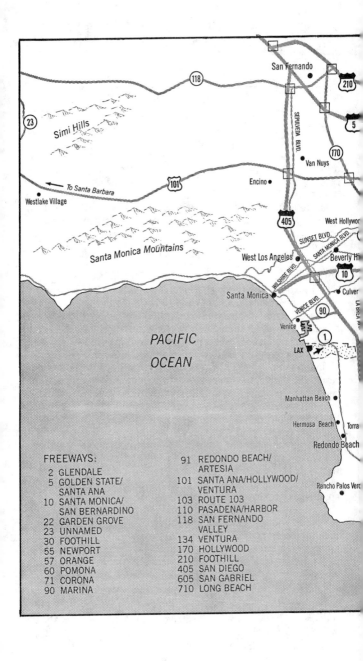

FREEWAYS:

2	GLENDALE
5	GOLDEN STATE/ SANTA ANA
10	SANTA MONICA/ SAN BERNARDINO
22	GARDEN GROVE
23	UNNAMED
30	FOOTHILL
55	NEWPORT
57	ORANGE
60	POMONA
71	CORONA
90	MARINA
91	REDONDO BEACH/ ARTESIA
101	SANTA ANA/HOLLYWOOD/ VENTURA
103	ROUTE 103
110	PASADENA/HARBOR
118	SAN FERNANDO VALLEY
134	VENTURA
170	HOLLYWOOD
210	FOOTHILL
405	SAN DIEGO
605	SAN GABRIEL
710	LONG BEACH

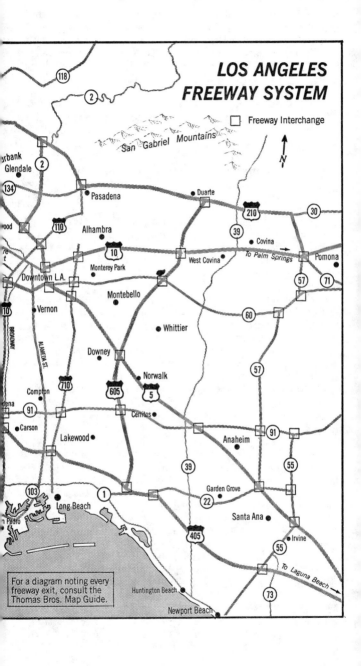

LOS ANGELES FREEWAY SYSTEM

□ Freeway Interchange

usual rate—so many dollars per day and so many cents per mile, including gasoline. But if you're really going to tour, then you'll do better to seek an unlimited-mileage arrangement or else one that provides sufficient free mileage to make your trip economical. On the freeway those few "cents per mile" tend to mount rapidly into dollars. It's amazing how easily you can roll up 100 miles in one day.

My first words of advice on this topic are *plan ahead*. If you intend to rent a car during your vacation, before you leave home check your policy or call your insurance agent to determine the limits of your coverage. Does your insurance cover collision damage to the rented car? If not, you may want to pay the added cost for the collision (or loss) damage waiver. As of this writing, most rental firms make customers liable for damage up to the total value of the car. The waiver currently averages $10 to $12 per day. It's becoming increasingly difficult to keep up with the changes many rental companies are making. One such change is a shift of responsibility to renters for theft of vehicles or damage caused by vandalism (previously covered by the company). To avoid liability for damage or theft, as well as collision damage, renters must buy what is now called the loss damage waiver (formerly the collision damage waiver).

Taking it from the top, assuming that you rent from one of the well-established companies, large or small, the odds are that the car won't be a clunker. You're obviously going to check the cost, daily or weekly, and the charge for mileage as well as optional insurance and taxes. And since not all rental companies are located at the airport, ask about pick-up and drop-off—you may need a taxi or shuttle ride to or from the terminal. Those are the basics.

If you plan to get the car at one location and return it to another, ask about the drop-off charge, if any. And if you rent the car at a weekly rate and decide to return it early, you may be charged at the much higher daily rate. *Ask!*

Then before you drive away, check the registration—make certain it's still in effect. Finally, make sure that the company has an emergency phone number and one for emergency road service, and take these numbers with you.

Car rentals of specific-size vehicles, including vans, are usually easier to obtain from the big rental-car companies. Each of the companies below has an office at Los Angeles International Airport, Burbank, and Long Beach Airports, as well as offices throughout Greater Los Angeles—**Avis** (tel. toll free 800/331-1212), **Budget** (tel. 800/527-0700), **Hertz** (tel. 800/654-3131).

If you need something special to create a memorable impression, Budget Rent-A-Car rents exotic cars. Budget has offices for rentals of these beauties in Beverly Hills (tel. 213/274-9173), Marina del Rey (tel. 213/821-8200), and on La Cienega Boulevard in Los Angeles (tel. 213/659-3473). These rentals are not for the budget-conscious traveler—they may require hefty credit-card deposits—but consider that you may be sitting where a "star" sat

BUSES

If you don't drive, you can reach most of the sightseeing centers in Greater Los Angeles by bus. The network of local and express buses is operated by the **Southern California Rapid Transit District (RTD)**.

The line's **Ticket Office** is at 419 S. Main St., Los Angeles, CA 90001 (tel. 213/626-4455), where you can obtain maps and schedules from the rack, or by writing or telephoning. You can also dial the number for detailed information on a given trip from point to point. A free pamphlet entitled "Self-Guided RTD Tours" is available; it outlines how to take public transit to such places as Farmers Market, Disneyland, Beverly Hills, Universal Studios, and Griffith Park attractions. There's also a convenient office in ARCO Towers (515 S. Flower St.) just adjacent to the Visitors and Convention Bureau.

The basic bus fare is $1.10 for all local lines. Express lines utilizing freeways have higher fares. Those visitors over age 65 (Medicare card must be shown to driver) qualify for a 55¢ fare during off-peak hours. Drivers carry no change, so exact fare is required. In addition, for those riders who travel into counties other than Los Angeles (for example, to Disneyland) there are extra charges.

If you're planning a lengthy stay in Los Angeles, you might consider the economical monthly passes: $42 to $102 (depending on the distance you're traveling) for unlimited riding on local lines, $10 for the same privilege for senior citizens.

For information on **airport buses,** see the "Getting There" section earlier in this chapter.

TAXIS

In widely spread-out Los Angeles, this is a last-resort transportation option. Taxis start their meters at $2 (for the first two-tenths of a mile) and charge $1.50 for each additional mile. There is no charge for luggage. If you should need a cab, call the **Independent Cab Co.** (tel. 213/385-8294), **Checker Cab Co.** (tel. 213/624-2227), or the **Yellow Cab Co.** (tel. 213/221-2331).

III

LOS ANGELES FAST FACTS

This chapter organizes, in alphabetical order, certain basic information intended to make your trip in and around Los Angeles as enjoyable and hassle-free as possible.

AREA CODES: Exactly like "all Gaul," Los Angeles will be divided into three parts (by the telephone company) as of February 1, 1992. **Area code 213** will continue to include most of downtown Los Angeles and surrounding communities such as Hollywood and Montebello. **Area code 818** encompasses much of the San Fernando Valley, and as of this moment Glendale and Pasadena. The **new code, 310** (created because Pacific Bell is running out of telephone numbers), will include Los Angeles International Airport (LAX) plus the western, coastal, southern, and eastern portions of the county. Communities such as West Los Angeles, San Pedro, and Whittier also will be part of the 310 area code. If you are in one area code and wish to call another, you must begin with the **prefix "1-"** then dial the area code. Should you dial a number with the wrong area code, an operator will intervene and provide the correct code.

BABYSITTERS: If you're staying at one of the larger hotels, the concierge can usually recommend organizations to call. Be sure to check on the hourly cost (which may vary depending on the day of the week and the time of day) as well as any additional expenses such as transportation and meals for the sitter. You also might try the **Baby Sitters Guild,** 1622 Bank St. (P.O. Box 3418), S. Pasadena, CA 91031; they've been in business since 1948. From Los Angeles and west call 213/469-8246; from the San Gabriel Valley, 818/441-4293. The Guild (licensed by the State of California) provides mature, bonded babysitters on call 24 hours.

BANKS: Banking hours are generally from 10 a.m. to 3 p.m. weekdays; some are open Saturdays till noon. However, if you need to cash a check, your hotel may be your best resource, depending on the amount involved.

CHARGE CARDS: Not all restaurants, stores, or shops in California accept all major credit cards, and some accept none. Therefore, check first if you expect to use plastic for a large expenditure—it can save annoyance and possibly some embarrassment. And if you're visiting from another state, you may be surprised to discover that in California you can charge packaged liquor purchases.

CHURCHES: Los Angeles has hundreds of churches and synagogues. Should you be seeking out a house of worship, your hotel desk person, or bell captain, can usually direct you to the nearest church of most any denomination. If not, the Pacific Bell *Yellow Pages* can usually provide the location and, frequently, the times of the services.

CLIMATE: From May through October, weather in Los Angeles warrants lightweight summer clothing, with a sweater or lightweight jacket for the occasional cool evening or super-cool restaurant. November through April temperatures are cooler, and generally require spring-weight clothing and a raincoat. However, even during the cooler months you can have a week or more of summerlike weather, in which case just shed the jacket or sweater. For information about average monthly temperatures, see the chart in the introduction to Chapter II.

CRIME: As in all cities having a large influx of tourists from within the U.S. and abroad, crime is a problem. Whenever you're traveling in an unfamiliar city or country, stay alert. To avoid an unhappy incident or an end to what might have been an enjoyable trip, use discretion and common sense. Be aware of your immediate surroundings. Take traveler's checks and leave your valuables in the hotel safe. Wear a moneybelt and don't sling your camera or purse over your shoulder; wear the strap diagonally across your body. These measures will minimize the possibility of your becoming a victim of crime. It's your responsibility to be aware and be alert even in the most heavily touristed areas.

CURRENCY EXCHANGE: Foreign currency exchange services are provided by the **Bank of America** at its branch at 555 S. Flower St. (tel. 213/228-2721), third floor. **Deak International** at the Hilton Hotel Center, 900 Wilshire Blvd. (tel. 213/624-4221) in downtown L.A., also offers foreign currency exchange services. Another Deak office is at the Bank of Los Angeles building, 8901 Santa Monica Blvd. (213/659-6092) in West Hollywood.

DENTISTS: Hotels usually have a list of dentists should you need one. For other referrals, you can call the **Los Angeles Dental Society** (tel. 213/481-2133).

DOCTORS: Here, again, hotels usually have a list of doctors on call. For referrals, you can contact the **Los Angeles Medical Association** (tel. 213/483-6122).

DRIVING: Advice and suggestions on this topic and on car rentals are covered in Chapter II.

EARTHQUAKES: There will always be earthquakes in California —most of which you will never notice. However, in the event of an earthquake, there are a few basic precautionary measures to take whether you're inside a high-rise hotel, out driving, or walking.

When you are inside a building, seek cover, do not run out of the building; move away from windows in the direction of what would be the center of the building. Get under a desk or table, or stand against a wall or under a doorway. If you are in bed, get under the bed, or in a doorway, or under a sturdy piece of furniture. When exiting the building, use stairwells, NOT elevators.

If you are in your car, pull over to the side of the road and stop. Do not stop until you are away from bridges or overpasses, and telephone or power poles and lines. Stay in your car.

If you are out walking, stay outside and away from trees or power lines or the sides of buildings. If you are in an area with tall buildings, find a doorway to stand in.

EMERGENCIES: For police, fire, highway patrol, or medical emergencies, dial 911.

EVENTS AND FESTIVALS: For a listing of special events in Los Angeles, drop by the **Visitors Information Center,** Monday through Saturday 8 a.m. to 5 p.m., downtown at 695 S. Figueroa St. (between Wilshire and 7th), Los Angeles, CA 90017 (tel. 213/689-8822); or in Hollywood at the Janes House, Janes House Square, 6541 Hollywood Blvd. (tel. 213/461-4213), Monday through Saturday 9 a.m. to 5 p.m. The other option is to write to the downtown center at the above address. For up-to-the-minute happenings, the Sunday edition of *The Los Angeles Times* has a **Calendar** section covering all entertainment, the arts, studio gossip, museums, etc., plus what's doing in Las Vegas and Laughlin.

FOOD: I don't know what the least expensive meal would be in Los Angeles, but there are lots of places to eat for less than $5. The problem is you can starve in the time it takes to get from one place to another. On the other hand, you can also spend as much as $75 for a meal, per person, without wine or even valet parking. Los Angeles has restaurants for everyone—Chinese, Italian, Indian, American, Japanese, Moroccan, French, French-California, California-French, Japanese-French, elegant pizza, Greek, Czech, Jewish, Tuscan, vegetarian, Vietnamese, Lithuanian, Mexican, etc. And the food ranges from good to superb. Some of these restaurants are located in hotels, most are not; I've tried to select some of the best in all price categories.

Not all restaurants are open daily. If you're planning an evening at one I haven't listed, call first and also ask if reservations are necessary. Check to see if they take plastic. Not all of the better restaurants do, and not all take every major credit card.

HAIR SALONS: First, ask at the hotel if there is a hair salon on the premises. If the hotel does not have one, they're usually glad to make a recommendation.

HOLIDAYS: Obvious holiday occasions and dates of major conventions are not the times to try for reservations on short notice. If you're not certain what events are in the offing, and you have specific vacation dates in mind, send for the annual list or call the Visitors Information Center. Also see "Events and Festivals" above.

HOSPITALS: To find a hospital near you, quickly, turn to the Community Access pages at the front of the Pacific Bell *Yellow Pages*. There you will find a list of hospitals, with their locations superimposed on a map of the city. This is an especially useful reference since Los Angeles is quite spread out and you probably won't know locations by address.

INFORMATION: The **Los Angeles Visitors Information Centers** are located in downtown Los Angeles and Hollywood. Addresses and phone numbers are given above under "Events and Festivals." As you might guess from the fact that it is a separate city, Beverly Hills has its own **Visitors and Convention Bureau** at 239 S. Beverly Dr. (tel. 213/271-8174, or toll free 800/345-2210).

LAUNDRY AND DRY CLEANING: Any one of the major hotels can take care of these services for you, but allow two days to do the job.

LIQUOR LAWS: Liquor and grocery stores can sell packaged alcoholic beverages between 6 a.m. and 2 a.m. Most restaurants, nightclubs, and bars are licensed to serve alcoholic beverages during the same hours. The legal age for purchase and consumption is 21 and proof of age is required. As I mentioned under "Charge Cards," in California you can purchase packaged liquor with your credit card; however, most stores usually have a minimum dollar amount for charging.

MEDICAL SERVICES: As I've already noted under the headings of "Doctors" and "Dentists," larger hotels will be able to direct you to medical help, or you can contact the professional societies mentioned for referrals.

NEWSPAPERS: *The Los Angeles Times* is widely distributed throughout the county. Its Sunday edition has a **Calendar** section, which is an excellent and interesting guide to the entire world of entertainment in and around Los Angeles, the arts, what's doing, who's doing it, what's coming to town, and new restaurants, among other things.

PETS: Hotels and motels generally will not accept pets. So if you're traveling with Homer the dog or Katie the cat, ask before making the reservations. Motel 6 (the budget category) does accept a typical pet in the room, but will not permit the animal to be left unattended.

POLICE: For emergency help dial 911. I stress the word "emergency"—this does not include misplaced earrings, missing shoes, flat tires, etc. However, theft, burglary, and other crimes should be reported immediately. For nonemergency service, call 213/485-2121, or in Beverly Hills, 213/550-4951.

RELIGIOUS SERVICES: Times are usually posted outside the places of worship, or are sometimes listed in the Pacific Bell *Yellow Pages* after the name of the church.

SPORTS (SPECTATOR):   Los Angeles has two major league baseball teams—the **Los Angeles Dodgers** (tel. 213/224-1400), and the **California Angels** (tel. 714/937-6700); two NFL football teams—the **L.A. Raiders** (213/322-3451), and the **L.A. Rams** (tel. 714/937-6767); two NBA basketball teams—the **L.A. Lakers** (tel. 213/674-6000), and the **L.A. Clippers** (213/748-0500), and now the superb **L.A. Kings** hockey team (tel. 213/419-3182). The L.A. Dodgers play in Dodger Stadium, located at 1000 Elysian Park, near Sunset Boulevard. The California Angels and the L.A. Rams call Anaheim Stadium home at 2000 S. State College Blvd., near Katella Avenue in Anaheim. The L.A. Lakers and the L.A. Kings hockey team hold court (or ice it, as the case may be) in The Forum at 3900 W. Manchester Blvd., at Prairie Avenue in Inglewood. Finally, the L.A. Raiders do their dirty work in the L.A. Memorial Coliseum at 3911 S. Figueroa St., and the L.A. Clippers play nearby in the L.A. Sports Arena at 3939 S. Figueroa.

And, finally, there's the Sport of Kings. Lovely **Hollywood Park** racetrack has thoroughbred racing from April through July and November through December. A computer-operated screen offers a view of the back stretch and stop-action replays of photo finishes. There's also a children's play area with modern playground equipment and an electronic games area. Hollywood Park is at 1050 S. Prairie Ave. in Inglewood (tel. 213/419-1500). Post time is 1:30 p.m., Wednesday through Sunday. **Santa Anita** racetrack, one of the most beautiful tracks in the country, has thoroughbred racing from October through mid-November and December through late April. During racing season, the public is invited to watch morning workouts daily from 7:30 to 9:30 a.m. Santa Anita also has a children's playground. Post time varies so be sure to call. Santa Anita is located at 285 W. Huntington Dr. in Arcadia (tel. 818/574-7223). Finally, there's **Los Alamitos Race Course** featuring quarterhorse racing from mid-November through January, and May through mid-August; harness racing is held from late February through April. Los Alamitos is at 4961 Katella Ave., in Los Alamitos (tel. 213/431-1361 or 714/995-1234).

STORE HOURS: Stores are usually open from 10 a.m. to 6 p.m. Monday through Saturday, closed Sunday. Many malls and department stores are also open on Sunday.

TAXES: California State Sales Tax is 7¼%, hotel tax is 12%.

TELEPHONE SERVICE: In addition to the usual telephone service, you can obtain weather information for Los Angeles (tel. 213/554-1212), time (tel. 213/853-1212), and information on local highway conditions (tel. 213/626-7231). And of course, there's the usual directory assistance (411), plus directory assistance that will enable you to ascertain telephone numbers of customers who have 800 numbers (tel. 800/555-1212).

TICKETS: Tickets to most concerts, theater events, and sports events, as well as numerous other happenings of interest to all, can be obtained through either Ticketmaster, at 213/480-3232, or Teletron, at 213/410-1062, for a per-ticket fee. They accept major credit cards and will mail tickets anywhere in the country two weeks prior to the event, or immediately if the event is occurring within two weeks. You can also pick up tickets at Ticketmaster and Teletron outlets. Call for locations.

TIPPING: You probably already know about tipping in restaurants and the usual 15% before tax. In some restaurants it will automatically be added to the cost of the meal, in which case you will see it listed above the total. If the service was excellent, 20% before tax would be appropriate. A 25% tip is proper if the meal is on the house. A 10% tip shows that you were unhappy with the service. If a captain or headwaiter is involved, they're usually tipped 5% to 7%. The wine steward gets 10% of the wine tab, but not less than $1. You do not tip the owner, manager, or chef.

If you're checking into a hotel with several bags, a tip of $5 is par for the course.

Valet parking can be a great convenience at those hotels and restaurants that have it. A tip of $1 is appropriate for the service, over and above the charge for parking, if any.

When you leave the hotel, a tip of $1 per day for the period of your stay, left for the maid, is a most reasonable amount and will be appreciated.

FINDING "A PLACE IN THE SUN"

You'll need a new concept of hotel living in greater Los Angeles. More than half of my hotel and motel recommendations are, in truth, miniature resorts, often with self-contained recreational facilities and swimming pools. Only a small selection are more conventional, chosen for the woman or man who is there strictly for business, wanting perhaps secretarial service but little distraction.

It's assumed you'll have a car with unlimited mileage (the bus system is difficult for visitors who select out-of-the-way places). The freeways make it possible to choose a hotel in a spot you would have rejected years ago. Signs are well placed, and maps make touring easy.

If you're with your family, combining business with holiday activities, there are many hotels to select to satisfy both needs. If you're interested in marinas, yachts, and the sea life, consider a hotel in Marina del Rey (which contains more pleasure boats than any other marina in the nation), just minutes from the airport (See Chapter X). Or, if you want to "go suburban," what about Pasadena, 20 to 45 minutes from downtown Los Angeles? At a Santa Monica hotel you'll be right on the beach. Those travelers with children will want to consider the Anaheim area, and may want to turn now to Chapter IX, which previews Disneyland and all the many attractions of Orange County. Many motels there have supervised playgrounds.

Nearly all of my selections quote daily rates, though the budget-conscious will find weekly prices lower at some hotels.

Those who prefer the most elegant address in Southern California will seek rooms in Beverly Hills or Bel-Air. These famous residential retreats of movie stars shelter some of the most expensive hotels in the West (the Beverly Hilton, the Regent Beverly Wilshire, and the Beverly Hills), and the Hotel Bel-Air is exceedingly posh. Hollywood is probably your most central and convenient location. Downtown hotels cater primarily to the business community.

The actual budget inns of Los Angeles are few and far between. Nevertheless, they do exist, and I've described them below—as well as a few offbeat places for those whose taste runs to the more unusual or atmospheric.

A word about how this chapter is organized. Since Greater Los Angeles is such a far-flung metropolis, encompassing many separate communities, I thought it best to break the city down into areas, then to discuss the different kinds of accommodations—deluxe or upper bracket, first class, moderate, and budget, in that order—within each sector. (For easy reference, see "Accommodations" in the index.) I'll lead off in downtown Los Angeles with a good selection of hotels and motels.

---

1. Downtown Los Angeles

THE UPPER BRACKET

The spectacular **Westin Bonaventure,** 404 S. Figueroa St. (between 4th and 5th streets), Los Angeles, CA 90071 (tel. 213/624-1000, or toll free 800/228-3000), is the creation of world-famous architect John Portman. The Bonaventure's five gleaming cylindrical towers not only revise the L.A. skyline, but contain what is probably the world's most futuristic hotel.

The 21st-century-look atrium lobby is the size of two football fields. Under a six-story skylight roof it contains a one-acre lake, hanging gardens, trees, splashing fountains, and very attractive places to eat and drink. Eleven escalators (accented by hundreds of tiny lights) and 12 glass-bubble elevators rise from this level, the latter seemingly right from the reflecting pools. The entire hotel is so designed that views, inside and out, from any vantage point, are thrilling. Guests enjoy the panorama of Los Angeles day and night while being whisked to their rooms in outdoor elevators, from their rooms (a full floor-to-ceiling window wall in each), and from the rooftop restaurant and revolving cocktail bar. And the sweeping interior architectural shape is equally dramatic; you can sit, practically suspended in midair, in one of the "pods" overlooking the bustling lobby.

As for the 1,500 rooms, they're located on the upper floors, and no bedroom is more than six doors from an elevator. The rooms are everything you'd expect from a first-class hotel—sophisticated and elegant with floor-to-ceiling views of the city.

There is, of course, no shortage of dining facilities. The Sidewalk Café and the Lobby Court sprawl over the lobby area. The former is open from 6 a.m. to 1 a.m.; the latter serves breakfast, lunch, and cocktails to diners seated in comfortable leather banquettes under large fringed umbrellas (it's open Monday to Saturday 11 a.m. to 1:30 a.m. and Sunday from noon to midnight).

The Flower Street Bar, a rich mixture of marble, brass and mahogany, has become the new downtown "hot spot" for cocktails.

Beaudry's (named for the famous 19th-century mayor), also on the lobby level, offers gourmet fare in posh surroundings; 18 intimate dining areas are created by shimmering gold-mesh curtains sheltering plush brown velvet circular booths. Beaudry's offers such tempting dinner entrees as lobster ragoût in a puff pastry graced with an excellent Nantua sauce. Entrees at lunch cost $13 to $18; at dinner they range from $19 to $30.

There's also a very fine Japanese restaurant here, Inagiku, on the sixth level, with areas for teppanyaki cooking, tatami rooms, a tempura bar, sushi bar, and regular table seating. Elegant dining with a view (from every table) is featured at the 35th-floor Top of Five Restaurant; the Bona Vista cocktail lounge a floor below revolves to offer 360° panoramic views. Finally, there's even a Bagel Nosh on level four, and a Carl's Jr. on level six.

There's also entertainment nightly in various lounges and restaurants throughout the hotel.

Rooms are priced at $150 to $210 single, $160 to $240 double; suites begin at $390.

Even if you don't stay at the Bonaventure, it's an attraction in itself; come by for a look around, a before-theater drink in the revolving cocktail lounge, or dinner in one of the hotel's fine restaurants.

The **Biltmore,** 506 S. Grand Ave. (between 5th and 6th streets), Los Angeles, CA 90071 (tel. 213/624-1011, or toll free 800/421-8000, or 800/252-0175 in California), has been unrivaled as the *grande dame* of L.A.'s deluxe hotels since it opened in 1923. Over the years it has played host to royal personages and Hollywood royalty—everyone from English princes to John Wayne.

Always a beautiful hotel, the Biltmore today is looking better than ever following a $40-million renovation that enhanced its architectural heritage while incorporating harmonious modern touches (such as the prints by Jim Dine in the guest rooms) and up-grading to state-of-the-art mechanical systems. The entrance on Grand Avenue features a *porte cochère* where valet parking is available.

The rooms are spacious and high-ceilinged, lavishly appointed, and attractively decorated in luscious tones of pale yellow, gray lilac, rose, and light green. Traditional French furniture houses the desk and TV. All rooms are, of course, equipped with every modern amenity and the Biltmore offers a few luxurious extras like the availability of 24-hour maid service and room service, hand-delivered messages, and a multilingual concierge staff to help you with all travel and sightseeing arrangements. The Biltmore Health Club, featuring an elegant Roman spalike pool, steam room, sauna, Jacuzzi, Nautilus equipment, and weights, is open daily for hotel guests and members.

Once the lobby of the hotel, the spectacular Rendezvous Court now serves as a lovely palm lounge where you can enjoy afternoon tea or evening cocktails while listening to the delicate sounds of the fountain. Overhead is the ornate cathedral-like vaulted ceiling, hand-painted by the Italian artist Giovanni Smeraldi. His work is best seen in the main Galeria—the marble walkway that extends the full width of the hotel. Twin staircases from the Rendezvous Court lead to the Galeria via an arched alcove.

The Biltmore's dining facilities include the prestigious Bernard's, which offers an exalted environment of oak paneling, fluted columns, and hand-painted beamed ceilings, further embelished with the soft strains of a harp. The cuisine is a combination of classic French and the best of regional American dishes. At dinner, you might begin with an appetizer of Westcott Bay oysters. Entrees, priced at $23 to $35, include specialties such as grilled medallions of veal served with morilles, or breast of chicken served with a fresh citrus sauce; lunch is a bit less costly, with entrees from $18 to $26. The hotel's Court Cafe is open for breakfast, lunch, and dinner, and features regional American cuisine in a warm Mediterranean cafelike atmosphere.

The Grand Avenue Bar offers a cold lunch buffet, and in the evening it showcases top-name jazz entertainment.

Rates for singles are $140 to $210; doubles $160 to $240; suites start at $390.

Unique on the downtown scene is the **New Otani Hotel and Garden,** 120 S. Los Angeles St. (at 1st Street), Los Angeles, CA 90012 (tel. 213/629-1200, or toll free 800/421-8795, 800/252-0197 in California). It's the city's only Japanese hotel complete with an authentic half-acre Japanese garden and a Japanese-style health club for men and women offering Japanese baths and shiatsu massage in addition to the usual club facilities. The garden is highlighted by ancient stone lanterns, cascading waterfalls, and ponds.

Most of the 440 rooms are basically Western in decor, though they do feature extra-deep tubs. About 80 rooms have Japanese-style windows and are decorated in muted beige tones. And in addition

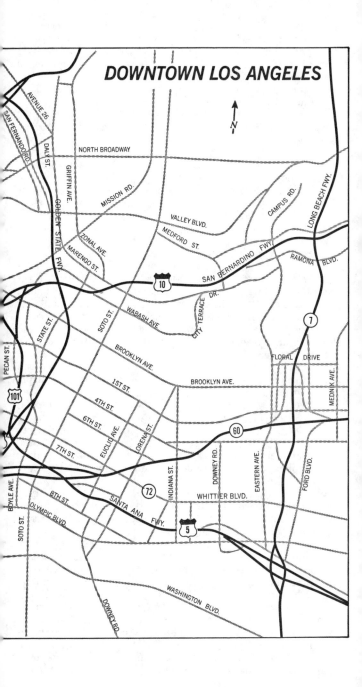

DOWNTOWN LOS ANGELES

to the expected luxury-hotel amenities, they offer desk-level outlets for electric typewriters, extension phones and radio speakers in the bathrooms, refrigerators, special audio channels with information about L.A. (in English and Japanese), smoke detectors, and digital alarm clocks. Most of the rooms are decorated in three different color schemes—plum, orange, and yellow/gold—and furnished in a restrained, elegant contemporary motif.

Facilities include access to a two-story shopping arcade in the adjacent Weller Court mall, 24-hour room service, lots of parking space, and service desks to cater to your every need; there's even a concierge to help you get a babysitter, rental car, theater tickets, and airline tickets, or make tour arrangements, etc. Golf and tennis are available nearby.

The New Otani's answer to the hotel coffeeshop is the Canary Garden, serving breakfast, lunch, and dinner. It offers a wide range of fare, from a bagel with lox and cream cheese to salmon teriyaki. And it's the only place I know that offers a green-tea–ice cream shake.

For Japanese classical haute cuisine there's the lovely Thousand Cranes, overlooking the garden, and offering daily Japanese breakfasts, and Japanese buffets on Saturday and Sunday for $35 per person (including tax and tip). Regular dinner entrees here range from $22 to $33; they include sashimi, teriyaki, tempura, and other Japanese dishes. Tatami seating is available.

Commodore Perry's, named for the famous naval officer who forced Japan to open trade with the West, aptly features American/Continental specialties.

Singles pay $125 to $165 at the New Otani, and doubles run $145 to $185; Japanese suites, with Oriental furnishings, tatami-mat bedrooms, and deep whirlpool baths, begin at $375.

Hyatt Regency Los Angeles, Broadway Plaza, 711 S. Hope St. (at 7th Street), Los Angeles, CA 90017 (tel. 213/683-1234, or toll free 800/228-9000), is a dazzling jewel in the Hyatt crown. It's an integral part of the adjoining skyscraper, the Broadway Plaza business and shopping complex. The ultramodern lobby contains a garden plaza, lounges, sidewalk café, and boutiques under a two-story skylight ceiling; a bank of wide escalators takes you to multi-level reception areas and poolside gardens. Wood paneling, natural brick, old-fashioned streetlamps, and lots of greenery add a warm touch. Informal banjo, mariachi, steel band, and organ concerts are sometimes presented here during the day.

Conceived with the executive in mind, 487 ultra-contemporary rooms await you. All are oversize, with extra-large beds. Each room has an excellent view for a downtown hotel, color TV, deep pile carpets, and bold textures. Singles go from $145 to $165; doubles and twins, from $170 to $190; suites from $275.

On the garden level is Joint Venture, offering nightly entertainment, where glistening mirrors reflect the shining Plexiglass in a million prismatic images. In addition to regular meals, a Sunday champagne brunch is served here for $20 per person. Pavan, the Hyatt's gourmet restaurant, features Continental cuisine for lunch and dinner, Monday through Saturday. Dining at the rooftop Angel's Flight is thrilling: You get a circular panoramic view of the city in an hour. The Sun Porch is designed to look like a Paris street, and there's the Lobby Bar, complete with a natural-wood piano bar, for cocktails.

In addition to all the above-mentioned facilities, the Hyatt offers guests tennis and health club privileges at the nearby Los Angeles Racquet Club.

The **Los Angeles Hilton and Towers,** 930 Wilshire Blvd. (at Figueroa Street), Los Angeles, CA 90017 (tel. 213/629-4321, or toll free 800/445-8667), enjoys a prime position at the point where Wilshire Boulevard commences, near the entrances to major freeways.

Personal service is paramount in this huge, 900-room hotel. Every convenience and luxury is at hand, from 24-hour maid service and room service to in-house movies on your color TV, and laundry chutes. There is a writing desk in each room, individual heat and air-conditioning controls, and double-panel glass windows to minimize outside noise. The furnishings are contemporary in tone, with subdued colors—mauve, seafoam green, gray, and camel. Nonsmoking rooms are available, as are rooms specially equipped for handicapped guests. For any and all, there is an outdoor swimming pool surrounded by tables for dining and drinking.

The premium Towers rooms (15th and 16th floors) have separate check-in facilities and a staff serving only the Towers guests. The rooms have deluxe furnishings plus such amenities as two-line telephones and newspaper delivery each morning. The Towers lounge serves complimentary Continental breakfast, provides the latest Dow Jones reports (assuming you really want to know), has two television sets, reading material, and games. There is also a daily cocktail hour, with complimentary hors d'oeuvres and beverages.

The Hilton has a fitness center located on the west side of the main lobby near the entrance to the pool.

The public rooms include four restaurants and a cocktail lounge. There's the 24-hour Gazebo coffeeshop; the City Grill with its California cuisine, including Sonoma lamb and fresh Pacific seafood for lunch; Minami of Tokyo which, not surprisingly, serves Japanese dishes and sushi for dinner nightly, luncheon weekdays. And there is the Lobby Bar serving cocktails and snacks, and featuring musical entertainment. But above all, there is Cardini's, for superb northern Italian cuisine. The decor is ultra-contemporary with marble floors, elegant arches, and columns in Mediterranean blues and pastels. As to the cuisine, emphasis is on light pastas and a good selection of fish and veal dishes. But look beyond—there are such first-course beauties as bufala mozzarella garnished with sun-dried tomatoes, and such enticing entrees as linguine with lobster, and swordfish with baby artichokes and calamata olives. At the end, pay attention to the pastry tray for just a few more gorgeous calories. Dinner for two, without wine, will be about $60 to $100. Lunch will, of course, be less.

The room rates depend on placement, size, and furnishings. A single can be rented for $150 to $175. Double- and twin-bedded rooms are in the $170 to $195 range.

The Hilton also has about two dozen shops on the premises, and the adjacent Citicorp Plaza holds a three-level shopping mall.

The **Sheraton Grande,** 333 S. Figueroa St. (between 3rd and 4th streets), Los Angeles, CA 90071 (tel. 213/617-1133, or toll free 800/325-3535), is certainly among the most glamorous hotels in downtown Los Angeles. The hotel's contemporary elegance is evident as you enter the building. The lobby and lounge are two stories high, spacious and airy, with skylights and lush green plants. There's piano entertainment here daily, and every afternoon tea is served from 3 to 5 p.m.

A 14-story structure, the Sheraton Grande has 470 deluxe rooms—including 15 suites—that feature accommodations with a residential feel, decorated in muted colors with bright accents. All rooms contain color TV, direct-dial phone, and marble baths with tub/shower combination. Amenities include 24-hour room service, butler service, valet parking, pool, sundeck, health club, a multilingual concierge, and four movie theaters.

The hotel's gourmet dining room is Ravel, serving California cuisine. The Back Porch is an informal dining area situated on a terrace overlooking the pool; three meals a day are served here. The hotel also boasts a new bar and eatery, Moody's.

Rates at the Sheraton Grande are $180 to $210 single, $200 to $235 double. Suites cost $475 to $975.

BUDGET

The Hotel Stillwell, 838 S. Grand Ave., between 8th and 9th Streets (tel. 213/627-1151), is conveniently situated in the downtown area. It's just a short distance to the Ahmanson Theatre and Dorothy Chandler Pavilion in the Civic Center featuring a variety of theatrical and musical events. It's also close to the Museum of Contemporary Art, Little Tokyo, Olvera Street, Union Station, and a variety of exceptional restaurants. (See Chapter VI.)

The main floor of the Stillwell is imposing in size, but what the lobby lacks in warmth is made up for by the pleasant personnel. The hotel has 250 recently renovated rooms (nonsmoking available) that can accommodate guests traveling alone or with children. The decor is simple and comfortable—soft blues and grays, floral prints on the spread, and attractive framed prints of flowers. The space is reasonably light, but if you want a room that will be flooded with sunlight, ask for a corner room. All rooms have a shower/tub, TV, phone, and individually controlled air conditioning.

Adjoining the hotel is an elegant-looking restaurant serving Mexican food. Also off the lobby is Hank's Bar and Grill, a cozy, friendly pub with all sorts of memorabilia. And to the rear of the hotel is Gill's Cuisine of India.

Single rooms range from $33 to $43, twin/doubles from $43 to $53, suites from $69 to $89. A note of caution regarding parking in front of the hotel—despite loading-zone designations, they are for vehicles with commercial plates only, so it's wise not to leave the car unattended, even briefly. You may come back to find a parking ticket under your windshield wiper.

2. Hollywood

FIRST CLASS

Hyatt on Sunset, 8401 Sunset Blvd. (two blocks east of La Cienega Boulevard), Hollywood, CA 90069 (tel. 213/656-1234, or toll free 800/233-1000), is one of the most noted hotels along the famed "strip," with 13 floors encasing 262 bedrooms. About 75% of them overlook the Los Angeles skyline; the other quarter, the Hollywood Hills. This recently renovated link in a chain is close to Restaurant Row on La Cienega Boulevard and the nightlife along Sunset Strip. Rooms, decorated in subdued earth tones, are

---

"Privacy for the Harassed"

Château Marmont, 8221 Sunset Blvd. at Marmont Lane, Hollywood, CA 90046 (tel. 213/656-1010), is a Château-style apartment hotel nestled on a cliff just above Sunset Strip. Remodeled and expanded a few years ago, it still is the home center for many a visiting film celebrity and entertainment industry mogul. There isn't enough space to list all the famed who have lived here (and still do on occasion). Carol Channing met her mate here; Howard Hughes once maintained a suite; Boris Karloff stayed here for many years; Greta Garbo used to check in using the name of Harriet Brown; John and Yoko once maintained a suite here, as have Sophia Loren and Sidney Poitier. More recently the Château has sheltered Richard Gere, Al Pacino, Robert De Niro, Lauren Hutton, and Bianca Jagger. And it's no secret that John Belushi died here.

Actors, producers, and writers often gathered in the great baronial living room/lobby furnished with grandiose Hollywood antiques. However, even if the hotel is full, the lobby may be empty. Otherwise you'd find them lounging around the egg-shaped swimming pool, edged with semitropical trees and shrubbery. You can get almost any kind of accommodation here, including lanai-style bungalows out back.

The rooms are homey and charming, and all are equipped with color TV, direct-dial phone, and bath. Some 53 of the 62 units have a complete, fully equipped kitchen. Rooms without kitchen are priced at $110 a night, single or double. Studio apartments with kitchen are $140 for one or two people, one-bedroom suites run $170 to $190, and two-bedroom suites, $235. Cottages are $140 a night; penthouse suites, $235 to $450; bungalows, $320.

There are many, many restaurants in the area. Hotel room service is available daily from 6:30 a.m. to midnight, offering such fare as wine and beer, cold meat and cheese platters, salads, fruit, sandwiches, etc.

One British guest said it best: "The Château offers tolerance for the eccentric and privacy for the harassed."

equipped with direct-dial phone, color TV with in-room movies, dressing area, and tub/shower baths. Most also have a private balcony. Singles cost from $125 to $155, and doubles run from $145 to $175, with suites ranging from $350 to $550. Special weekend rates are available. Facilities include a heated rooftop swimming pool, valet or self-parking, and the Silver Screen Restaurant and Jazz Club for dining and entertainment.

Holiday Inn, 1755 N. Highland Ave. (between Franklin and Hollywood Boulevard), Hollywood, CA 90028 (tel. 213/462-7181, or toll free 800/465-4329), is a 23-story "mini-skyscraper" in the heart of Old Hollywood. It features a revolving rooftop restaurant called Windows on Hollywood, for dining and dancing with a view. On the second floor guests may lounge around a swimming pool, surrounded by a sundeck. There's also a coffeeshop called Show Biz Café, open for breakfast, lunch, and dinner, and the Front Row Lounge, for cocktails.

It is, in reality, a glorified motor lodge (there's a garage on the premises with free parking). The accent is on the comfortable, well-equipped, redecorated bedrooms, 470 in all, complete with air conditioning, remote control cable color TV, direct-dial phone, clock radio, and a digital safe. Singles are $93 to $124; doubles, $110 to $141. An extra person in the room pays $12, and children 18 or under stay free with their parents.

BUDGET

One of the best of the budget category is the pleasant and centrally located **Hollywood Celebrity Hotel,** 1775 Orchid Ave., near Hollywood Boulevard and Highland, Hollywood, CA 90028 (tel. 213/850-6464, or toll free 800/222-7017, 800/222-7090 in California). While you may be the only guest staying at the hotel, you still receive star treatment.

The Hollywood Celebrity has 39 spacious, comfortable units, all with art deco treatment, air conditioning, cable TV, radio, and phone. A complimentary Continental breakfast, delivered to your room, is included in the rates as is a bottle of wine on arrival, the morning newspaper, and valet parking.

Singles are $65, doubles $70 to $75. You can bring a pet (of reasonable size), but that requires a $100 deposit. On the other hand, an extra person is only $8.

3. Beverly Hills

THE UPPER BRACKET

The **Beverly Hills Hotel and Bungalows,** 9641 Sunset Blvd. (at Rodeo Drive), Beverly Hills, CA 90210 (tel. 213/276-2251), has a history intertwined with that of the power and glory of the film colony. The hotel has been home base or else a home away from home for everybody from kings, queens, and presidents of vast economic empires to international film and television stars. Many of these personages have selected one of the hotel's exclusive bungalows, set in lush, semitropical gardens.

Keyed to luxury living, the pink stucco hotel enjoys a site on a 12-acre parkland. No wonder the Rockefellers, the Whitneys, the Astors, the Vanderbilts, plus the more "average" well-heeled American, have preferred its charms. You'll know why when you see the iridescent turquoise pool of the Pool and Cabaña Club, the patio offering al fresco dining, a set of championship tennis courts, the coffee room and the world-famous Polo Lounge.

There are hundreds of stories about the Beverly Hills Hotel, enough to fill a book by Sandra Lee Stuart called *The Pink Palace*. It's where W. C. Fields ordered a table for two—himself and a man-eating plant . . . where Gable and Lombard trysted . . . where Howard Hughes once kept a complex of bungalows, one for a food taster . . . and where Tallulah Bankhead fell fully clothed into the pool and was rescued by Tarzan (Johnny Weissmuller). It was the backdrop, too, for Neil Simon's play *California Suite*.

Then there's The Dining Room for gourmet dinners. (You'll find this award-winning restaurant discussed under "The Top Restaurants," Chapter V.)

Each of the 325 accommodations (which include 21 bungalows and garden suites) is custom-designed in the Hollywood style, with tropical overtones. Of course, there is everything in the way of amenities: color TV, VCRs, telephones, room service, and, in many cases, a patio or terrace and even a wood-burning fireplace. The rates are determined by the size of the room, its view, and its furnishings. Single and double rooms range from $185 to $295 for singles, $230 to $320 doubles; suites, from $395 to $1,100; bungalows from $495 to $3,100.

The **Regent Beverly Wilshire,** 9500 Wilshire Blvd., at Rodeo Drive (tel. 213/275-5200, or toll free 800/421-4354), is the *grande dame* of Beverly Hills—reflecting a revival of the regal comforts offered in the tradition and elegance of the grand hotels of the world. The Beverly Wilshire has cosseted international royalty; the rich; the incredibly rich; film, TV, and stage personalities; U.S. Presidents; corporate giants; and impressarios. It also houses Tiffany and Buccellati.

Magnificently redone, Regent Beverly Wilshire reopened in April 1990 with the very posh tone that has always been part of her beauty and charm. The spacious lobby reflects that elegance with its French Empire furnishings; French and Italian marble floors; rare Brocatelle gold, marble-lined columns; mahogany and ebony Front and Concierge desks; the restored bronze and crystal chandelier; hand-wrought sconces; and two paintings by Verhoven.

El Camino Real, the Beverly Wilshire's private street of cobblestones and gas lights that separates the Beverly and Wilshire wings, leads to your disembarking area. Following arrival, you're met by a guest relations officer, dressed in quintessential sartorial conservativism, who personally escorts you to your accommodations. No need to clutter up the lobby with luggage, it is recorded by computer and arrives by a separate lift.

Guest rooms, for the most part, are larger than the average hotel room. Many Wilshire Wing rooms have nearly doubled in size, while those on the Beverly side around the pool are more compact but very comfortable with terraces at pool level and balconies above. All blend light and space beautifully with four lovely color themes —wheat, a gentle rose, soft peach, and a delicate celery green. Accommodations are warm, comfortable, and beautifully appointed with a mix of period furniture providing the ultimate in a relaxing or working environment. Each guest room has three phones with a two-line phone on the desk. There is color cable TV in every living room, bedroom and bath. Special double-glazed windows ensure absolute quiet from the outer world. As to the baths—they are the ultimate: All are lined in marble, with a deep soaking tub, a separate glass-enclosed shower just about large enough for a small cocktail party, a large vanity, and lighting that totally surrounds you. Amenities include fresh flowers in each room, plush deep-pile white bathrobes, white scuffs, scales, hairdryers, and toiletries created for the hotel. The hotel also has steward service on every floor (a concept imported from Regent's Hong Kong property), and 24-hour concierge service. A call system in each room has silent buttons by the door and bed to summon stewards for such services as light refreshments and one-hour pressing.

There are three places to dine in the hotel. The Cafe, on the Wilshire and Rodeo Drive corner, where M. F. Kreiss' Drugstore once was, specializes in classic down-to-earth meals. It's an elegant, updated version of the old-fashioned soda fountain with black and white striped marble floors and Roman shades. Floor-to-ceiling windows make it a great spot for people watching, or simply collapsing after a hard day of shopping on Rodeo Drive. This is where you'll find two eggs any style, a Belgian waffle smothered in berries, lox and eggs, blintzes, hamburgers, a sampler of mini-sandwiches including a hot dog, reuben and hamburger, several excellent salads, chili, and a choice of daily special entrees. The Cafe also has a superb fountain menu from yogurt sundaes to (are you ready?) chocolate, marshmallow and honey ice cream with coffee sauce and biscuit leaves. The Cafe is open from 6 a.m. to midnight.

The Lobby Lounge is an elegant European-style salon for tea served from 3 to 5 p.m., light menus, late night dinner fare, and cocktails—a place "to be seen." The Lobby Lounge features much the same menu as the luncheon and late night selections of the Cafe; there's also live entertainment in the evening.

The Dining Room is done in the Directoire style with lush woods and soft fabrics. There is also a glass-walled kitchen that gives a view of the chefs at work. Luncheon offers a lengthy list of appetizers, soups, sandwiches, salads, and entrees, served from 11:30 a.m. to 3 p.m. My choices (in season) are the cold poached salmon for lunch or the Texas blue crab omelete with lobster sauce. For dinner, given a substantial appetite, I'd begin with the black mussel soup or

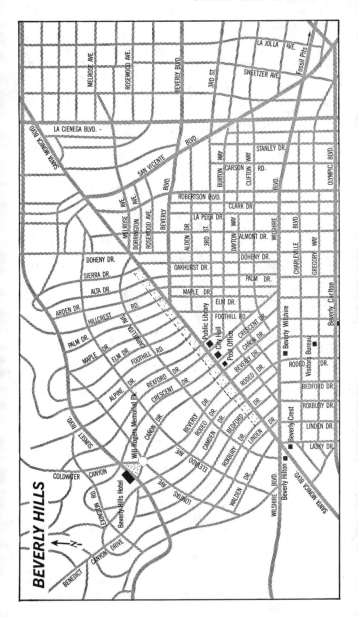

angel hair with basil and tomato, and move on to the grilled veal medallions with wild mushrooms and tarragon. Assuming that you have the zest for it all, dinner for two will range from $90 to $110, without wine. The Dining Room is open from 11:30 a.m. to 10:30 p.m. Reservations are suggested.

As to other activities on and around the Beverly Wilshire, you might fling yourself into the Fitness Salon where you can work out while you watch the sensible folk lounge and snack in the sun by the lovely Italian villa–style pool, or relax their limbs in one of the two hot tubs, each with different temperatures. Following all this, you might choose a stretch in the sauna or steam room, a massage, and for a final touch a facial, manicure, and pedicure.

There is no simple explanation as to what is a "grand hotel." Suffice it to say that it is rather like that which describes "old money"—class, elegance, a comfortable ease with status. And that's much of what the Regent Beverly Wilshire is all about.

For single or double occupancy the rate for Superior Rooms is $255, Deluxe Rooms $325, one- and two-bedroom suites $400 to $1,500, the Presidential Suite $3,000. There is no charge for children 14 years and under when they occupy existing bedding in the same room as their parents. Baby cribs are available at no charge.

A scheduled airport van to or from LAX is $12 per person; but if you want to make a grand entrance or exit, a chauffeured limousine or sedan one way from the airport will be provided for approximately $90 including tax and gratuity.

L'Ermitage, 9291 Burton Way (near Foothill Drive), Beverly Hills, CA 90210 (tel. 213/278-3344, or toll free 800/424-4443), opened in 1976 on a residential street. A gracious establishment, conceived along the lines of a small European luxury hotel, it offers suites (only 112 of them), a restaurant reserved for hotel guests, and a plush rooftop spa and pool in a garden setting. It is extremely popular with top executives and entertainment industry celebs.

Guests are escorted to their suites by an assistant manager and are pampered from the moment they arrive. The spacious, elegantly furnished rooms feature parquet entrances, sunken living rooms, fireplaces, kitchenettes stocked with complimentary soft drinks, wet bars, color TVs, spacious dressing areas and powder rooms. All townhouse suites have fully equipped kitchens. There's an extra phone in the bath, not to mention such niceties as exclusive L'Ermitage toiletries and custom soaps for gentlemen and ladies. A full-time concierge is on hand to help you out in any way.

The dining room, Café Russe, is adorned with the paintings of Braques, Renoir, and de la Peña, no less, among others (I'm talking original art!). A strolling guitarist adds to the relaxed ambience. An *intimate* bar adjoins. In addition, 24-hour room service (including candlelight meals with an accompanying musician) is available.

Guests at L'Ermitage enjoy a morning paper at no charge. Luscious strawberries and brown sugar are delivered to each suite at 4 p.m., and complimentary caviar is served each afternoon in the elegant top-floor bar. Other thoughtful touches include overnight shoeshine and complimentary limousine service. There is a rooftop garden that features a mineral water spa, heated pool, and private solarium.

All this luxury doesn't come cheap, but would you expect it to? One-bedroom executive suites are $225 to $295, one-bedroom townhouse suites run $335 to $545, two-bedroom townhouse suites are $455 to $625, and a three-bedroom townhouse is $1,500.

The **Beverly Hilton,** 9876 Wilshire Blvd. (at Santa Monica Boulevard), Beverly Hills, CA 90210 (tel. 213/274-7777), is a world unto itself. Lodged in a wedge-shaped area in the heart of Beverly Hills, it offers deluxe rooms, many having balconies and overlooking an Olympic-size pool and surrounding hillsides. In all, there are 592 air-conditioned rooms with all the comforts, including in-room movies on your color TV. The different rates depend on size and placement, with the stiffer tabs assessed for the rooms overlooking the pool or those on a higher level. Singles range from $155 to $195; doubles, from $175 to $215. A plus is that there is no charge for children (of any age!) occupying the same room as their parents.

The Beverly Hilton's prize-winning L'Escoffier restaurant is renowned for the quality of its French cuisine as well as for its service. L'Escoffier has a prix fixe dinner at $61. A la carte entrees are $25 to $35. The Mr. H. Restaurant offers international cuisine buffet in a traditional setting, with Jacobean chairs, crystal chandeliers, and paneled damask walls. An extensive buffet is served at lunch for $14 and at dinner for $27. Champagne Sunday brunch, by the way, is a Beverly Hills tradition here, and is served for $25. There is also a branch of Trader Vic's on the premises, with à la carte entrees from $14 to $35.

FIRST CLASS

Beverly Rodeo, 360 N. Rodeo Dr. (a few blocks north of Wilshire Boulevard), Beverly Hills, CA 90210 (tel. 213/273-0300, or toll free 800/421-0545, 800/441-5050 in California), was conceived by Max Baril as "a smart little European hotel." It's his personal pride, and he's incorporated a lot of glamour into this intimate 100-room hotel in the heart of the Beverly Hills shopping area, near such prestigious stores as Gucci, Giorgio, Van Cleef & Arpels, Saks, and I. Magnin. A liveried attendant opens the door, and you're ushered into a lobby that is both provincial French and Californian. The bedrooms have floral-print bedspreads and drapes, baths with marble-topped sinks and extra phones, and provincial furnishings. All are air-conditioned and have color TV and AM/FM radio; some have a balcony and a refrigerator. Rates for standard rooms range from $130 to $160; deluxe, from $150 to $180; and executive rooms, from $160 to $190. The more expensive tariffs are charged for courtside accommodations with balconies. Of course, more opulent suites are available as well, priced from $255 to $400. Adjoining a charming inner courtyard is the Café Rodeo, open for breakfast, lunch, and dinner, and just great for people-watching along Rodeo Drive.

If there's no room at this inn, you can try a sister hotel, the **Beverly Pavilion,** 9360 Wilshire Blvd., Beverly Hills, CA 90212 (tel. 213/273-1400, or toll free 800/421-0545). Accommodations are similar; prices are a bit lower. There is also an excellent restaurant—Colette—on the premises.

Beverly Hillcrest, 1224 S. Beverwil Dr. (at Pico Boulevard),

Beverly Hills, CA 90035 (tel. 213/277-2800, or toll free 800/421-3212, 800/252-0174 in California), is a luxuriously styled establishment at the edge of Beverly Hills, close to the San Diego and Santa Monica Freeways. The hotel is dramatic and sumptuous, a multi-million-dollar plaza structure, with bedrooms boasting roomy lanai balconies. Part of the drama is the 12-story ascent via a blue-steel-and-glass outside express elevator to the Top of the Hillcrest for cocktails, dining, and dancing with a view.

The guest accommodations are unusually spacious, each with its remote-control color TV, air conditioning, and refrigerator, plus genuine marble sinks (and a phone) in the bathroom. A decorator has definitely been at work, giving each room style and flourish. Some rooms have half-canopied beds, and the furnishings are a mixture of French and Italian pieces. Rates range from $125 to $135 single, $135 to $150 double, $215 to $345 for a suite. Special weekend rates are also available.

For a spectacular view, visit the cocktail lounge and dining room. On the lower level is Portofino, a plush, candlelit Italian restaurant with dark-paneled and exposed brick walls. Lunch and dinner are served at moderate prices. The menus offer excellent and varied selections. Off one of the plazas, the swimming pool is surrounded by sunbathing areas, palm trees, and a terrace for refreshments.

MODERATE

The **Beverly Crest Hotel,** 125 S. Spalding Dr. (just south of Wilshire Boulevard), Beverly Hills, CA 90212 (tel. 213/274-6801, or toll free 800/247-6432), has exceptionally well-planned bedrooms, many overlooking a courtyard with a swimming pool—a favorite spot for sunbathing and cool drinks.

Guest rooms, although a bit on the small side, are decorated in lovely shades of blue, peach, or orange. They have a very contemporary look with black lacquer or white furnishings and include all the familiar amenities, such as color TV with cable service, AM/FM radio, direct-dial phone, room service from 7 a.m. till 11 p.m., self-controlled air-conditioning and heating, and a bath with a tub-shower combination. You can park your car at an undercover garage at no extra charge.

Adjoining the pool patio is the Venetian Room Restaurant and Bar, serving three meals a day in a tasteful atmosphere. The hotel is within walking distance of some of the high-quality department stores of Beverly Hills.

Single rooms are $98 to $110; doubles $110 to $120.

4. Century City

THE UPPER BRACKET

Century Plaza Hotel, 2025 Ave. of the Stars, off Santa Monica Boulevard), Century City, CA 90067 (tel. 213/277-2000, or toll free 800/228-3000), is a superstar, built in 1966 on a 180-acre site once occupied by Twentieth Century—Fox Studios. In the center of Alcoa's skyscraper city, it was designed by the celebrated architect Minoru Yamasaki. Everything seemingly is larger than life, built for tomorrow. Occupying a commanding position adjoining Beverly Hills, the hotel contains 20 floors (5½ miles of corridors!), has a new 30-floor tower, and boasts a dramatic formal entrance.

The hotel, together with its $85-million tower completed at the end of 1984, has a total of 1,072 rooms. The tower's 30th floor is occupied by an 8,000-square-foot Plaza Suite. (Where else but in Los Angeles would you find one of the largest and most expensive suites in the world?) In total, the Century Plaza is enormous—it appears roughly the size of New York's Grand Central Station.

The tower alone houses 322 rooms, with only 14 exceptionally spacious rooms per floor. All have private balconies. In addition to the usual amenities, each has a wet bar and refrigerator, three conveniently located phones, an all-marble bathroom with separate soak tub and shower, double vanity and washbasins, and a heat lamp. As you might expect, the TV is contained in an armoire; writing desks have travertine marble tops, and there's a live tree (did you expect plastic?) or lovely green plant in each room.

All tower rooms receive a complimentary newspaper each morning, soft drinks and ice each afternoon, deluxe bath amenities such as robes and oversized bath towels, twice-daily maid service, and 24-hour room service featuring items from La Chaumiere. There's complimentary town-car service to and from Beverly Hills for shopping.

The 750 accommodations, apart from the tower (including 76 suites), are attractively decorated in a garden motif with teal-blue or forest-green carpeting. Here, too, your color TV is discreetly hidden in an oak armoire, which doubles as a desk and provides extra drawer space. All rooms have clocks, AM/FM radios, individually controlled heating and air conditioning, big closets (with plenty of hangers for a change), marble-topped refrigerators, balconies, and three phones—table, bedside, and bath.

The Lobby Court, open from 11 a.m. to 2 a.m. for cocktails, is a rendezvous and setting for important interviews. It's extremely comfortable with velvet- and leather-upholstered armchairs and Italian carpeting. Breakfast, lunch, dinner, and Sunday brunch are served in the sunny, window-walled Garden Pavilion overlooking reflecting pools, fountains, and tropical gardens. Café Plaza is a provincial-style coffeeshop adorned with French travel posters. Also located in this hotel is the award-winning Japanese restaurant Yamato, about which more in the upcoming dining chapter. The newest restaurants are in the tower—La Chaumiere, which blends California and Continental cuisine and presents it beautifully in a setting reminiscent of a fine European club, and The Terrace for classic California dining. As with Yamato, there's more on La Chaumiere in the dining chapter.

Other services and amenities that contribute to the luxurious ambience of the Century Plaza are two large outdoor heated pools, three Jacuzzis, a children's pool, and a sundeck amid fountains and lily ponds; tennis and health club privileges across the street; extra security precautions; a full complement of shops, airline desks, car-rental desks, etc.; and concierge service to help with all your travel-$190 double; suites begin at $215. In the tower, singles are $215 to $230; doubles, $240 to $255; suites begin at $950. The Plaza Suite is $3,500.

The ABC Entertainment Center is directly across the street from the hotel. The complex features an 1,850-seat Shubert Legitimate Theater, two ultramodern cinema theaters, and several fine restaurants.

5. West Wilshire

FIRST CLASS

Beverly Hills Comstock, 10300 Wilshire Blvd. (off Comstock Street), Los Angeles, CA 90024 (tel. 213/275-5575, or toll free 800/343-2184), caters to the carriage trade. It offers mostly suites opening onto the courtyard pool area; all contain either private balconies or patios.

The large rooms are decorated in either California modern with lots of chrome and glass or in a more traditional style with wingback chairs and sofas. Most have fully equipped kitchens, and all offer color TV, direct-dial phone, and tub/shower bath. You'll pay from $100 to $150 daily for a one-bedroom kitchen suite, $225 to $280 for a two-bedroom kitchen suite. Monthly rates are available.

Le Petit Café, open 7 a.m. to 10 p.m., serves breakfast, lunch, and dinner, with a full-service bar. Also on the premises is a gift shop; free parking is available for guests.

6. Westwood

FIRST CLASS

Holiday Inn Westwood Plaza Hotel, 10740 Wilshire Blvd. (at Selby Avenue), Westwood, CA 90024 (tel. 213/475-8711, or toll free 800/465-4329). For standard, reliable accommodations—or, as they say of themselves, "no surprises"—you can always count on a Holiday Inn. This one has 302 attractively furnished rooms, each with two double beds, bath with tub and shower, direct-dial phone, and color TV. Many offer a nice view. Facilities include a swimming pool and whirlpool on a sundeck lined with chaise lounges. There's also a restaurant, the Café Le Dome, open daily from 6:30 a.m. to

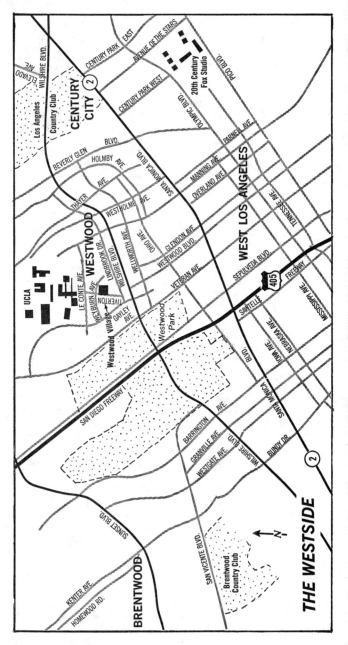

10:30 p.m., offering Continental cuisine. The Café Le Dome Cocktail Lounge (popular with L.A.'s basketball and football teams, many of whom stay at the hotel) adjoins.

Single rooms are $105 to $115; doubles, $115 to $125; suites, $170 to $400. Kids 18 or under can stay free in a room with their parents, and guests can park free.

MODERATE

Royal Palace Westwood, 1052 Tiverton Ave. (just north of Wilshire Boulevard), Los Angeles, CA 90024 (tel. 213/208-6677, or toll free 800/631-0100, 800/248-6955 in California), is right in the heart of Westwood Village, near the U.C.L.A. campus, with an abundance of shops, restaurants, movie theaters, and other nighttime entertainments. The Royal Palace Westwood is also across from what will soon be the Dr. Armand Hammer Museum, which will house his complete $30 million art collection. Its location—near Wilshire Boulevard, the San Diego Freeway, Beverly Hills, Santa Monica, and the airport—just couldn't be better. All rooms have new Acme units with stove, refrigerator, and stainless counter tops. Some also have microwave ovens, and the bathrooms contain marble vanities. You get color TV with three entertainment channels, a full-length mirror, and direct-dial phones. Doubles range between $63 and $91, and singles, between $57 and $84; suites are $110, and an extra person in a room is $8. There's a homey lounge, exercise room and free off-street parking.

---

7. West Los Angeles/Brentwood

THE UPPER BRACKET

The Bel-Air Summit Hotel (formerly the Bel-Air Sands), 11461 Sunset Blvd. (at the San Diego Freeway), Los Angeles, CA 90049 (tel. 213/476-6571, or toll free 800/421-6649, 800/352-6680 in California), is just minutes from Beverly Hills, Westwood Village and U.C.L.A., Century City, and 10 miles from LAX.

The 162 large, air-conditioned rooms and suites are decorated in subtle colors and understated European decor. All rooms have remote control color TVs, VCR, radios, built-in hair dryers, refrigerators, electronic security keys, and direct-dial phone. There are two heated pools and a tennis court on the premises.

The hotel's dining room is the Bel-Air Bar and Grill. Breakfast, lunch, dinner, and a fabulous Sunday brunch are served here, the last including champagne.

Rates are $125 to $170 for singles, $145 to $225 for doubles; suites start at $265.

MODERATE

Los Angeles West TraveLodge, 10740 Santa Monica Blvd. (at Overland Avenue), Los Angeles, CA 90025 (tel. 213/474-4576, or toll free 800/255-3050), is within easy access of U.C.L.A., Beverly Hills, and Century City, and offers a small swimming pool, plus comfortable rooms equipped with direct-dial phones, tub and/or shower baths, color TVs, clocks, and in-room coffee makers. All rooms have refrigerators. There's plenty of free parking. Rates are $56 to $70 single, $63 to $85 double or twin, $6 for an extra person in the room.

---

8. Bel-Air

THE UPPER BRACKET

Hotel Bel-Air, 701 Stone Canyon Rd. (off Sunset Boulevard), Bel Air, CA 90077 (tel. 213/472-1211), is the country club of the deluxe hotels in the Greater Los Angeles area and recipient of the Mobil five-star award. Removed from the commercial areas, it lies in the foothills of the exclusive residential Bel Air section above Sunset Boulevard, surrounded by the rising Santa Monica mountains and some of the most prestigious estates of Southern California. In fact, staying here is like a visit to a private estate where Spanish architecture prevails, and there are covered arcades leading from one building to the other. Everything seems surrounded by semi-tropical plants—banana, orange, and lemon trees, bamboo and palm.

A large oval-shaped swimming pool is set in the midst of the gardens and is surrounded by a flagstone terrace. In a stone-and-flower-edged pond, white swans glide by (best viewed from an arched stone bridge).

The public rooms are richly traditional, with a lavish use of fine antiques. A fire is kept burning in the entrance lounge, especially nice on nippy evenings. There are 92 rooms and suites, all decorated in elegant style by five top designers. Some have patios or terraces overlooking the pond. Rates vary according to the size, furnishings, and location. Amenities include two direct-dial phones (one in the bath), cable color TV, and radio. Rooms range from $195 to $360; suites, from $390 to $1,300.

In the wood-paneled, clublike lounge, you can relax over cocktails in comfortable armchairs and listen to piano music. Drinks are also served in the flower-scented bougainvillea court. The traditional interior dining room at the Bel-Air is one of L.A.'s loveliest restaurants. At lunch you can come by for cold dishes like lobster sausage with basil oil, grilled salmon with lemon vinaigrette, as well as sandwiches, egg dishes, and full entrees—most of them Italian or seafood selections. At dinner there are such entrees as Muscovy duck with tangerine-essenced sauce, and loin of lamb Wellington baked in filo, ranging from $20 to $35.

---

9. Sherman Oaks

FIRST CLASS

The **Valley Hilton,** 15433 Ventura Blvd., Sherman Oaks, CA 91403 (tel. 818/981-5400, or toll free 800/248-0446, 800/356-

6196 in California), is well situated in the heart of the valley, at the crossroads of two major freeways, San Diego (Hwy. 405) and Ventura (Hwy. 101). It boasts a heated rooftop swimming pool, Jacuzzi and sundeck, plus the use of a fitness center one block away (hotel guests pay a $5 daily use fee). The Valley Hilton has 216 spacious rooms, attractively decorated and with new and remodeled bathrooms. Accommodations are equipped with color TVs, direct-dial telephones, "pollen-free" heat and air conditioning, and private balconies. Fine dining is available at the ground floor Orion Café and Lounge. Especially popular is the sumptuous Sunday brunch. The Valley Hilton is near NBC, Universal Studios, Magic Mountain, Griffith Park, Hollywood, and Beverly Hills. Singles are $95 to $130, doubles $120 to $145. Be sure to ask about special discount plans.

10. Van Nuys

MODERATE

Carriage Inn, 5525 Sepulveda Blvd., Van Nuys, CA 91411 (tel. 818/787-2300, or toll free 800/854-2608, 800/542-6082 in California), is on "motel row," near the San Diego Freeway (Hwy. 405) at Burbank Boulevard. It's a super structure, with a seemingly endless maze of accommodations. In the middle is a small swimming pool, a Jacuzzi, a coffeeshop and dining room, and a cocktail bar, which features nightly entertainment. The 185 air-conditioned rooms are spacious, designed skillfully in a contemporary fashion, with color TVs, direct-dial phones, tub/shower baths, and small sitting areas. Singles and doubles are priced at $65.

11. Studio City

MODERATE

Sportsmen's Lodge, 12825 Ventura Blvd. (at Coldwater Canyon Avenue), Studio City, CA 91604 (tel. 818/769-4700, or toll free 800/821-8511, 800/821-1625 in California). Movie, TV, and recording industry people all know about the Sportsmen's Lodge. Out in the Valley, it is so near to many of the studios that actors often make it their second home. Mel Tillis, Brooke Shields, Mr. T., John Denver, and Charlton Heston are among the many celebs who have stayed here. A major asset is its adjoining restaurant, one of the finest in the San Fernando Valley. The rooms are set back from the busy highway, and many of them open onto a central playland-garden center. A bridge, a pond, rock gardens, a waterfall, lush semitropical plantings, a swimming pool—everything makes for a romantic setting. Although built some years ago, the rooms have been refurbished, and most of them have private lanai balconies or patios. Each has direct-dial telephone and color TV. Regular rooms are $90 to $100 single, $100 to $110 double; poolside executive studios are $146 single, $151 double. Suites begin at $275. Airport limousines ply the route to and from the hotel and the Burbank airport.

12. Pasadena

FIRST CLASS

The **Pasadena Hilton,** 150 S. Los Robles Ave. (at the corner of Cordova Street), Pasadena, CA 91101 (tel. 818/577-1000, or toll free 800/445-8667), is a 13-story hostelry crowned by a rooftop restaurant. Fifteen minutes from downtown Los Angeles, it's only a block and a half south of Colorado Boulevard, famed for its Rose Parade. Rooms were recently redecorated in soft earth tones. Some have beds with elaborate high headboards; all have spacious bath, refrigerator, and color TV with in-room movies.

Singles range from $108 to $135; doubles, from $123 to $150. The higher figures are for accommodations with king-size beds and balconies. One-bedroom suites cost $250 to $375. You can dine in Skylights, overlooking the entire San Gabriel Valley, or dance and enjoy live entertainment in the adjoining Slicks Night Club. Breakfast is served in the ground-level French-style Café Madagascar, and a lobby bar called Fanny's is a favorite rendezvous during Happy Hour. Other facilities include an outdoor swimming pool and parking; tennis and golf are nearby.

The **Huntington Hotel,** 1401 S. Oak Knoll (at Wentworth Drive, about three-quarters of a mile north of Huntington Drive), Pasadena, CA 91109 (tel. 818/792-0266, or toll free 800/822-1777), had reigned supreme with conservative dignity since 1907 as one of the great old hotels of Southern California. Families from the East used to come out for the winter in their private railway cars. There are 23 landscaped acres, which include the Japanese and Horseshoe gardens. The hotel was built by Gen. Marshall Wentworth, who wanted to embody "a dream." Henry H. Huntington, the Pacific Electric Railway tycoon, acquired it in 1914 and renamed it "The Huntington."

The main hotel is closed; however, the Huntington is now being operated as a small, quaint country inn and handsome cottages on or about the grounds are available. One-bedroom accommodations range from $165 to $250.

MODERATE

The **Saga Motor Hotel,** 1633 E. Colorado Blvd. (between Allan and Sierra Bonita), Pasadena, CA 91106 (tel. 818/795-0431), is about a mile from the Huntington Library and reasonably close to Pasadena City College, Cal Tech, and the Jet Propulsion Lab. It's also well within striking distance of the Rose Bowl. But the bottom line is that the Saga has, by far, the most attractive rooms I've seen for the price. The very inviting, sunlit, and spotlessly clean reception area reflects this—there are lovely wicker armchairs with orange cushions, teal carpeting, a TV, ficus trees, and greenery (albeit not from Mother Nature), and a very helpful desk person.

The rooms are comfortable and nicely decorated—beige carpeting, light walls, brass beds, blue and white checked spreads, and a blue and white tile bath with both shower and tub. Amenities include cable color TV and, of course, a phone. A number of the rooms are located in a single-story building surrounding a pool; the remainder are in a small three-story building with some rooms overlooking the pool and others a quiet street at the rear of the building. My preference would be a room by the pool. The pool is heated year round and is surrounded by a wide sundeck with comfortable chaises.

There also is a large suite available on the third floor, comfortably furnished with a couch and oversize cocktail table, a small refrigerator, dining table for two, handsome upholstered club chairs, and a king-size brass bed. It has a small balcony with just enough furniture to relax in and have a mid-day or after-dinner libation.

Single rates are $55, doubles, $57; one or two persons with a king-size bed $59, including a refrigerator; suite as described above is $75. Complimentary coffee and doughnuts are included in the rates.

13. Airport Hotels

FIRST CLASS

One of the nicest airport hotels is the **Sheraton Plaza La Reina,** 6101 W. Century Blvd. (near Sepulveda Boulevard), Los Angeles, CA 90045 (tel. 213/642-1111, or toll free 800/325-3535). Its 810 guest rooms are tastefully decorated, with predominantly dark-green and burgundy color schemes, brass accents, upholstered rattan furnishings, and upholstered headboards that coordinate beautifully with the bedspreads and drapes. A live plant in every room is a nice touch. The carpeted baths have marble countertops and tub/shower combinations. Other amenities include direct-dial phone, color TVs with three free entertainment channels, and built-in digital alarm clocks. A complimentary newspaper is provided daily. Other features include an outdoor heated pool and spa, exercise rooms with Universal gym equipment, a unisex beauty salon, self-service laundry, and several boutiques and gift shops. There's a 24-hour shuttle bus service between the airport and the hotel, and scheduled trips are provided to the Manhattan Village Shopping Center and the beach. A car-rental agency is also located on the premises.

Restaurant facilities are overseen by European-trained René Lannoy, and the results happily are far above what one might expect at an airport hotel. Facilities include the Plaza Brasserie, an airy, contemporary café, open from 6 a.m. to midnight, and Landry's, open for lunch and dinner, where the focus is on steak, chops, and seafood, including a sushi bar. Drinks (and some great hors d'oeuvres) can be enjoyed in Zeno's or in the Plaza Lounge in the lobby. Room service is available around the clock.

Singles at the Plaza La Reina are $100 to $145; doubles, $120 to $165; suites begin at $300.

Los Angeles Airport Marriott, 5855 W. Century Blvd., Los Angeles, CA 90045 (tel. 213/641-5700, or toll free 800/228-9290), is also near the International Airport. It offers more than 1,000 guest rooms, each with bedside remote-control color TV, AM/FM radio, digital alarm clock, climate control, and oversize beds. Ironing boards, irons, and hair dryers are readily available. Accommodations display a warm use of textiles and colors, and most of them are commodious enough to have sitting areas. Many have private balconies or lanais. Singles go for $110 to $160, and doubles run $120 to $180. Suites begin at $275. The Marriott has a gigantic free-form pool plus a whirlpool and a "swim-up bar" and cabaña for refreshments, as well as a health club and concierge desk.

Dining is an event. There are many restaurants and lounges from which to choose. The rooftop lounge, the Hangar Room, offers entertainment and a panoramic view. The Fairfield Inn is a coffeeshop with live trees creating a garden ambience. The Lobby Bistro serves buffet breakfasts, lunches, and dinners featuring a "California Lite" menu low in sodium, cholesterol, and calories. The Capriccio offers Continental cuisine and exhibition cookery in a Mediterranean atmosphere. Gammons is the Marriott's million-dollar luxury lounge for dancing. It has a natural look with more than 100 plants overhead, and its facilities include two dance floors, comfortable conversation pits, four backgammon areas, a large bar, and an immense TV screen for patrons to view sporting events and other programs of special import.

Finally, the Marriott provides courtesy limousine service to and from the airport and has parking space for over 1,000 cars.

RESTAURANTS OF LOS ANGELES

Los Angeles is one of the world's premier restaurant cities, almost as diverse in its range of ethnic eateries as New York. Its restaurants are exciting and utterly delightful, many of them taking advantage of the fine Southern California climate with outdoor seating, the rest creating unique and imaginative interiors with more aesthetic sophistication than gimmickry.

In the last decade or so Angelenos have become more knowledgeable about their food. They eat well and love to discuss restaurants and what appears to be a continually changing chef scene. Dining places are a major part of the star system and the status scene—you are where you eat, what you eat, and more important, you are where you are seated. Almost every plush dining establishment has its "A" tables and its social-outcast sections. Unless you're rich and famous, you might as well decide you're above such snobbery; after all, no matter where you sit the food's the same. And no matter where you go, if it's good—from sleazy-but-great hamburger joints to bastions of haute cuisine—you're likely to see the stars. Part of the fun of L.A. dining is stargazing—it adds glamour, and glamour is a big element in L.A.'s dynamic dining experience.

The restaurants I've chosen below offer great food, ambience, and overall enjoyable dining—at all price ranges and in a wide variety of ethnic categories.

1. The Top Restaurants

The yardstick was demanding, but the following restaurants qualified as some of the finest in Greater Los Angeles. They're expensive—but worth it! Expect to pay at least $70 per person for a complete meal, though your tab could run much higher. These restaurants offer not only some of the best food in the city, but some of the most charming and/or spectacular settings as well. Let a meal at one of these restaurants be a night on the town. And don't necessarily plan to do anything else that evening, even if you can afford it, as you may want to linger a while. Reservations are, of course, imperative at all the restaurants in this category. If dinner tabs are too high for your budget, check to see if the restaurant that appeals is open for lunch, when you can get by for half the price or less.

The unrivaled citadel of haute cuisine in Los Angeles since its opening in 1975 is **L'Ermitage,** 730 N. La Cienega Blvd., just north of Melrose Place (tel. 213/652-5840).

The owner, Dora Fourcade, has further enhanced the reputation of L'Ermitage for its cuisine and exquisite interior design. Since its inception, the restaurant has maintained its rigorous standards, ensuring that only the very finest ingredients go into the preparation of any dish. The wine list (all 12 pages) also reflects this pursuit of quality.

The delicate pastel-colored dining area here is a masterpiece of understated elegance, reminiscent of private dining rooms in plush Parisian homes. Tables are set with flowers, Christofle silver, and Villeroy and Boch china. Luscious pastries and cheeses are displayed in glass and silver carts made by Christofle. Lavish floral arrangements, Persian rugs on parquet floors, and a wood-burning fireplace create a warm and sparkling atmosphere. In addition to the interior rooms, there's a patio in back with a fountain and plants under a domed glass skylight.

The menu changes seasonally. Since the light pastry at L'Ermitage is not to be believed, you would do well to begin with an hors d'oeuvre of puff pastry filled with seasonal selections, perhaps tender stalks of young asparagus. On a recent visit, the entrees included roasted squab on a bed of green cabbage and fresh foie gras; Maine lobster with green onions and julienne of mushrooms served with potato purée; and striped bass à la Viennoise with mushrooms and fresh tomatoes served with saffron angel hair pasta.

Whatever you order, pace yourself to leave room for an unforgettable dessert, like poached pear in red wine and black currant sauce served with a delectable homemade vanilla ice cream set in a delicate pastry shell, or a wonderful apple tart served on a very thin and flaky crust. L'Ermitage has one of the best cheese selections in Los Angeles. Still, the ultimate treat would be one of the wonderful dessert soufflés, Grand Marnier or chocolate.

Expect dinner to cost about $65 to $70 per person. L'Ermitage is open Monday through Saturday for dinner from 6:30 to 10 p.m. Reservations are suggested.

Jimmy Murphy, former maître d' at the prestigious Beverly

Hills Bistro, went out on his own a few years ago with **Jimmy's,** 201 Moreno Dr., near Santa Monica Boulevard in Beverly Hills (tel. 213/879-2394). Well, not exactly on his own; Johnny Carson and Bob Newhart were among his backers.

His restaurant is a beauty, from the Baccarat crystal chandeliers to the Limoges china table settings. The predominant color is a muted gray-green enhanced by exquisite fabrics used as wall coverings. One wall of windows overlooks a garden terrace where you can dine al fresco under white canvas umbrellas. And, of course, there are plentiful arrangements of fresh flowers on the tables and in Chinese urns here and there.

The decor is matched by the high quality of the cuisine. A dinner here might begin with an hors d'oeuvre of assorted shellfish, or perhaps you'd prefer the pheasant pâté with truffles. It's not easy to choose the entree when the likes of lobster in cognac sauce, filet mignon sautéed with cognac, green pepper, and cream, and filet of sole with orange butter are among the offerings, at $22 to $30. Leave room for one of the pastry chef's dessert masterpieces—you'll see them sumptuously displayed around an ice sculpture as you come in.

If Jimmy's is too pricey for you at dinner, come for lunch when you might make a meal of the cold lobster salad or salad niçoise with a glass of wine, perhaps followed by an order of Camembert and a pot of espresso. Entrees and lunch salads cost $15 to $22.

Lunch is served weekdays from 11:30 a.m. to 2:45 p.m., and dinner Monday to Saturday from 6 p.m. to midnight, with piano bar entertainment from 8 p.m. Reservations are essential.

Le Restaurant, 8475 Melrose Pl., off La Cienega Boulevard, West Hollywood (tel. 213/651-5553), is a stylish remake of an old-fashioned stucco bungalow. Drive up slowly or you may miss it.

The front garden is enclosed by terracotta walls, and you enter through a black wrought-iron gate, passing pear trees on either side. Inside there are several intimate dining rooms, which have been occupied by such stars as Kirk Douglas, Valerie Harper, and Dinah Shore.

Diners sit on bentwood chairs at pink-covered tables set with Limoges china. Plants are suspended from a skylight ceiling and exquisite flower arrangements are placed here and there. Lattice-work adorns the treillage room; elsewhere oak-paneled walls are hung with delightful watercolors by C. Terechkovitch. Tables are divided from one another by etched-glass panels.

The menu is classically French haute cuisine. Dinner entrees range between $20 and $34. You have 19 scrumptious hors d'oeuvres from which to choose. Perhaps lobster bisque or foie gras de Strasbourg. Main dishes include such delights as whitefish à l'estragon. For dessert, *les pâtisseries du chef* are most recommended.

Dinner is served Monday through Saturday from 6 to 10:30 p.m.

The Windsor, 3198 W. 7th St., corner of Catalina Street, in mid–Wilshire Los Angeles (tel. 213/382-1261), is the restaurant that—deservedly so—has won awards for excellence for more than 35 years in a row. It may have something to do with having the same uncompromising owner all that while. At night, the area surrounding it is relatively dead, but don't let that deter you, it's well worth the trek downtown. Upon entering you step down into a sunken restaurant, the domain of owner Ben Dimsdale's Continental cuisine. The atmosphere is sort of clubby English, with rich walnut paneling, stained glass windows, and an impressive display of oil paintings. At your table you'll be presented with a lavish à la carte menu with loads of selections. And there's a wine list to match. Whatever you choose will be excellent, and served to you tableside from a cart in the traditional manner.

Dinner is served Monday through Saturday from 4:30 to 11 p.m. You might begin with an hors d'oeuvre of smoked salmon, a beautifully presented seafood platter, or marrow bordelaise. Specialties include steak Diane, veal chop Florentine *en croute,* tournedos of beef, and a considerable list of pastas. Entrees range in price from $16 to $30. For dessert it's a hard choice between baked Alaska and soufflé Grand Marnier, or a variety of delectable pastries. In total, dinner for two averages about $80, without wine. However, there is a complete pre-theater dinner served from 5 to 7:30 p.m. for $25. À la carte lunches, served weekdays from 11:30 a.m. to 3:30 p.m., are less expensive, and a full meal can be had for $20. The de jour lunch is excellent at $17.50. Tuesday through Saturday evening, soft piano music adds to your dining pleasure. Reservations are a must.

Chasen's, 9039 Beverly Blvd., at Doheny Drive, Los Angeles (tel. 213/271-2168). According to Pauline Kael, Orson Welles threw a temper tantrum at Chasen's and "inspired" Herman J. Mankiewicz to write *Citizen Kane.* This is but one of the legends spinning around this long-enduring favorite, which began as a chili parlor, then went on to become a theatrical tradition. Movie stars *still* dine here, which is why you may see a line of photographers near the door.

The warm personal style of Maude Chasen, widow of the restaurant's founder, creates a pleasant atmosphere. The main dining room has beamed ceilings, rich wood paneling, soft lighting, and plush red tufted-leather booths. The menu has ascended the culinary scale since chili days; Chasen's now serves a wide selection of Continental dishes. You might begin a meal with an ounce of beluga caviar, escargots bourguignonne, or assorted seafood on ice. A wide choice of entrees includes Chasen's special hobo steak (not listed on the menu), veal bone chop, or rack of lamb, for $29 to $30. (Everything is à la carte.) And they're still famous for their chili (said to be the world's most expensive)—Liz Taylor has it sent to her. You can finish up with banana or strawberry shortcake, for which Chasen's is also renowned.

Open for dinner only, from 6 p.m. till 1 a.m. nightly, except Monday. Chasen's now accepts only American Express.

The Bistro, 246 N. Canon Dr., at Dayton Way, Beverly Hills (tel. 213/273-5633), has been for over 25 years one of L.A.'s most "in" places for private parties, as well as for the movie and society colony. The restaurant is like a stylized version of the justly famed Grand Véfour in Paris, with elegance and charm. Large floral displays adorn the oak bar, mirrored walls alternate with lovely hand-painted panels of classical motif, food is lushly displayed, and a rosy glow emanates from multishaded chandeliers, art nouveau torches, and candles. If your table isn't ready, you can always perch on a bar stool near the entrance.

You'll find some of the finest soups in town—not only the superb lobster bisque for which the restaurant is well known, but some other interesting beauties such as cream of watercress and an outstanding mussel soup. When it comes to appetizers, two choices you don't want to overlook are the papillote of salmon and pheasant pâté. Expect entrees to arrive just as ready to be photographed as is much of the clientele. Items change daily, but some of the more interesting entrees are the duck or quail salad, or shrimps and scallops on angel hair pasta with caviar sauce. And if you haven't already surmised it, all the pasta is homemade and fresh. Other choices might include eastern lobster on a bed of tagliatelle noodles, grilled salmon, or goujonette of sole. Throughout dinner, The Bistro assumes a rather comfortable, romantic atmosphere with the soothing, gentle sounds of piano music.

Typical dinner offerings are in the range of $24 to $35. Dinner is served Monday through Saturday from 6 to 10:30 p.m. Reservations are essential, as are jackets.

The **Bistro Garden,** 176 N. Canon Dr., off Wilshire Boulevard (tel. 213/550-3900), is a lovely, comfortable part of the L.A.-Very-Important-People restaurant scene. It's the place to see and be seen—headquarters for the "movers and shakers" and adorned by the "beautiful people." The ambience is appropriately gardenlike and in one corner there's a piano for quiet evening entertainment. During the summer, there is a lovely outside garden where, weather permitting, you can dine under striped umbrellas amid trees and flowering plants.

Lunch at the Bistro Garden features many cold dishes such as papaya filled with shrimp and a salad of cold lobster and vegetables; other choices are omelets, hamburger, and broiled shrimp with mustard sauce. Entrees cost $15 to $24. Don't pass up those desserts on the piano. Variety is always the order of the day. Dinner might begin with an appetizer of pâté maison or marinated herring, and continued with an entree of linguine with clam sauce, paprika goulash, or roast rack of lamb for two, for $22 to $32 per person.

The Bistro Garden is open Monday through Saturday from 11:30 a.m. to 3:30 p.m. for lunch, from 6:30 to 10:30 p.m. for dinner. Dinner only is served on Sunday from 6:30 to 10:30 p.m. Reservations are always essential.

There's a new Bistro Garden, bigger and brighter, at 12950 Ventura Boulevard in the Valley (tel. 818/501-0202).

The Beverly Hills Hotel has had a long-standing relationship with the world of entertainment so it's no surprise that **The Dining Room,** the hotel's new restaurant, 9641 Sunset Blvd. (tel. 213/276-2251), features celebrities in its decor and on its menu. Famous personages are featured in black and white photographs around the room, and their favorite dishes grace the menu.

The Dining Room is an elegant beauty done in soft pastels with comfortable booths, banquettes, and armchairs, with sufficient space between tables to make conversation comfortable. Tables are set with fine china and tableware, candles, and pleasant floral arrangements blending with the pink and green hues long associated with the hotel.

What does the menu list as favorite dishes of celebrities? Delectable selections include Johnny Carson's Lake Superior whitefish, Sophia Loren's vitello tonato, Elizabeth Taylor's chili, and Liza Minnelli's salade de Provence. My choice just happens to coincide with that of James Stewart (actor and poet), who also recognizes the gustatory beauty of sand dabs.

The Dining Room also offers the chef's style of California cuisine with light sauces, California products, the freshest ingredients, including herbs from the hotel's own herb garden, and grilled meats and fish. There is a lengthy list of cold appetizers, among which is a choice of 12 to 15 from the hors d'oeuvres cart. Among the hot first courses is the very popular escargots baked in baby russet potatoes with hot garlic butter. Seafood choices include baked lobster, blackened swordfish, poached salmon, and sautéed sea bass. Meat specialties from the broiler come with your choice of sauce, or you may prefer those featuring the chef's special touch, such as medallions of veal sautéed with creamed chanterelle mushrooms or pan-fried prime sirloin steak prepared with fresh cracked black pepper in a cream and cognac sauce. Entrees range from $19 to $35. Dinner averages $50 to $60 per person without wine.

Complimentary after-dinner truffles accompanied by chocolate-dipped strawberries should not deter you from at least a glance at the dessert choices. There is, of course, Frank Sinatra's favorite creamy New York–style cheesecake, but it is also worth asking about the soufflé maison.

The Dining Room has an excellent selection of domestic and international still and sparkling wines priced from $18 to $250. Particular emphasis is on the California chardonnays and cabernets. California wines by the glass are $4 to $6.50.

The Dining Room is open for dinner Monday through Saturday from 6:30 to 10 p.m. There is unobtrusive piano music throughout dinner. In keeping with the tradition of the Beverly Hills Hotel, telephones are available at each table. Reservations are necessary, as are jackets.

La Scala & Boutique Restaurant, 410 N. Canon Dr., between Santa Monica Boulevard and Brighton Way (tel. 213/275-0579, or 550-8288), is a petite beauty. On the spur of the moment, several years ago Jean Leon created a delightful gourmet boutique and restaurant in Beverly Hills. They fast became the chic celebrity-packed Beverly Hills dining spots. Since then, La Scala and the Boutique have merged, but the patrons are still as fascinating and the cuisine as delicious as ever. Somehow, regardless of their individual style, most of the customers have the look of people in The Business.

The restaurant is easily identified by "La Scala" on the spotless white bowed awnings. And inside faux orange trees are the focal point among dark woods, red leather booths, amber mirrors, soft spot lighting, and fresh flowers. To the rear, you may notice the kitchen behind the glass partition and a small bar with a few seats. And directly above are a number of those Gerald Price caricatures of famous Hollywood faces. Wine bottles are placed strategically around the booths to remind you of the excellent cellar. At noon the clientele arrives in suits, dresses, short-sleeve shirts, warm-up suits, whatever. For dinner, it's less of an eclectic mix. The noise level is minimal, allowing for easy conversation, even though the restaurant is relatively small. If you have a choice, however, seating to the rear is preferred to avoid those grouped at the entrance waiting for tables.

What to eat? For lunch, you might begin with the delicious bean soup with aromatic virgin olive oil, otherwise described as *fagioli alla Toscana con olio santo.* Follow that with the luncheon specialty, Leon's chopped salad (which half the restaurant is usually enjoying). If you want more than a sandwich or a cold plate, two of the best main dishes are the cannelloni "Gigi" and the grilled shrimp marinara. A piece of cheesecake, or some of the delicious homemade ice cream with berries or chocolate, rounds out the meal. Entrees are between $10 and $15. Most salads and soups are in the vicinity of $7 to $10.

As for dinner, you might begin with the extraordinary marinated salmon with white truffle, or, less extravagantly, with prosciutto and melon. Pasta dishes are featured. One of the house specialties is spaghetti *alla checca* with chopped tomatoes, virgin olive oil, garlic, and basil. Beautifully prepared main courses include grilled shrimp or langoustines with white wine, duck sausage with cannelli beans, and spring chicken with rosemary and white wine. There are also specials that change nightly. Entrees range from $11 to $19. A soothing end to the meal is the tiramisu, a rich delight whose key ingredient is mascarpone cheese.

La Scala & Boutique Restaurant is open Monday through Saturday from 11:30 a.m. to 11:30 p.m. There are no reservations for lunch, except for groups of six or more. Reservations are recommended for dinner.

---

2. Hollywood

Dar Maghreb, 7651 Sunset Blvd., with its entrance on Stanley Avenue (tel. 213/876-7651). Save this one for a special occasion—it's not just a meal, it's a ritual Moroccan feast. The magic begins the moment you set foot in Dar Maghreb and find yourself transported from the prosaic world of Sunset Boulevard to a marble-floored patio with an exquisite fountain under an open sky. A kaftaned hostess leads you to the Rabat or Berber Room. The former has high ceilings, painted traditionally in geometric designs. The floors are covered with handmade Rabat carpets upon which silk cushions are strewn. Low sofas line the walls.

The Berber Room is more rustic, done in earth tones, with raw wood-beamed ceilings and Berber rugs on the floor. Both rooms are lovely and authentic to the most minute detail; Berber and Andalusian music play in the background, and there is belly dancing nightly. Your waiter, attired in an authentic servant's costume, can answer any of your questions about the decor, furnishings, or food.

The meal is a multicourse feast, including a choice of chicken, squab, quail, shrimp, lamb, or rabbit, eaten entirely with the hands and hunks of bread (no silverware is given). Everyone in your party partakes of the same dish and, lest you feel squeamish, a server comes and washes everyone's hands in rose-scented water before the meal begins. There are six dinners offered, priced at $19 to $28 per person.

A typical dinner—the Marrakechi Feast—begins with Moroccan salads of cold raw and cooked vegetables: tomatoes, green peppers with cucumbers, eggplant, and carrots in delicious dressings. You scoop up the salads with fresh-baked bread, and they're so good that you'll be tempted to fill up on them. Resist this impulse —more good things are on the way.

Next comes b'stila, an appetizer of shredded chicken, eggs, almonds, and spices in a flaky pastry shell, topped with powdered sugar and cinnamon. This is followed by a tajine of chicken and then couscous with lamb and vegetables. There is also a second entree of lamb and honey. Portions are huge, and it's best to eat slowly, lingering over each course. A bottle of wine helps slow things down, and has an enhancing effect generally. Dessert is a bowl of several kinds of fresh fruit and Moroccan cookies.

At this juncture, the server comes and washes your hands again, using hot towels perfumed with rose water. Dessert is accompanied by mint tea, the pouring of which is quite a performance. I'm always in a state of blissful relaxation after a meal at Dar Maghreb, and like to lean back on the cushions with an after-dinner drink and enjoy leisurely conversation. Dinner is served nightly from 6 p.m. Reservations are recommended.

The **Musso & Frank Grill**, 6667 Hollywood Blvd., a few blocks west of Cahuenga (tel. 213/467-7788), is billed as the oldest restaurant in Hollywood. Everybody goes there and they're all treated with the same efficient brusqueness. It's the kind of place people return to again and again for the comfortable, rich ambience, superb service, and consistently good food that's been served here for over 70 years.

The setting is traditional—beamed oak ceilings, red leather booths, mahogany room dividers (the kind with coat hooks), and soft lighting emanating from wall sconces and chandeliers with tiny shades.

The menu is grand, and everything—soups, salads, bread, vegetables—is à la carte. Try the shrimp Louie, perhaps along with some Camembert that comes with crusty bread and butter. For heartier fare, there's the veal scaloppine marsala, roast spring lamb, or broiled lobster. There's a new menu each day. Entrees average $10 to $30. Sandwiches and omelets are also available. There's an extensive liquor and wine selection on the back of the menu.

The grill is open Monday through Saturday from 11 a.m. to 11 p.m.; closed Sunday.

Emilio's, 6602 Melrose Ave., at Highland Avenue (tel. 213/935-4922), is an award-winning Italian restaurant with a celebrity clientele. True Italian regional cuisine is served in an abundance of atmosphere, what with a central fountain bathed in colored lights, Italian music in the background, brick archways, marble columns, and stained-glass windows. Somehow, it all combines to create a romantic ambience, enhanced by very good food and very Italian waiters. I particularly like to sit in the balcony area, overlooking the scene below.

At Emilio's, forget your budget and your diet; plan to order lavishly and savor every bite. You might begin with the antipasti ($5 to $10) of mussels blessed with spicy tomato sauce and garlic, or the scallops with oil and garlic. As to your second course ($10 to $24), the *brodetto Adriadico* (a fisherman's stew) is heartily recommended, as are the veal entrees. However, there is a magnificent pasta selection, all homemade and prepared with delectable sauces. The choices are difficult. It's hard to ignore the linguine with shrimp and lobster cream sauce, or the rondelli stuffed with ricotta, mortadella, and spinach, and sauteed with mushrooms and cream. If you want to ease up on calories, try the homemade noodles with sun-dried tomatoes, baby corn, carrots, and peas. From time to time, you may find roast suckling pig or osso bucco on the menu.

The other desserts here are probably wonderful, but I've never been able to resist the creamy zabaglione ($14 for two). And do not miss Emilio's cappuccino—it's incredible.

Emilio's is open for lunch Thursday and Friday from 11:30 a.m. to 2:30 p.m., and dinner nightly, and offers a country-style Sunday buffet, from 5 p.m. to midnight.

Ristorante Chianti & Chianti Cucina, 7383 Melrose Ave., at Martel Avenue (tel. 213/653-8333), was founded in 1938 by the well-known New York restaurateur Romeo Salta. Then syndicated news columnist Ed Sullivan discovered Chianti and wrote an entire column praising the place. Walter Winchell, Louella Parsons, Clark Gable, W.C. Fields, Groucho Marx, and many others flocked to Chianti, and it's been a popular haunt ever since. It is considered the oldest northern Italian restaurant in Los Angeles, though Chianti Cucina did not arrive on the scene until 1984. The restaurant operates as a single entity, but it offers two completely different dining experiences and menus.

Ristorante Chianti is traditional Italian in appearance—quiet, intimate, complete with red velvet seating and sepia-tone murals—but the food is tastefully contemporary. A variety of hot and cold appetizers range from fresh handmade mozzarella and prosciutto, or the lamb carpaccio with asparagus, to my favorite, marinated grilled eggplant filled with goat cheese, arugula, and sun-dried tomatoes. As to entrees, the homemade pasta is exceptional yet deliciously untraditional: black tortelloni filled with fresh salmon and blessed with lobster sauce, and giant ravioli filled with spinach, ricotta, quail eggs, and touched with shaved black truffle, for example. Other entrees include fresh fish and prawns, poultry, and a fine selection of meats such as the veal scaloppine with porcini mushroom sauce, a grilled veal loin chop, a superb filet mignon with

Pasta and Puccini

Sarno's Caffè Dell'Opera, 1714 N. Vermont, near Hollywood Boulevard (tel. 213/662-3403), is a joyous place where robust Italian cuisine is served and, as you may have guessed, opera is sung. Owner and host Alberto Sarno, once an aspiring opera singer himself, runs a charming little establishment, darkly lit and cluttered, crammed with tablesful of happy customers.

The food here is terrific, and very much like the ambience— robust, unpretentious, and delightful. Among the specialties are the traditional veal parmigiana, chicken cacciatore, and fresh river trout in white sauce. There's also a wide variety of pasta dishes, all served al dente; fettuccine Alfredo and tagliatelle are two of the standouts. A substantial antipasto is $9. Pasta dishes cost $8 and $10, and Italian meat dishes—complete with salad, French roll, and beverage—cost $10 to $12. Lunches are lighter, and about half the price. Pizza is $10 to $12, depending on the heaped toppings. For those with a really hearty appetite, there are complete dinners for $13 to $17, including soup, salad, roll, vegetable, pasta, beverage, and dessert. If you want something light, there are salads and sandwiches for $6 to $9. And of course there's plenty of vino and a host of Italian coffees to choose from. Pastries and spumoni are excellent.

About 7:30 each evening, the fun begins. Alberto, the waiters and waitresses, and anyone else who's so inclined take turns singing opera, old Italian favorites, and American ballads and show tunes. There's a piano in the front dining room/bar that accompanies many of the singers. Regulars and newcomers are quick to join in the fun, humming and singing along. It all adds up to a delightful evening, in the company of strangers who, by evening's end, seem more like friends.

Sarno's is open seven days a week: Sunday to Thursday from 11 a.m. to 11 p.m., Friday and Saturday till 1 a.m.

marsala and gorgonzola sauce, or a deliciously seasoned rack of lamb.

On the other hand, the bright, bustling, attractive Chianti Cucina is the contemporary Italian—designed to allow patrons to feel that they're dining right in the kitchen, much as honored guests are traditionally allowed to do in restaurants in Italy. The Cucina menu changes frequently but consistently features exceptional antipasti, pasta, and a fine entree selection though somewhat more limited than that for the Ristorante Chianti. Among the first courses, my choice for the day was the smoked duck with pearls of mozzarella and steamed spinach lightly touched with a Mediterranean dressing. And for carpaccio lovers, there's beef filet with alfalfa sprouts and a bit of parmesan. The pasta dishes range from the lobster- and shrimp-filled tortelli seasoned with saffron in a lovely cream sauce, to the simple pasta dumplings with roasted pepper sauce, basil, and parmesan. The entrees always include seafood such as fresh fish of the day, or for the hearty eater there's the osso buco braised with vegetables and wine, or perhaps the roasted rabbit stuffed with lamb loin, rosemary and garlic. Entrees at both restaurants average $13 to $19, antipasti $6 to $8.

As for desserts on either menu, you can always have fresh berries in season or the elegant cannoli, but why pass up the magnificent tiramisu?

An award-winning wine list is an additional bonus. There is also a full bar.

Ristorante Chianti is open nightly from 5:30 to 11:30 p.m.; Chianti Cucina is open Monday through Saturday from 11:30 a.m. to midnight, Sunday from 5 p.m. to midnight. Reservations are essential.

Tom Bergin's Tavern, 840 S. Fairfax Ave., just south of Wilshire Boulevard at Barrows Drive (tel. 213/936-7151), is headquarters for L.A.'s Irish community and, like many an Irish bar, a famous gathering place for sports writers, athletes, and rabid fans. The tavern celebrated its 50th anniversary in 1986—remarkable for any Los Angeles restaurant.

This was the first L.A. restaurant to charter buses to pro football games—they still do, and hold 230 seats to the games reserved five years in advance. I always thought this kind of place existed only in New York and Dublin, but Bergin's has been going strong since 1936. Actors Bing Crosby and Pat O'Brien were early friends of the house.

The dimly lit pub has photos and paintings of Bergin's friends plastered all over richly wood-paneled walls, not to mention some 1,000 cardboard shamrocks attached to the beamed ceiling above the bar. Jack Ohlsen, general manager emeritus, dreamed up the idea of hanging shamrocks to please Saint Patrick—each one bears the name of a favorite customer.

Irish coffee is a house specialty. But you can also sit down to a hearty dinner in a rather charming candlelit dining room where curtained windows, green-clothed tables, and a fireplace create a homey warmth. At dinner a mesquite-charcoal-broiled New York steak with

---

The Best Hot Dog in Town

Pink's Hot Dogs, on the northwest corner of La Brea and Melrose Avenues (tel. 213/931-4223), near the heart of old Hollywood, is the kind of place you wouldn't expect to find in a guidebook. Yet its beef chili dogs at about $2 are justly famous, served with infinite skill. Some 4,000 of these delicious dogs are sold daily between the hours of 7 a.m. and 2:30 a.m. Outdoor tables are placed at the corner, although most people line up and stand while they eat their treats. Pray the bulldozers stay away from this little nugget of a place!

onion rings, garlic-cheese toast, salad, and potato is served. More traditional Irish fare, served with soup or salad and garlic-cheese toast, is Dublin-style corned beef and cabbage with a steamed potato, or chicken Erin, simmered in cream and cider sauce, with bacon, leeks, mushrooms, and rice pilaf. Entrees cost $10.75 to $18.75. Burgers and salads are also listed, and for dessert you can sample the pieman's wares—fresh fruit pies—or imbibe the Bailey's Irish Cream cheesecake.

Lunch is less expensive, with entrees like Irish pot roast served with soup or salad, potato, and garden vegetables ($9.25). You can also get "pub grub," served at the bar, for $5.75 to $7.95.

For the record, Bergin sold the tavern in 1973 to two trusted regulars, Mike Mandekic and T. K. Vodrey, both of whom he knew would stick to traditions.

Bergin's serves lunch from 11 a.m. to 4 p.m. weekdays, and dinner from 4 to 11 p.m. daily. The bar is open till 2 a.m.

Golden Temple, 7910 W. 3rd St., near Fairfax Avenue (tel. 213/655-1891), diagonally across from Farmer's Market, oversees a busy intersection. The interior is rather plain, but hanging plants and stained-glass panels add color. There is a small patio where you can dine.

The chef prepares a special homemade soup and entree each day. It may be a delicious lentil-vegetable soup with chunks of fresh vegetables, followed by lasagne with spinach noodles and a fresh tomato sauce with herbs, or another of their delicious vegetarian entrees. Regular menu items include light fare at $5 to $8, like the Santa Fe enchiladas—two corn tortillas layered with natural cheese, onion, and a mild salsa; it's topped with guacamole and sour cream, and served with refried beans. On the other hand, you might prefer a vegetarian burger topped with sautéed mushrooms and scallion sauce, served with a baked potato and sour cream, and a steamed vegetable plate with rice and sesame sauce. Servings are large, and dinner—priced at $7 to $10—includes soup or salad and homemade bread. If you're not too hungry, you could easily make a meal of a bowl of soup and a guacamole salad or Chinese spring rolls with sweet-and-sour sauce. Fresh juices include carrot, pippin apple, watermelon, and pink grapefruit. Homemade desserts are prepared daily (the aroma as you enter is heavenly) and can be purchased to go.

The lunch menu is similar, but prices are lower.

The Golden Temple is open Monday through Saturday for lunch from 11:30 a.m. to 4 p.m., and for dinner from 5:30 to 10 p.m. weeknights, to midnight on Saturday.

Proximity to CBS Studios alone would probably guarantee **Roscoe's House of Chicken 'n' Waffles,** 1514 N. Gower St., off Sunset Boulevard (tel. 213/466-7453), a celebrity clientele. Its devotees have included Jane Fonda, Stevie Wonder, Eddie Murphy, Flip Wilson, Alex Haley, and the Eagles. The setting is very simpático, with slanted cedar and white stucco walls, changing art exhibits, track lighting overhead, lots of plants, and good music in the background.

Only chicken and waffle dishes are served for $4 to $8 though that includes eggs and chicken livers. A chicken-and-cheese omelet with french fries accompanied by an order of homemade biscuits makes for a unique and delicious breakfast, for $7. A specialty is a quarter of a chicken smothered with gravy and onions, served with waffles or grits and biscuits. You can also get chicken salad and chicken sandwiches. Homemade cornbread, sweet-potato pie, homemade potato salad, greens, and corn on the cob are all available as side orders, and there's wine or beer to have with your meal.

Roscoe's is open Sunday through Thursday from 9 a.m. to 11 p.m., Friday and Saturday till 3 a.m. Cash only. There's another Roscoe's in Los Angeles (mid-city) located at 4907 W. Washington Blvd., at La Brea (tel. 213/936-3730).

At Fairfax and Third Avenues, near West Hollywood and just east of La Cienega, the **Farmer's Market** (tel. 213/933-9211) is the world's most glorified "cafeteria" and indoor/outdoor grocery store. It is jam-packed with produce—not only the home-grown California stuff (those sun-ripened oranges, grapefruits, and dates), but imported goods as well (pickled Georgia freestone peaches, Norwegian cod roe, even beef-blood pudding, and Japanese pinhead gunpowder—a type of green tea, each leaf rolled into a pellet). Wheeling around wooden carts along with Beverly Hills matrons is only part of the adventure. (For shopping recommendations, see Chapter VII.)

The market dates from 1934, when 18 farmers, some of them right out of *Grapes of Wrath*, started hauling in fresh produce on the spot and selling it from the backs of their trucks. Who knows when the first Jane Darwell predecessor decided to fry a chicken, bake some raisin bread, and whip up an old-fashioned potato salad the way the folks back home in Oklahoma like it? Eventually, tables were set up under olive trees, at which customers could consume the prepared food.

You can still dine al fresco at the many outdoor tables, first having selected a meal from the 30-or-so food stalls. The variety is staggering. Your selections might include fresh fruit juices; barbecued beef, chicken, ribs, or Texas chili; tacos, tamales, enchiladas, and the like; waffles; a choice of hundreds of cheeses; smoked fish; blintzes; hot roasted chestnuts; fruit salads, vegetable salads, seafood salads; roast meats; seafood entrees; pizza; fish and chips; burgers; stuffed cabbage; falafel; Italian fare, from eggplant parmigiana to lasagne; nuts; dried and fresh fruits; a bottle of wine to complement your meal; and every dessert you've ever had or dreamed of. You can also dine indoors at regular restaurants like **Du-Par's** (tel. 213/933-8446)—especially famous for their pies—but I prefer the opportunity to concoct wild international combinations of food.

Farmer's Market is open from 9 a.m. to 6:30 p.m. Monday through Saturday, 10 a.m. to 5 p.m. on Sunday. The market begins to get crowded around 11 a.m. so I suggest that you begin your excursion when it opens and sustain yourself with a warm doughnut and a cup of cappuccino, or any one of a dozen freshly squeezed juices. Then peruse your options and definitely schedule some time for browsing, sampling, and buying before or after you stop to dine.

---

3. Sunset Strip/West Hollywood

With its boutiques, swank nightclubs, colony of film agents, and plush apartments, Sunset Strip (Sunset Boulevard in West Hollywood) provides all the extremes of everything from drop-in hamburger joints to some of the finest restaurants in Los Angeles. We have already pointed out one of them—Le Restaurant—discussed at the beginning of this chapter.

One of the hottest restaurants in the L.A. area continues to be **Spago,** 8795 Sunset Blvd., with its entrance at 1114 Horn (tel. 213/652-4025). It's the brainchild of Wolfgang Puck, and gorgeously designed by Barbara Lazaroff in white, pink, mauve, and peach with exotic flowers galore. Across the front of the restaurant is a huge picture window, offering a panoramic view of the city. Out back is an enclosed garden patio. The kitchen is open to the diners' view, so you can watch as the chef prepares your meal, to be cooked in the wood-burning oven in the dining room. Pizza is a specialty, though it bears little resemblance to your local parlor variety. You can have a pizza with artichokes, shiitake mushrooms, eggplant and garlic, or duck sausage, tomatoes, basil, and shiitake mushrooms. Or with lox and cream cheese! There's also pasta, like angel-hair noodles with goat cheese and broccoli, or black pepper fettuccine with Louisiana shrimp, toasted garlic, and basil ratatouille, or ravioli filled with lobster. Entrees include roast baby lamb with braised shallots and herb butter, and grilled chicken with garlic and Italian parsley. Entrees range from $20 to $26. Be sure to save room for dessert—the pastry chef prepares some 18 varieties nightly, and these are displayed on the kitchen counter. The food is superb, the place is noisy, and the celebrities are many. You'll enjoy every minute of it.

Spago is open nightly from 6 to 11:30 p.m. Due to its popularity, it's necessary to make reservations *three to four weeks in advance.*

The **Shanghai Winter Garden,** 5651 Wilshire Blvd., corner of Hauser Boulevard (tel. 213/934-0505), is where you'll find surroundings as elegant as the very fine food. It's one of my favorite Los Angeles Chinese restaurants. Tables are covered in cheerful pink; an archway depicting a phoenix and dragon, set in an intricately carved teak wall, separates the dining areas; Chinese paintings and woodcarvings adorn the walls; and overhead are large tasseled Chinese lamps. It all combines to create a very graceful effect, and the ambience is enhanced by taped Chinese music.

The menu offers a wide selection—more than 100 entrees to choose from including a classic Peking Duck (order one day in advance). Among the specialties are diced fried chicken sautéed with spinach; shrimp with bamboo shoots and green peas in a delicious

Beansprouts Alfresco

The Source, 8301 W. Sunset Blvd., at Sweetzer Avenue (tel. 213/656-6388), is a small Sunset Strip establishment where natural, mostly vegetarian fare is enhanced by ingenious simple spicing, and every dish served seems brimming over with vitamins and vitality. This is the typical-of-L.A., bean-sprouts-on-everything eatery that Woody Allen used in *Annie Hall* to depict his skeptical East Coast view of Southern California. And items like the magic mushrooms with scallions, bean sprouts, Swiss chard, grated cheddar, and haziki seaweed are no doubt of the variety for which he'd substitute a pastrami on rye any day. Ditto the eggplant with grated mushrooms and olives, sautéed in garlic butter, topped with grated cheddar, pignole nuts, and tomato sauce, and served with brown rice. Much, but not all, of the food is vegetarian; chicken and fish are served. All of the entrees cost $9 to $11 and come with homemade soup or salad and a basket of whole-wheat rolls and butter. For dessert, there's carrot cake, not to mention brown-rice pudding with dates, cinnamon, cream, and raisins. Also available are large, meal-in-themselves salads, sandwiches, crêpes, soup, vegetarian burgers and hamburgers, for $5 to $7. Drinks range from yogurt shakes to the Hi-Potency Drink (orange juice, banana, wheat germ and honey; or with milk and molasses). Of course there's always beer or wine. Woody Allen notwithstanding, everything served is as yummy as it is good for you, and the patio with its umbrella tables is one of L.A.'s most congenial dining spots.

Open Monday through Friday 8 a.m. to midnight, Saturday and Sunday 9 a.m. to midnight.

---

sauce with crisp sizzling rice; crispy duckling made with five spicy ingredients and served with Chinese bread; and crushed white meat of chicken sautéed with diced ham, pine nuts, and green peas. Entrees are priced at $10 to $25. For dessert, fried banana or apple serves four. As you can see, this is a place for culinary adventures. Shanghai Winter Garden also offers daily lunch specials—eggroll, fried rice, and entree—for about $10.

Shanghai Winter Garden is open Monday through Saturday for lunch from 11:30 a.m. to 3 p.m., for dinner nightly from 4 to 10:30 p.m. Reservations are accepted.

On the one hand there's "gringo food"—fiery, lots of cheese, sour cream, beans, tamales—on the other there's the fine and delicious Mexican cooking of **Antonio's,** 7472 Melrose, West Hollywood, CA 90046 (tel. 213/655-0480). Antonio's is the picture of a very sedate and proper Mexican restaurant—no reds, yellows, and greens here, rather the quiet tans and browns reminiscent of a Spanish heritage. The warmth comes from the very gracious welcome and attention you will receive, and the hospitable guidance you'll get if you've never had authentic Mexico City–style cuisine. For those concerned with calories, unlike its "gringo-style" counterpart, the true cuisine of Mexico City is delicious, perfectly seasoned, high in protein, low in cholesterol, and lean on the calories, which may account for the number of celebrities and dignitaries who dine here. These beautiful figure-flattering dishes feature a variety of fresh seafood and meats with exotic vegetables, and the majority of entrees are steamed, rather than fried. If fiery tonsil-torture is not your idea of a fine dining experience, you're going to savor the skillful blends of herbs and spices that distinguish the subtle, imaginative Mexican cuisine at Antonio's.

Dinner entrees ($13 to $19) are light and unusual, such as costillas de perco en chipotle, or to rephrase it—flavorful spareribs served in a chile and herb sauce. Antonio's chayote relleno is a delicate dish, featuring the tasty chayote squash filled with lean ground beef, ricotta cheese, and spices in a light tomato sauce.

The menu changes daily, but fresh fish is available at all times. When I ate there, the catch of the day was delicious, steamed with a colorful bouquet of beautifully seasoned vegetables. As a matter of fact, if you've never truly enjoyed fish, Antonio's can completely change your attitude. Chicken is served for a variety of tastes— Guadalajara-style in tamales stuffed with assorted fresh vegetables, or chicken stewed in a delicate green sauce of tomatillos, green peppers, and exotic spices. All entrees are accompanied by green corn tortillas. If you're really counting, most dishes have fewer calories than a hamburger.

Antonio's offers the opportunity to explore and discover a delicious variety of tastes—cabbage leaves stuffed with a mixture of ground beef, chorizo, and herbs graced with chipotle sauce. Half orders of evening specials are available for the undecided.

All this is not to say that if you crave cheese enchiladas, a hamburger, tacos, or enchiladas with guacamole, you won't find it; but the true beauty of dining at Antonio's rests with the simple seafood, meat, and chicken dishes combined with the freshest of vegetables and the extraordinary seasonings.

A cozy wine room, lined with vintage bottles, is available for a small dinner party.

Antonio's serves lunch Tuesday through Friday from noon to 3 p.m.; dinner from 5 to 11 p.m.; Saturday and Sunday from 2 to 11 p.m.

A second Antonio's has opened on Santa Monica's "restaurant row" at 1323 Montana Ave. and 14th Street (tel. 213/395-2815).

Perhaps the granddaddy of all the beef establishments is **Lawry's The Prime Rib,** 55 N. La Cienega Blvd., just north of Wilshire Boulevard (tel. 213/652-2827). Here, in a simulated atmosphere of an oversize old English inn, you'll be served some of the finest prime ribs in Los Angeles. You can ask for a before-dinner drink at a pewter-topped, wood-paneled bar. In all, the restaurant suggests a huge, furnished country home with Persian-carpeted oak floors and valuable oil paintings on the walls. Some Angelenos think of Lawry's as their private club.

The restaurant does one thing—roast prime ribs of beef—and it does it fantastically well! The management doesn't dissipate its energies trying to offer a variety of dishes.

There are four beef cuts, sliced to order at your table, each super-delicious: the "English" cut, the "Lawry" cut, the "California" cut, and the "Diamond Jim Brady" cut, for $16 to $25. The ribs are served with Yorkshire pudding, creamed corn, mashed potatoes, and whipped, creamed horseradish. With each dinner comes the house salad on its iced "spinning bowl," with a French sherry dressing. There is, in addition, a good wine list, featuring many California labels. For dessert, there's chocolate pecan pie.

The restaurant is open for dinner Monday to Thursday from 5 to 11 p.m., on Friday and Saturday from 5 p.m. to midnight, and on Sunday from 3 to 10 p.m. Reservations are accepted but not essential.

---

4. Downtown L.A.

Downtown Los Angeles has a seemingly incongruous group of restaurants. Most Angelenos head downtown to sample Chinese and Japanese food in an ethnic setting; however, a few of the choices that follow are for nostalgia fans, holdovers from Los Angeles of yesteryear. All are purveyors of great food.

Music Center Restaurants, 135 N. Grand Ave. (tel. 213/972-7211), are in the Dorothy Chandler Pavilion at the Los Angeles Music Center. As might be expected, the restaurants in this busy group of concert halls and theaters are geared to serve the needs of diners who are often in a rush to make a curtain. If you are interested in a more leisurely meal, plan accordingly, and come before or after the rush.

Otto Rothschilds Bar and Grill (tel. 213/972-7322), located on the ground floor of the Dorothy Chandler Pavilion, celebrates the visual history of the motion picture industry and its stars in an unparalled exhibit. Photographs of stage and screen celebrities, taken by Otto Rothschild over a period of forty years, adorn the walls of this handsome eatery. It's one of the most convenient and attractive downtown spots in which to have breakfast, lunch, dinner, or an after-theater meal. As to breakfast, the restaurant opens at 7 a.m. and offers the traditional egg-plus-whatever repasts as well as some very exceptional omelets including one with crab, avocado, and mushrooms; or you might prefer a "country scramble" of eggs, grilled ham, and country gravy; or the prime New York steak and eggs combination. But after you've decided, take a second look at the menu and the description of the carameled apple pancakes filled with sliced apples and dusted with a hint of cinnamon. How can you resist? Breakfast tabs range from $6 to $10. There's nothing commonplace about lunch, either, whether you opt for the crab and cheddar sandwich grilled on sourdough or Otto's shredded Oriental chicken salad. I, personally, tend to be partial to the appetizers and light entrees such as the Szechuan grilled chicken tenderloins with two dipping sauces, or the prime rib chili served with corn chips. Regular entrees might include the Garden Fettuccine with wild mushrooms, asparagus, sun-dried tomatoes, broccoli, and zucchini; tempura shrimp served with a pungent fruit sauce; or the pan-seared chicken breast served over wild mushrooms. Light entrees average $8, regular entrees about $10. Among the dinner entrees, there are excellent choices from the list of prime meats, seafood, and pastas. A herb-roasted prime rib is served with whipped cream horseradish sauce; the rack of lamb (which I can rarely resist) comes crusted with Dijon herb crumbs; or, if you take your seafood spicy, try the colossal Cajun broiled shrimp. Dinner entrees range from $16 to $28. The after-theater menu is designed to fit the appetite, offering light entrees such as the smoked ham and cheddar omelet, a Rothschild burger, or a salad; and more substantial items such as the prime rib sandwich, pasta, fresh fish, or even the herb-roasted prime rib of beef; all from $12 to $19. The restaurant is open weekdays from 7:30 a.m. to 11 p.m., weekends 11:30 a.m. to 10 p.m. Reservations are essential. The elegant **Pavilion** (tel. 213/972-7333) on the fifth floor of the Dorothy Chandler Pavilion is more formal and the Continental dinner fare (about $17 to $31 including an appetizer buffet) matches the sumptuous decor. Lunch is served Monday through Saturday 11:30 a.m. to 2 p.m., dinner 5:30 to 8:30 p.m. Sunday dinner is served from 5:30 to curtain time, which varies depending upon the performance. A harpist plays nightly. Reservations, especially for before-theater dining, are essential; make them when you get your theater tickets. The **Backstage Cafe** (tel. 213/972-7525), with the same hours as Otto Rothschilds, has cafeteria-style service and offers a variety of light snacks and sandwiches.

The **Pacific Dining Car,** 1310 W. 6th St., at Witmer Street (tel. 213/483-6000), is just a few short blocks from the center of downtown Los Angeles. The restaurant has been authentically decorated to evoke the golden age of rail travel. Walls are paneled in warm mahogany with brass luggage racks (complete with luggage) overhead. Old menus and prints from early railroading days line the walls, and brass wall lamps with parchment shades light some tables.

The atmosphere is warm and friendly, but the main reason for going to any restaurant is the food, and in this the Pacific Dining Car excels. Steaks are prime, aged on the premises, and cooked over a mesquite-charcoal fire. At dinner, top sirloin, a New York steak, fresh seafood, veal, and lamb are all served for $22 to $37. For starters the calamari is excellent, but weight-watchers might prefer the beefsteak-tomato and onion salad.

Prices at lunch are lower, at $19 to $29, and the menu items are basically the same with the exception of hamburger, salads, and linguini. I have consistently enjoyed a perfectly charbroiled boneless breast of chicken, with choice of potato or tomato. There's an outstanding wine list. Desserts are simple fare such as apple pie. Breakfast here is served from 11 p.m. to 11 a.m.

A Budgeteer's Haven

The oldest restaurant (established 1930) in downtown Los Angeles is **Vickman's,** 1228 E. 8th St., off Central Avenue in the produce market (tel. 213/622-3852). During Depression days Vickman's sold a beef dip sandwich for 10¢, less than today's tax on the same item. Nowadays, prices are of course considerably higher, though still low by current standards. Practically unchanged, however, is the decor (or lack thereof): creamy walls, linoleum tile floors, fluorescent lighting, big Formica tables, and wooden booths ranging the walls. For some reason there's a huge scale in one corner. The Vickman's managers are always on the scene making sure the service and food are up to snuff. It is, and their clientele is so loyal it amounts to a cult.

They come for hearty breakfasts, perhaps a Spanish omelet, fresh-baked danish pastries, or the market omelet with fresh mushrooms and shallots, for $6 to $8. Fresh-squeezed orange juice is also available. At lunch there are blackboard specials like cold poached salmon with caper sauce, stuffed pork chops, and boiled chicken. On the other hand, you could order a bagel with cream cheese and lox, a chopped liver sandwich, or a bowl of chili and beans. Leave room for a big hunk of home-baked fresh-fruit (strawberry, peach, etc.) pie with gobs of real whipped cream. It's all cafeteria style with no table service.

Vickman's is open weekdays from 3 a.m. to 3 p.m., on Saturday from 3 a.m. to 1 p.m., and Sunday from 7 a.m. to 1 p.m. No dinner. No credit cards. No reservations.

Open 24 hours a day, seven days a week. Reservations are definitely advised for lunch and dinner. Great food!

Langer's, 704 S. Alvarado St., at 7th Street (tel. 213/483-8050), is a Jewish deli run by the Langer family since 1947. Here the walls are lined not with the usual portraits of stars but with oil paintings of the family—Al Langer cutting pastrami; his wife, Jean, on the other side of the counter buying it; portraits of the Langer grandchildren, etc. It's a big, roomy place with both counter seating and plenty of comfortable brown-leather booths, and the two-window corner location makes it light and airy. Your appetite is whetted as soon as you enter, not only by tantalizing deli aromas but by all the strudel, halvah, salamis, lox, knishes, etc., piled behind and atop the big glass counter.

Since it's not a kosher deli, you can add Swiss cheese (60¢ extra) to your pastrami on rye. (But then how can you improve on the perfection of Langer's pastrami?) You can also order potato pancakes with sour cream and apple sauce or cheese blintzes. There are specials every day, such as stuffed kishka and hot gefilte fish, but even without them the menu is quite comprehensive. Sandwiches and egg dishes cost $6 to $10; hot entrees are $7 to $14. Homemade cakes and pastries for dessert range from apple strudel to strawberry shortcake; they're displayed in a revolving glass case.

Langer's is open seven days from 6:30 a.m. to 11 p.m. There's validated parking a block away at Westlake Avenue and 7th Street.

The **Original Pantry Cafe**, 877 S. Figueroa, at 9th Street (tel. 213/972-9279), has to be one of the most unique restaurants in all of L.A. It has been open 24 hours a day for over 60 years—that's over ½ million hours. And it never closes; they don't even have a key to the front door. The decor is well worn, but let's face it—if you'd been working 24 hours a day for 60 years, your decor might be a bit worn, too. There are shiny cream-colored walls with old patined oil paintings and globe lamps overhead. Big stainless-steel water pitchers and bowls of celery, carrots, and radishes are on every Formica table. In addition to the bowl of raw veggies, you get a big portion of homemade creamy coleslaw and all the homemade sourdough bread and butter you want—a meal in itself before you've even ordered. When you do order, you'll be amazed at the bountiful portions of delicious food set before you by waiters in long flowing aprons.

A Pantry breakfast might consist of a huge stack of hotcakes, big slabs of sweet cured ham, home fries, and a bottomless cup of freshly made coffee, all for under $5. A huge T-bone steak, home fried pork chops, baked chicken, and macaroni and cheese are served later in the day for $6 to $10.

The Pantry is a memorable original—don't miss it.

Philippe The Original, 1001 N. Alameda St., at the corner of Ord Street (tel. 213/628-3781), is where you'll find good old-fashioned value and quality in everything they serve. Don't leave L.A. without stopping here. Philippe's has been around since 1912, which is more than you can say for most restaurants, and they have the best French-dip sandwiches on the lightest, crunchiest French rolls you'll ever sink your teeth into (about $3). There's nothing stylish about the place—it's democracy in action: You stand in line while your sandwich is being assembled with whatever goodies you want on the side, and you carry it to one of several long wooden tables where there are movable stools. French-dip sandwiches consist of roast beef, roast pork, New Zealand lamb, breast of turkey, or ham. In addition, at $1.20 to $2.35 Philippe's serves homemade beef stew prepared daily from fresh vegetables and choice beef, chili and beans, two different soups daily, and pickled pigs' feet (they prepare and serve close to 200 pounds a week), which I love. Desserts include New York–style cheesecake, cream and fruit pies, puddings and custards, and their own baked apples.

Philippe's serves a hearty breakfast from 6 till 10:30 a.m. daily including, as you might expect, eggs with bacon, smoked ham or sausage, fried potatoes, and homemade biscuits; omelets; pancakes; and their special cinnamon-dipped French toast. All the egg dishes can be topped with their zesty homemade salsa. And coffee is included with most breakfast items.

Everything they make at Philippe's is delicious, up to and including the doughnuts and coffee. The only changes I've noticed in the 40-plus years since I first discovered their gastronomic joys are a little less sawdust on the floor and shorter hours. Coffee is still a dime! Beer and wine are available.

Philippe's is open for breakfast, lunch, and dinner daily from 6 a.m. to 10 p.m. Cash only. There's free parking in the rear and a lot across the street.

NEW CHINATOWN

New Chinatown is a miniature Asian community just a few blocks from Olvera Street, three blocks north of Sunset Boulevard. A small slice of Hong Kong, it replaced the former Chinese section, where Union Station now stands. In many ways, it's far superior to the old. Between North Broadway and North Hill Street, it centers on a colorful open plaza, with narrow, traffic-free lanes, lined with shops and restaurants.

Little Joe's, 900 N. Broadway, at College Street (tel. 213/489-4900), is a holdover from the days when this part of town was predominantly Italian. It started the same year that Jolson's *The Jazz Singer* was released: 1927. Like the flicks, it grew until it now

---

The Best Hamburger in the World

Cassell's Hamburgers, 3266 West 6th St., at New Hampshire Street (tel. 213/480-8668), Los Angeles, in the Wilshire district just west of the downtown area. On one thing Angelenos agree: Cassell's serves just about the best burger in a town where the competition is rough! For over 30 years they have been creating what is undeniably a gastronomic triumph. The ambience—yellow Formica tables with bridge chairs and linoleum floors—is nil, the owner preferring to put his profit into the hamburger, not the decor, and making the Cassell hamburger a legend in its own time.

For about $5 are served a sumptuous, all prime USDA-graded steer beef (imported almost daily from Colorado) burger, the cost including all the fixings you desire: two kinds of lettuce, homemade mayonnaise, roquefort dressing, freshly sliced tomatoes, onions, pickles—all on a help-yourself basis. You can also have all the peaches, pineapple slices, cottage cheese, and delicious homemade potato salad you want. You can order your burger medium, rare, well done, or "blue," which is merely whisked over the fire. The beef is ground fresh every day. Have some freshly made lemonade (with only top-grade lemons, of course) to accompany your meal. Although I could never resist the burgers, good homemade sandwiches are an option. After you've received your order at the pickup counter, just sit down and savor every bite. It's reassuring to know that, in spite of fame, Cassell's has refused all franchise offers.

Cassell's is open only for lunch, Monday through Saturday from 10:30 a.m. to 4 p.m.

occupies an entire brick-built, converted hotel with six dining rooms. Step inside from the streets of Chinatown and you're in another world—the dining areas are adorned with murals of Rome and Venice, seating is in roomy, comfortable booths, and soft lighting emanates from lanterns overhead. The ambience is warm and simpático.

The portions served are wholesome and large, the flavors aromatic. For those who are famished, the lead-off recommendation is a six-course dinner ranging in price from $15 to $22 and including antipasto, followed by the soup of the day, a choice of spaghetti or homemade ravioli, then an entree with vegetables and potatoes, topped off with dessert. Entrees might be anything from veal scaloppine to halibut steak; all are also available à la carte for $10 to $18. There's an extensive list of salads, seafood, pasta, and broiled meats. At lunch choices are $6 to $13 and range from an order of homemade ravioli to a sausage sandwich to heartier entrees like prime rib.

Little Joe's is open Monday to Saturday from 11 a.m. to 9 p.m. Reservations are taken.

Grand Star, 943 Sun Mun Way, off North Broadway between College and Bernard streets (tel. 213/626-2285), is owned by Frank and Wally Quon and their mother, Yiu Hai Quon (born in 1897), recently a TV personality. There are four complete meals priced at $10 to $16 per person. The latter is the gourmet selection, including spicy shrimp in a lettuce shell, wonton soup, spicy chicken wings, Mongolian beef with mushrooms, lobster Cantonese, barbecued pork with snow peas, fried rice, tea, and dessert. If there are four or five in the party Mama Quon's chicken salad is added, plus larger portions of all else. You can also order à la carte items ranging from dumplings flamed in rum to lobster sautéed in ginger and green onion for $8 to $14. Steamed fish, priced according to size, is a specialty, as are the cashew chicken, Mongolian beef, and Chinese string beans.

On the street level, the Grand Star looks more Italian than Chinese: It's dimly lit with black-leather booths and big bunches of dried flowers here and there. I prefer to sit upstairs, where tables are covered with red cloths and the family's exquisite collection of Chinese embroideries adorns the walls. Entertainment, usually a female vocalist, with piano accompaniment, is featured at cocktail time and on most evenings. Open daily for lunch and dinner, 11:30 a.m. to 10 p.m. Monday through Wednesday, to 11 p.m. Thursday, to midnight Friday, noon to midnight Saturday, to 10 p.m. Sunday.

Grandview Gardens, 944 N. Hill St. between College and Bernard streets (tel. 213/624-6048), is especially famous for dim sum. You can order drinks in the cocktail lounge, which is guarded by a huge gold Buddha at the door. The long dining room has a peaked beamed ceiling and burnt-orange walls lined with Chinese paintings. Especially on weekends its tables are crowded with Chinese families partaking of dim sum delicacies. Generally there are three items to a plate, and each plate is priced at about $1.50. Pastries filled with barbecued pork, curried beef turnovers, ribs in black-bean sauce, steamed buns with chicken and mushrooms, lotus-bean pastry, stuffed duck feet, fried dumplings, and steamed noodle rolls are among the many offerings. In addition to dim sum there are about 150 à la carte listings ranging from sweet-and-sour pork to lobster with ginger and onion, $6 to $15. Low-priced family dinners are also served.

Grandview Gardens is open daily from 10 a.m. to 10 p.m.; dim sum is served from 10 a.m. to 3 p.m. There is validated parking.

LITTLE TOKYO

Little Tokyo is a portion of downtown Los Angeles, close to City Hall, between Alameda and Los Angeles Streets. Here you can find restaurants providing authentic Japanese meals. Roughly, the area is confined to about three blocks, with gift shops and restaurants interspersed with banks and clothing stores.

Horikawa, 111 S. San Pedro St., off 1st Street (tel. 213/680-9355), is popular with Japanese businessmen for its sushi bar and teppan-yaki grill, and its very attractive dining areas. At the entrance of this tranquil restaurant is a small fountain such as you might find in a Japanese garden. The separate Teppan Grill Room has beamed white walls hung with reproductions of works by the Japanese artist Shiko Munakata. And the walls of the main dining room are covered with soft sepia-and-white photomurals of famous Kyoto gardens.

You can begin your dinner at Horikawa with a sushi sampler or seafood teriyaki. Complete dinners, priced at $35 to $75, might include shrimp tempura, sashimi appetizer, *dobin-mushi* (a seafood and vegetable soup served in a mini-pot), *kani* (crab) salad, filet mignon *tobanyaki* (served on a sizzling mini-cooker), rice, tea, and ice cream or sherbet. You can also order à la carte. In the Teppan Room you might opt for filet mignon and lobster tail served with fresh vegetables, in the $18 to $30 range. Most luncheon entrees in either room are in the $10 to $15 range.

Apart from the above, what sets this restaurant apart are the kaiseki dinners—an extraordinary dining experience usually including a ten-course dinner, five-course lunch; dinners require two days' notice. The courses vary and are best discussed in advance once you know the number in your group; ask to reserve one of the lovely tea house rooms. Ryotei dinners (served tea house–style, usually 11 to 13 courses) are $110 per person. Courses are usually selected by the chef according to the tastes of the diners.

Horikawa is open for lunch weekdays only from 11:30 a.m. to 2 p.m.; for dinner Tuesday to Thursday from 6 to 10 p.m., on Friday to 10:30 p.m., Saturday 5:30 to 11 p.m., and on Sunday from 5:30 to 9:30 p.m. Reservations are advised at dinner.

Tokyo Kaikan, 225 S. San Pedro St., between 2nd and 3rd streets (tel. 213/489-1333), is one of the most popular Japanese restaurants in Little Tokyo, and it's also among the most attractive. The interior is designed like a rustic Japanese country inn, with much use of raw woods, rattan, and bamboo, enhanced by straw baskets, pottery, and farm implements. Overhead are brightly colored globe lights.

In addition to the regular menu, there are three different food bars specializing in tempura, shabu-shabu, and sushi. You might begin dinner with yakitori appetizer—cubed fruits skewered and fried with chicken and scallops. Entrees include beef sukiyaki, beef teriyaki, and shrimp or vegetable tempura. All are served with soup and rice. For dessert the green-tea sherbet is delicious and refreshing. A complete dinner of hors d'oeuvres, soup, sunomono, sashimi, and beef sukiyaki is one of several available for $16 to $22. Full lunches are $9 to $15, though you can also order à la carte.

Tokyo Kaikan is open Monday through Friday from 11:30 a.m. to 2 p.m. and 5 to 10:30 p.m., on Saturday from 6 to 10 p.m. only. Reservations recommended.

FOR THE BUDGET

Clifton's Brookdale Cafeteria, 648 S. Broadway, at 7th Street (tel. 213/627-1673), is one of a chain of economy cafeterias that has kept the less prosperous of Los Angeles nourished for five decades. (The original owner, Clifford Clinton—not Clifton—was famous for years for offering a 5-cent "maintenance" meal in pre-inflation days.) Clifford Clinton founded the business on what, today, would seem to be a very unique principle: "We pray our humble service be measured not by gold, but by the Golden Rule." During the Depression he kept thousands from starving by honoring an extraordinary policy: "No guest need go hungry. Pay what you wish, dine free unless delighted."

Those shopping or sightseeing downtown can enjoy a huge, economical meal that might consist of split-pea soup ($1.10), hand-carved roast turkey with dressing ($4), baked squash with brown sugar ($1.15), and Bavarian cream pie ($1.50)—not a bad meal for under $8, and you could eat for a lot less. Entrees cost $3 to $7, vegetable side dishes and soup are under $2, and salad platters and sandwiches run $2.50 to $4. There are over 100 à la carte items at modest prices. However, since there is a charge for everything, including bread and butter, you must limit choices to make your meal economical. It's all fresh, delicious, and homemade, too; even the baking is done on the premises. Fresh bakery items are sold at the front counter.

Clifton's Brookdale is open Monday through Thursday from 6 a.m. until 7:30 p.m., Friday through Sunday to 8 p.m. There is another Clifton's, downtown at 515 W. 7th St. at Olive (tel. 213/485-1726), open Monday through Saturday from 7 a.m. to 3:30 p.m.

---

5. Beverly Hills

In addition to those restaurants discussed below, you'll find some excellent Beverly Hills restaurants—The Bistro, La Scala & Boutique, and The Dining Room in the Beverly Hills Hotel—discussed in the earlier section on "Top Restaurants."

Trader Vic's, 9878 Wilshire Blvd., at Santa Monica Boulevard in the Beverly Hilton (tel. 213/274-7777), creates an interesting nautical look with Chinese prints, ship's models, and tropical shells, right in the hotel. Gone are the dugout canoes, fishnet, and glass buoys. What once was the Captain's Cabin has been expanded. And the dark bar is now a somewhat more sophisticated lounge. But don't despair, all has not been abandoned at sea. There are still the pleasant rum drinks with the cute little umbrellas.

As to the menu—the puupuus (otherwise known as hors d'oeuvres) include an absolutely delicious crisp calamari. The padang prawns sate are also worthy of serious consideration. The shrimp are gently sautéed, skewered, blessed with a sate-chili butter, then finished via a short trip to the broiler.

You might begin your meal with an order of barbecued spareribs from the Chinese oven or a Cosmo salad of fresh mushrooms, celery, and artichoke with the special mustard dressing. Two excellent entrees are the barbecued squab and the Indonesian lamb roast, trimmed and marinated, served with a peach chutney. On the other hand, if matured beef is your passion, Trader Vic's has a chateaubriand for two.

For dessert, there's Mud Pie or the Aloha Ice Cream—vanilla in mango sauce topped with banana chips.

Entrees are about $16 to $30, appetizers about $7 to $12, and desserts in the neighborhood of $5. Trader Vic's is open daily from 5 p.m. to midnight. Jackets and ties are required for men. Reservations are necessary.

Nate 'n' Al Delicatessen, 414 N. Beverly Dr., off Brighton Way (tel. 213/274-0101), offers an alternative to chic and expensive dining in the heart of this posh shopping area. It's a bustling Jewish kosher-style deli that has been an institution in Beverly Hills since 1945. Attesting to the quality of the food is the fact that it's always mobbed and probably half the folks are deli-maven New Yorkers. Some of the crowd is waiting to take out food from an appetite-whetting glass counter up front stocked with chopped liver, stuffed cabbage, creamed herring, and every kind of deli meat, but there's usually a line for tables too.

All the bread is fresh-baked. The extensive menu lists a wide variety of hot entrees like cheese blintzes with sour cream and apple sauce or roast turkey with potatoes, cranberry sauce, and a vegetable, for $8 to $13. Those with hearty appetites might want to start with an appetizer of chopped liver or gefilte fish. Sandwich offerings encompass everything from pastrami on rye to French-dip roast brisket of beef on an onion roll dipped in natural gravy, for $6 to $9—and they're all huge. Like everything else, desserts are numerous; I suggest the blueberry cheesecake.

The decor is unpretentious, and seating is in comfortable leather booths. Open Sunday to Friday from 7:30 a.m. to 8:45 p.m., on Saturday till 9:30 p.m. No reservations are accepted, and during busy meal hours there's always a line.

R.J.'s The Rib Joint, 252 N. Beverly Dr., between Dayton Way and Wilshire Boulevard (tel. 213/274-7427), bills itself as an "authentic American gourmet restaurant." Unlike most typical Beverly Hills eateries, where the slim and chic nibble daintily at endive salads and kiwi tarts, R.J.'s is more like the old Mama Leone's in New York, "where strong appetites are met and conquered." I'd hate to see the appetite that wasn't conquered by a meal here.

Heralded by a green-and-white-striped awning, R.J.'s offers a casual and comfortable interior in which to partake of its gargantuan meals. It has sawdust on the floors, lots of plants, and fans overhead. Exposed brick and raw pine walls are cluttered with historic photos of Beverly Hills and of oldtime actors and actresses. Over the bar on a platform is a pianist playing nostalgic American tunes. And a considerable amount of room is taken up by a 75-foot salad bar (more like the spread of your friendly greengrocer) and dessert display. There's additional seating up on a balcony.

Your dinner begins with as much as you like from the most sumptuous salad bar you're ever likely to encounter. It's easily a meal in itself, which it can be for about $10. Otherwise its 40 or so offerings are included in the price of your entree along with sourdough rolls and butter. As for the entrees, they come in immense servings and include steaks, beef and pork, ribs grilled over oakwood and mesquite charcoal, a bucket of clams, chili, hickory-smoked chicken, crispy duck, and lobster, for $15 to $30. Doggy bags are permitted, and it's likely you'll take home enough for one or two extra meals. The quality of food served matches the amazing quantity. Everything is fresh and natural, and the butter-laden desserts are baked on the premises. A wedge of chocolate cake, which is about a foot tall, is sufficient dessert for a party of four. Ditto the chocolate-chip cookie experience—a gigantic cookie topped with mounds of vanilla ice cream and smothered in hot fudge and real whipped cream. The well-stocked bar at R.J.'s is also worthy of mention (over 500 brands). Only premium liquors and fresh-squeezed juices are used in drinks; they carry over 50 varieties of beer from all over the world, and the house specialty is an ice cream daiquiri. Lunch, by the way, is less expensive at $9 to $15.

R.J.'s is open Monday through Thursday from 11:30 a.m. to 11 p.m., Friday and Saturday to 11:30 p.m., Sunday from 10:30 a.m. to 10 p.m.

Prego, 362 N. Camden Dr., at Brighton Way (tel. 213/277-7346) is attractive, bustling, and a great place for a very special kind of gourmet pizza. When Prego arrived on the restaurant scene, it was an instant success with its combination of elegance and simplicity. It is still a success. It's a lovely place, all brick, white, and wood, with unusual modern art on the walls and sprays of seasonal flowers to add another touch of beauty. Music from Italy plays softly in the background.

Prego is basically a trattoria. The food is prepared in an open kitchen by expert chefs. There are lots of antipasti to choose from, like focaccia al formaggio (layers of thin Italian bread and stracchino cheese) and insalata Prego (romaine lettuce, carrots, celery, bell pepper, mushrooms, and vinaigrette). For an entree, you have a choice

Eggs and Crafts:

The Egg and The Eye, 5814 Wilshire Blvd., between Stanley and Curson avenues just east of Beverly Hills (tel. 213/933-5596). At first, the name seems merely a pun on the old Claudette Colbert movie *The Egg and I.* But, in actuality, The Egg and The Eye is perhaps the finest omelet house in Los Angeles. Across from the La Brea Tar Pits, it is housed on the second floor of an exhibition center for the Craft and Folk Art Museum. (All items on display are also for sale.) Either before or after your meal, you can enjoy the gallery collection. The omelets are expensive, but well worth the money, considering their quality. You're faced with a choice of 37, ranging in price from $7 to $12, the latter filled with caviar and sour cream. In addition to dessert omelets, there's a very good homemade cheesecake with strawberry sauce. Non-omelet entrees like curry chicken salad and scallops Créole are also served, in about the same price range. With all meals comes a basket of black raisin bread.

Open Tuesday through Friday from 11 a.m. to 2:30 p.m., Saturday and Sunday from 10 a.m.; closed Monday. Reservations are a must.

of homemade pasta, like ziti with fresh tomato and basil or lobster-filled pasta, or grilled dishes like fresh fish, lamb with sage, rosemary, and butter, or Italian sausage with spinach. Everything is good. And then there are the pizzas—gourmet creations like the Puttanesca (my favorite), with tomatoes, black olives, capers, mozzarella, artichokes, and oregano; or Dell'Adriatico, with prawns, tomatoes, mozzarella, garlic, and basil. Entrees range from $10 to $19. For dessert, there's assorted fruits and cheeses, pastry, and a variety of ice cream dishes like semifreddo al caffè—white-chocolate ice cream with espresso and whipped cream.

Prego is open Monday through Saturday from 11:30 a.m. to midnight, and on Sunday from 5 p.m. to midnight.

Twin Dragon, 8597 W. Pico Blvd., at Holt Avenue (tel. 213/657-7355), is just a stone's throw south of Beverly Hills. This is the domain of owner-chef Mr. Yu-Fan Sun and his brother, manager James Sun. The restaurant is large and comfortable with Chinese instruments and shell paintings decorating the walls, colorful antique tasseled lamps overhead, and a gorgeous saltwater fish tank over the bar.

The menu is extensive, in good Chinese-restaurant tradition. I highly recommend the spicy diced chicken with peanuts, braised shrimp spiced with chili peppers, and the fresh asparagus with prawns. Meat and seafood entrees cost $9 to $17 (Peking Duck is $24 and requires 24-hour advance notice), vegetable dishes $5 to $7. It's a good idea to put yourself in the hands of the chef, who will prepare specialties that don't appear on the menu.

Twin Dragon is open daily from 11:30 a.m. to 10 p.m., till 11 p.m. on Friday and Saturday. They take reservations for more than five, and often there's a wait at dinner.

The **Cheesecake Factory,** 364 N. Beverly Dr., off Brighton Way (tel. 213/278-7270), is a dilemma of sorts. They serve great food and superb desserts. My advice is to go there very hungry when you're not counting calories. For those whose sweet tooth is acting up, relief is here in the form of a profusion of delicious baked goods—every conceivable variation of a cheesecake (over 40 concoctions, including the incredible white chocolate raspberry truffle, fresh strawberry, coffee brownie chunk, and Kahlua almond fudge). On the other hand, there's also chocolate fudge cake, carrot cake, and much, much more. Prices average $4 to $7 for a portion of sheer bliss.

The Cheesecake Factory is also a reasonably priced restaurant with a substantial list of delicious dishes. There's mouth-watering barbecue-style chicken and ribs, spicy specialties such as cashew chicken and shrimp Jambalaya, Louisiana blackened fish, and steak. You can also get a whole breast of chicken served in several styles: teriyaki, fajitas, dijon, and grilled lime. For the vegetarian, there's a combination of fresh vegetables sautéed with curry, wine, and spices, and covered with melted jack cheese, or prepared Oriental-style with a special sauce, spices and nuts, and served over rice. Plus there are over 15 varieties of fresh pasta dishes, wonderful hot sandwiches, great omelets, salads, and burgers. Entrees range from $6 to $16.

The desserts are all on display up front, so you can fantasize while waiting for a table. There's often a wait, but I assure you it's worth it. The atmosphere is casual and friendly. They don't take reservations, but your patience will be rewarded. The Cheesecake Factory has a good selection of wines and beers as well as a full bar.

They're open daily, on Monday through Thursday from 11 a.m. to 11 p.m., on Friday and Saturday to 12:30 a.m., on Sunday from 10 a.m. to 10 p.m.

There's another Cheesecake Factory at 4142 Via Marina, in Marina del Rey (tel. 213/306-3344), which has the same fabulous desserts and food, plus full bar service. Days are the same as above; however, Monday through Saturday, it's open from 11:30 a.m. to 11:30 p.m. Sunday they're open from 10 a.m. to 11 p.m. Other Cheesecake Factory locations are at 605 N. Harbor Dr. in Redondo Beach (tel. 213/376-0466), and at 6324 Canoga Ave. in Woodland Hills (tel. 818/883-9900).

6. Century City

UPPER BRACKET

Yamato, 2025 Ave. of the Stars, off Santa Monica Boulevard, in the Century Plaza Hotel (tel. 213/277-1840), is one of my favorite Japanese restaurants. In a lavish setting, adjacent to Beverly

Hills, you can enjoy authentic regional food, prepared and served with infinite care—truly an art! Much attention was given to Yamato's creation, and decorative objects were collected from all parts of Japan. Two massive carved Buddhist temple dogs—at least four centuries old—grace the foyer. They stand as "guardians against evil." The elaborately carved overhead beams, 350 years old, are from Kyoto, and the fusumas—made into decorative panels—are 250 years old.

You have a choice of dining in the Occidental style, at tables with bamboo chairs, or you can enter the tatami rooms, where you eat on traditional floor mats, surrounded by sliding screens. The latter is like your own private dining room, its decor enhanced by a Japanese flower arrangement, painting, or scroll, and soft light filtering in through the shoji screens. An additional dining area upstairs has tables and tatami rooms overlooking a Japanese garden.

Under the thatched and beamed roof of the main dining area is a sushi bar, a very popular dining section where you can order raw-fish appetizers adapted to Western palates. A five-course gourmet dinner—"planned with the emperor in mind"—includes shrimp tempura and beef teriyaki. A family-style multicourse dinner can be ordered for two or more. Dinners range from $12 to $35 per person. From the hibachi, you can order such delights as a charcoal-grilled, basted sirloin beef teriyaki. Among the seafood choices is poached salmon with cucumber. Desserts include mandarin orange sherbet. A large selection is also available at lunch, when prices are lower.

Open for lunch weekdays from 11:30 a.m. to 2:30 p.m., and for dinner Monday to Saturday from 5 to 11 p.m., on Sunday from 4:30 to 10 p.m. Reservations are advised; specify if you want a tatami room.

Harry's Bar and American Grill, 2020 Ave. of the Stars, on the Plaza Level of the ABC Entertainment Center (tel. 213/277-2333), is an authentic replica of its namesake in Florence. They even made a mold of the rich oak wainscotting and transported it here to copy. The bar is very European with its high walnut counter and tall wooden stools. The intimate dining areas have the wonderful pink light characteristic of Florence. All of the artwork on the walls—dozens of framed paintings, posters, and tapestries—comes from Italy, hand-picked by owners Larry Mindel and Jerry Magnin. And somehow they've also managed to transport the air of excitement of the *original* Harry's, which was in Venice, not Florence. It was a hangout of Ernest Hemingway, whose wife Mary once recalled: "You dumped your bags in your hotel . . . and then headed for Harry's. That's where you were going to see whoever was in Venice." "Whoever" in those halcyon days might have been Orson Welles (downing 24 finger sandwiches and a bottle of champagne in a matter of minutes), Prince Rainier, Noël Coward, or even Winston Churchill.

But enough of legend and lore, Harry's is one of the most simpático restaurants in town, and offers, to quote Mindel, "damned good food." At dinner, the food is authentic Northern Italian with superb Venetian and Florentine dishes. The menu represents a most agreeable selection of specialties including homemade duck prosciutto, beet pasta with gorgonzola and pine nuts, and veal scaloppini with balsamic vinegar and mustard. As you might guess, all pasta is homemade. For seafood lovers, there is always the special catch of the day. Entrees range from $17 to $25. At lunch you might opt for a pasta salad, a hamburger, steak sandwich, or grilled double lamb chops for $10 to $24.

Open Monday to Friday from 11:30 a.m. to 3 p.m. and from 5:30 to 10:30 p.m.; Saturday and Sunday from 5 to 10:30 p.m. Reservations essential.

La Chaumiere, 2025 Ave. of the Stars, off Santa Monica Boulevard, in the Century Plaza Hotel (tel. 213/277-2000), is the new restaurant in the tower of the hotel. The decor is elegant country French and the food is a blend of Continental and California cuisines. As you enter, you'll first notice the fine wood paneling, brass fixtures, and large French tapestry. La Chaumiere thankfully has the peace and order of a private club. Unlike a number of popular restaurants, your normal speaking voice can actually be heard by your dining companion.

For dinner, you might begin your meal with a marvelously creamy avocado soup with white wine and chunks of king crab ($7), or the coquille of shrimp, scallops, and morels with a brandy crayfish sauce ($9). Several excellent entree choices include an exceptional eggplant pirogue—it's rather like an eggplant boat—filled with shrimp, mussels, and crab, graced with a superb crayfish sausage, and topped with a Créole mustard sauce ($26). Or you might be seduced by the delicate poached filet of sole with smoked salmon in a creamy watercress sauce ($22). If you yearn for meat, last but far from least are the flavorful and incredibly tender tournedos of veal with morels and Calvados ($29). And then there's dessert—the white-chocolate mousse quenelles with orange sauce are positively immoral ($6).

If the above prices are too rich, go for lunch when entrees start at $13. La Chaumiere is open for lunch Monday through Friday from 11:45 a.m. to 1:30 p.m., for dinner nightly from 6 to 9 p.m. Reservations are necessary.

Hy's, 10131 Constellation Blvd., across from the ABC Entertainment Center (tel. 213/553-6000), is among the most attractive restaurants in Los Angeles and is one of the city's best spots for dining and dancing.

The restaurant is entered via a massive *porte cochère.* Inside, the arched balconies, alcoves, and cascading tiers of tiny lights create an intimate atmosphere in the two-level dining rooms. Large tables, set aside for privacy, are draped in crisp ivory linens accented with soft pastel touches.

If you've just about been California-cuisined to death, Hy's would be a superb choice for your next meal. Their extensive menu showcases the excellent prime steak patrons have come to expect (aging, boning, and trimming of the dry-aged beef is done on the premises). But the restaurant also features excellent fresh seafood flown in daily from Hawaii and around the world, specialty salads, innovative pasta dishes and mouth-watering desserts. At lunch a good start would be the Norwegian smoked salmon or the soup du jour. Entrees afford a wide variety of choices, from the Mediterranean seafood salad, or salmon cakes with red bell pepper sauce, to the fettuccine with veal, shiitake, and oyster mushrooms. Luncheon entrees range from $11 to $17.

Dinner specialties are steak (T-bone, filet mignon, New York strip, Delmonico), prime rib, rack of lamb, veal, fresh seafood and Maine lobster. Hy's uses Hawaiian kiawe-wood charcoal to cook the beef with intense, even heat and lock in the very special flavor. A fine start to dinner would be the delicious blackened Cajun prawns or Hy's Caesar salad. You might then proceed to rack of lamb, steak au poivre, Norwegian salmon en papillote, or grilled chicken with cilantro pesto sauce. Hy's traditional basket of hot cheese and garlic bread accompanies all dinner entrees, which range from $16 to $32.

There's great live entertainment in the lounge on Monday, Friday, and Saturday nights; live music for their Happy Hour Tuesday through Friday, and on weekends from 9:30 p.m. till closing. The lounge features jazz every Monday night.

Hy's is open for lunch weekdays from 11:30 a.m. to 2:30 p.m., for dinner Monday through Saturday from 6 to 9 p.m. A late-night Gourmet Teaser Menu is served after 9 p.m. until closing. Reservations are necessary.

---

7. San Fernando Valley

San Fernando Valley, called simply "the Valley," has many small communities, including several motion picture and television studios.

STUDIO CITY

Sportsmen's Lodge, 12833 Ventura Blvd., at Coldwater Canyon Avenue (tel. 818/984-0202). Originally the attraction here was that you could catch your own trout in the ponds and streams around the restaurant. The ponds and streams (now swan-filled) are still there, providing an enchanting view, and the lovely grounds are perfect for after-dinner strolls. I like to dine in the Boulevard Room, where there's a fireplace.

The lodge does still offer the trout, stuffed with crabmeat. In addition to seafood, steaks, and veal, Polynesian and Asian dishes are featured: the shrimp and chicken teriyaki, for example. Other superb selections are the boneless breast of chicken Oscar and a filet mignon béarnaise with all the trimmings. Entrees cost $14 to $28.

If you take your meal before 6:30 p.m., prices are lower (they're also lower from 4:30 to 6 p.m. on Sunday). Sunday brunch between 11 a.m. and 2:30 p.m. is a tradition at the lodge, featuring soup or salad, a vegetable, coffee or tea, dessert, and an entree such as cheese blintzes or omelet aux foies de volaille (chicken livers) for $9 to $12.

Open Tuesday to Saturday from 5:30 to 10 p.m., on Sunday from 10:30 a.m. to 2:30 p.m. and 4:30 to 10 p.m. Closed Monday. Reservations suggested.

8. Pasadena

While sightseeing in the area, you may want to consider one of the following choices.

Miyako, 139 S. Los Robles Ave., between Green and Cordova Streets, in the basement of the Livingstone Hotel (tel. 818/795-7005), offers fine Japanese cuisine in an attractive setting. It gives you a choice of both tatami room and table service, and fresh flower arrangements are placed about discreetly. In the tatami room you can enjoy a view of a small Japanese garden, while attended by waitresses traditionally attired in kimonos. Subtle understatement is the order of the day.

I like to begin with a sashimi appetizer of seven tuna slices. A full Imperial dinner offers a combination of shrimp tempura, chicken teriyaki, and sukiyaki. Dinners and à la carte entrees cost $10 to $23. Lunches are priced around $7 to $14. Miyako is on the same street as the Hilton but has been around much longer—since 1959 under the same owner.

Miyako is open for lunch weekdays from 11:30 a.m. to 2 p.m., and for dinner Monday through Thursday from 5:30 to 9:30 p.m., Friday and Saturday to 10 p.m., on Sunday from 4 to 9 p.m. Reservations accepted.

Konditori Patio Restaurant, 230 S. Lake Ave., between Cordova Street and Del Mar Boulevard (tel. 818/792-8044), specializes in delicious open-faced Scandinavian sandwiches. They range in price from $5 to $10, and the 20 varieties include herring, shrimp, crabmeat, smoked salmon, Danish cheese, meat loaf, liver paté (country style), king crab meat, Danish ham, and roast beef. Baked fresh on the premises, the pastries and cakes are rich and good, and you can take them out into the garden, with its umbrella-shaded tables. Imported beer such as Copenhagen's Carlsberg is sold here. From 7:30 a.m. till 3 p.m. you can order a breakfast of eggs, Swedish pancakes, the omelets for which the restaurant is famous, or a Scandinavian salmon and herring platter, for $4 to $9. And Monday through Friday from 11 a.m. to 2 p.m. Konditori offers a full lunch at some extraordinary prices. The menu changes from time to time, but may include entrees such as hot Swedish meat loaf, hot poached salmon with dill sauce, Swedish meat balls, for $3.99 served with soup or salad, potatoes or fruit, a vegetable, and toast. The most expensive item is a petit New York steak with grilled onions for $4.99 including all the above embellishments.

The restaurant is open daily, till 5:30 p.m. Reservations are accepted. There are acres of free parking.

SIGHTS IN AND AROUND LOS ANGELES

No matter what the product—film or sightseeing attraction—Los Angeles has an inbred flair for the dramatic. Beginning in the 1920s, when Hollywood burst into its glory, the larger-than-life approach has been adopted by virtually every exhibitor or entrepreneur.

Ice cream parlors were hidden under the hoopskirts of a two-story-high cement version of Little Eva; Simon Rodia's Towers in Watts were made of scrap metal, tile, mosaics, and glass bottles; fake ruins of castles and missions were created by moonlighting studio carpenters to enhance real-estate values.

Faith healings required full-scale scenery and cast, as exemplified by the style of Aimee Semple McPherson. She would stage her life story nightly for an audience sometimes approaching 5,000. Of course, she'd have to omit mention of two or three of her husbands, as that autobiographical bit would not be appropriate for her later lecture on the "sins" of divorce. To illustrate that she was born on a farm in Canada, the curtain would open onto a pastoral setting, with Sister Aimee in a backyard swing—milk bucket dangling from her arm—and a cow in the background. She would then proceed to milk the cow and pass the full dippers to the audience who filed up to the stage. While ladling out the milk, she crooned love songs which she had written herself.

It's just in the Hollywood blood to put on a good show.

Hollywood premieres have always attracted worldwide attention. Of one in particular, Ezra Goodman wrote: "For the opening of Howard Hughes' aviation epic *Hell's Angels,* in 1930, he [Sid Grauman] had Hollywood Boulevard roped off for ten blocks, streetcars detoured, and 250 searchlights picking out 30 airplanes in the sky, while the Hollywood hills in the background were lit up with Hughes' name."

The same blockbuster tradition carries over into the sightseeing attractions in and around Los Angeles. Forest Lawn Cemetery achieves "the ultimate"—staging christenings, marriages, and deaths! Too many craftsmen had too much at stake to let the La Brea Tar Pits (an Ice Age fossil site) in Hancock Park remain empty after the bones were removed. The pits are filled with life-size replicas of the ancient beasts.

So, if you like the dry approach to sights, you've come to the wrong city!

For a complete listing of sights in and around Los Angeles, see the "Sights and Attractions" section in the index at the back of this book.

---

1. Downtown Los Angeles

Although Los Angeles began in and around the Old Plaza and Olvera Street, later development and growth pushed the heart of the city to another area, approximately seven blocks west, on **Pershing Square.** Opening onto the square (now tunneled with parking garages), the deluxe Biltmore Hotel was built, an auditorium for concerts and the Philharmonic Orchestra erected later. Elegant residences lined **Bunker Hill** in the late 19th century, the mansions reached via Angels' Flight, a unique cable car.

Then came the earthquake scare, and city planning authorities prohibited buildings more than 150 feet high. Foreseeing that such a limitation would seriously hamper certain businesses, companies began to head out along Wilshire Boulevard and into outlying areas. For a while, many parts of Los Angeles proper became relatively forgotten, falling into disrepair. Beautiful town houses gave way to slums. The 1884 Firehouse deteriorated into a flea-bag hotel.

Through skilled building techniques, the earthquake disaster potential ostensibly lessened, and the ban on tall structures was removed in 1957. Large-scale leveling of Bunker Hill began, despite strong protestations that landmark mansions were being destroyed. Starting in the mid-1920s, the **Civic Center** steadily grew, culminating in the 28-story City Hall.

The shimmering addition of the new $35 million **Music Center** in the '60s marked the beginning of a long-overdue renaissance for downtown Los Angeles. New office buildings and several major new hotels continued this massive restoration.

And now, at the heart of California Plaza on Bunker Hill in downtown Los Angeles you will find the magnificent **Museum of Contemporary Art (MOCA),** designed by the Japanese architect Arata Isozaki. MOCA is the only Los Angeles institution devoted exclusively to exhibiting art from 1940 to the present. (For more on the museum, see the "Music Center of Los Angeles County," below.)

The **Los Angeles Convention and Exhibition Center** occupies a 38-acre site at 1201 S. Figueroa St.

A WALKING TOUR OF OLD LOS ANGELES

People don't walk in Los Angeles. They drive automobiles. However, make one exception to that rule and visit **El Pueblo de Los Angeles Historic Park.** Though bogged down by a lack of funds, the old pueblo—the birthplace of the city in 1781—is continuously being restored as an historical landmark. A walking tour of this most interesting district is made easy if you go first to the Las Angelitas 'Docent Office, 130 Paseo de la Plaza, next to the Firehouse at 501 N. Los Angeles (call 213/628-0605 to make group tour reservations). Organized walking tours—at no charge—leave here Tuesday through Saturday at 10 a.m., 11 a.m., noon, and 1 p.m.

The tour begins on the **Old Plaza,** with its circular lacy wrought-iron bandstand. It was near here that Felipe de Neve, the Spanish governor, founded the pueblo. Opening directly on the square is the **Old Plaza Roman Catholic Church,** the city's oldest, dating from 1822. It's filled with paintings and ecclesiastical relics, and is open daily to visitors and worshippers.

But perhaps more so than the above, the block-long, colorful, traffic-free **Olvera Street,** one of the oldest in Los Angeles, forms a tangible link to the origins of the city, particularly its rich Spanish and Mexican heritage. Now transformed into a Mexican market, it is complete with colorful if touristy shops, cafés, and "puestos" with craftsmen such as silversmiths, glassblowers, leather artisans, and candlemakers.

The stalls and shops—open daily from about 10 a.m. to 8 p.m., to 10 p.m. in summer—display merchandise imported from across the border (see Chapter VII). The air is perfumed with spices. And the tiny open-fronted cafés offer Mexican food. There are three full-scale Mexican restaurants as well, Casa La Golondrina (see Chapter IX), Anita's, and El Paseo.

The star attraction on the street is the **Avila Adobe,** a long, low adobe building dating from 1818, making it the city's oldest. All the historic house museums are open every day except Monday (10 a.m. to 3 p.m. weekdays, to 4:30 p.m. weekends). Admission is free. Restored after the 1971 earthquake damage, it was built by Don Francisco Avila, and is graced with a front veranda and rear garden, brightened by a flourishing grape arbor and native plants. The original floors were made of packed earth, later topped by wood planking.

The **Pico House** (named after the last governor of Mexican California), built in 1870 on Main Street, was the first three-story building in Los Angeles, a prestigious hotel of the mid-Victorian era sheltering exhausted travelers from the East at the "end of the line." Here guests relaxed in comparative luxury (gaslight and bathtubs!), enjoying the enclosed courtyard with its sweet-smelling vines and flowers. The restoration of the façade has been completed as have the remaining buildings in the entire Pico–Garnier block. Plans are in progress for the buildings to house restaurants, museums, and offices.

The **Merced Theatre** is also undergoing restoration. If projected plans materialize, it will once more stage plays as it did in 1870.

Other famous buildings in the district include the Victorian **Sepulveda House**, now a museum, visitor's center, and bookstore; and the **Pelanconi House**, the latter built in 1855–1857, the time of the first two-story brick structures in Los Angeles, and now housing the Casa La Golondrina restaurant mentioned above.

In addition to the market and old buildings, there's usually some kind of Mexican-themed street entertainment—like mariachi bands, or Mexican folk dancers. And all Latin American holidays, as well as Mardi Gras, are celebrated with gusto.

At the end of the walking tour, you can stroll over to **Union Station**, 800 N. Alameda St., just east of the Plaza and Olvera Street. It has been declared a cultural monument—"one of the most beautiful buildings in Southern California." At the old terminal, movie stars would arrive grandly on the Santa Fe *Chief*, with their latest spouses. But this terminal was torn down in 1939 and replaced by the present one—the last "great" passenger terminal built in America. Covering 50 acres, it contains tile roofing, landscaped patios with benches and fountains, and arched passageways. Its architectural style has been described as "early California mission."

MUSIC CENTER OF LOS ANGELES COUNTY

With three theaters in one, the county-owned **Music Center**, 135 N. Grand Ave. (tel. 213/972-7211), offers Angelenos a proper forum for the performing arts. In many ways, the $35-million complex of buildings marks the coming of cultural age for the sprawling metropolis.

In large part the center owes its birth to the fund-raising efforts of Mrs. Norman Chandler, wife of the late publisher of *The Los Angeles Times*. Mrs. Chandler has been known for her civic and charity work, as well as for her beautification programs. The trio of theaters are named after Mrs. Chandler, the Ahmanson Foundation, and Mark Taper.

The public is invited to tour all three theaters: the **Mark Taper Forum,** the **Ahmanson Theatre,** and the 3,197-seat **Dorothy Chandler Pavilion.** The Music Center is the home of the Los Angeles Philharmonic, Joffrey Ballet, Los Angeles Master Chorale, and the Los Angeles Music Center Opera. The acoustically flexible theater, gleaming in glass with splashing fountains out front, is on six levels, including the fifth-floor Pavilion Restaurant. In another part of the building are Otto Rothschilds Bar and Grill and the Backstage Café. Free tours are conducted year round on Monday, Tuesday, Thursday, and Friday from 10 a.m. to 1:30 p.m. and on Saturday from 10 a.m. to 12:30 p.m. For tour reservations call 213/972-7483. Although the tour tickets are complimentary, the parking in the garages below isn't: during weekdays you pay a $10 deposit on entry. The cost is $1.50 for 20 minutes with a $10 maximum until 5 p.m. If you enter after 5 p.m., or any time on weekends or holidays, it's $5 maximum. On matinee days after 11 a.m., the cost is $1.50 for 20 minutes, $5 maximum. The garage is open until 11:45 p.m.

Of course, the best way to visit the Music Center of Los Angeles County is via a performance—either a recital, concert, drama, musical, ballet, dance program, opera, whatever. For details, you can refer to the daily newspapers, or call 213/972-7211.

NEW CHINATOWN AND LITTLE TOKYO

Neither is on the scale of its San Francisco equivalent. However, both offer a grouping of ethnic shops and restaurants that you might enjoy exploring. **New Chinatown,** bounded by North Broadway, North Hill Street, Bernard Street, and Sunset Boulevard, centers on a Chinese mall called Mandarin Plaza at 970 N. Broadway.

Little Tokyo is an area of just a few blocks close to City Hall between Alameda and Los Angeles streets and 1st and 3rd streets. It is the site of the city's only Japanese hotel, the luxurious New Otani; and of course many Japanese shops and restaurants are located here. Like New Chinatown it has a mall, this one called Japanese Village Plaza.

At present an hour or two is sufficient to explore either.

2. Wilshire Boulevard and Its Museums

In Los Angeles, Wilshire Boulevard is what Fifth Avenue is to New York, the Champs Élysées is to Paris, though the resemblance is stretched over several miles. Commencing its run in downtown Los Angeles, near Grand Street, it runs to Santa Monica. It is an impressive string of hotels, contemporary apartment houses, department stores, office buildings, and plush restaurants.

The realtors of the '30s named one strip—between Highland and Fairfax—*Miracle Mile*. Their ambitious label is increasingly being backed up by reality as new decorator stores and glass-and-steel office buildings locate here. Some of the most prestigious hotels in Southern California stand on Wilshire.

The boulevard passes through **MacArthur Park,** with its own lake, as well as **Lafayette Park.** Near the eastern edge of Miracle Mile is the Los Angeles County Museum in **Hancock Park,** site of the La Brea Tar Pits. The boulevard also runs through a portion of the Beverly Hills shopping section.

LOS ANGELES COUNTY MUSEUM OF ART

A complex of five modern buildings surrounding a spacious central court, the Los Angeles County Museum of Art at 5905 Wilshire Blvd. (tel. 213/857-6000), is considered one of the top museums in the country and the finest and largest in the West. A major expansion program has more than doubled its exhibition space.

The **Ahmanson Building,** built around a central atrium, houses the permanent collection of paintings, sculpture, graphic arts, costumes, textiles, and decorative arts from a wide range of cultures and periods from prehistoric times to the present. The museum's holdings on view in this building include Chinese and Korean art; Pre-Columbian Mexican art; American painting, sculpture, and decorative arts from colonial days to the mid-20th century; European painting, sculpture, and decorative arts from the Middle Ages through the early decades of this century; ancient and Islamic art; a unique assemblage of glass from Roman times to the 19th century; the outstanding Gilbert collection of mosaics and monumental silver; one of the nation's largest holdings of costumes and textiles; and an Indian and southeast Asian collection of art considered to be one of the most important in the world.

Major loan exhibits as well as galleries for prints, drawings, and photographs are found in the **Frances and Armand Hammer Building.** The **Robert O. Anderson Building** features 20th-century painting and sculpture as well as special exhibits. The **Leo S. Bing Center** has a 600-seat theater where lectures, films, and concerts take place, and the indoor/outdoor Plaza Café.

The **Pavilion for Japanese Art** was opened in September 1988. It was designed by the late Bruce Goff specifically to accommodate Japanese art, though certain elements of the museum are reminiscent of the Guggenheim Museum created by Frank Lloyd Wright—the curved rising ramp, the central treatment of light, the structure of the displays. An extraordinary touch by Goff was using Kalwall, a translucent material, for the exterior walls to allow a soft delicate entry of natural light much like that through shoji screens, at the same time performing the eminently practical function of screening out ultraviolet light. It is a serene touch that adds to the quiet beauty of the subjects. The Pavilion may very well be the only public museum where Japanese art can be seen in this light.

The museum now houses the internationally renowned Shin'enkan collection of the Edo period (1615–1865) Japanese paintings, rivaled only by the holdings of the Imperial Collection in Japan. It also displays the museum's collections of Japanese sculpture, ceramics, and lacquerware.

The Pavilion has on display the superb Raymond and Frances Bushell collection of netsuke (pronounced *net*-ski) from the 18th through the 20th century, though most were produced during the Edo period. You can see the amazingly detailed miniatures up close in their own gallery. These are figures carved from wood, ivory, and stag antler materials in all sorts of shapes of animals and people. Subjects are real, mythical, classic—goat groups, horse and mare, kissing geese, Buddhist priests, bandits, demon quellers, Dutchmen, etc. The design and detail of netsukes is even more amazing in light of their use and the limitations of their shapes. The Japanese used *inro,* sectioned boxes to hold money, tobacco, etc. A cord went from the top of the inro, under the kimono sash and through the netsuke to keep the inro from falling. Netsukes needed to be compact and free of sharp, protruding points that might catch on kimono sleeves, yet strong enough to support the weight of the inro. It's a rare collection that's sure to charm adults and children.

The museum offers a continuing program of outstanding special exhibitions (in 1990 there was the spectacular Impressionist and post-Impressionist collection of Walter H. Annenberg, in 1989 a magnificent Georgia O'Keeffe retrospective), films, lectures, guided tours, concerts, and a variety of educational events. Full admission (which admits visitors to specially priced exhibitions) is $5 for adults; senior citizens 62 and over, and students with ID, $4; children 6 to 17 years, $2; children 5 and under are admitted free. Free guided tours covering the highlights of the permanent collections are given daily.

There is a Plaza Café, as mentioned above, in the Leo S. Bing Center open Tuesday through Friday from 10 a.m. to 4:30 p.m., Saturday and Sunday to 5:30 p.m.

The museum is open from 10 a.m. to 5 p.m. Tuesday through Friday, till 6 p.m. on Saturday and Sunday. The second Tuesday of each month is free for all, except for admission to special exhibitions. The museum is closed every Monday, Thanksgiving, Christmas, and New Year's Day.

Parking at the Visitors Lot (turn north at the first block east of the museum) is $1 for 20 minutes, $5 maximum on Saturday and Sunday, $8 maximum during the week.

LA BREA TAR PITS/GEORGE C. PAGE MUSEUM

In **Hancock Park** is the richest fossil site inherited from the Ice Age (Pleistocene). A "natural history landmark," it is at 5801 Wilshire Blvd., to the west of La Brea Avenue, on the same grounds as the Los Angeles County Museum of Art. Beginning some 40,000 years ago, a bewildering variety of prehistoric reptiles, birds, and mammals, lured to the pits by the prospect of drinking water, became helplessly mired in the tar—and there they stayed, forever! Ironically, other predatory monsters, seeing them trapped, jumped into the oily muck to devour them, only to find that it was their "last supper." Although the existence of the site was known at least 9,000

LACM

9 1   2 1 3   8 5 7   6 0 0 0

Goya to Lautrec
Gm expressinats

special exhns

Fri hours   10-9?

any pavilns or bedgs
          closed - no

shop take CCds
      yes.
      10-9?
      in plaza level

years ago by the Native Americans, it wasn't until 1906 that scientists began a systematic removal and classification of the fossils. In subsequent years, more than one million specimens were brought up, most of them of the giant variety: ground sloths, huge vultures, mastodons (early relatives of the elephant), camels (in California?), and prehistoric relatives of many of today's rodents, bears, lizards, and birds. In one pit the skeleton of a Native American—dating from 9,000 years ago—was unearthed.

The current excavation, which began in 1969, has already uncovered more than half a million fossils, including many small plants and insects. Even freshwater shells have been found. All these discoveries have made the La Brea Tar Pits the world's best source of Ice Age fossils and what must be one of the most odorous.

A number of Angelenos have contributed to the construction of replicas of some of the animals in their original setting, and they stand today—fully life-size—to enthrall.

But the tar pits represent more than a museum of perfectly preserved plant and animal life. The discoveries made here have given scientists insight into ecological functions and requirements of many creatures still alive today. They have also spurred further research into paleontologic techniques that have made it possible to more accurately recover and date such fossils without damaging them.

In April 1977, as a result of the contribution of philanthropist George C. Page, the **George C. Page La Brea Discoveries Museum** was opened at the east end of the Hancock Park, 5801 Wilshire Blvd., two blocks east of Fairfax Avenue (tel. 213/936-2230 for recorded information, or 213/857-6311). It features over 30 separate exhibits, among them: reconstructed skeletons of the above-mentioned animals from the Pleistocene Epoch (Ice Age); the La Brea Story Theaters, twin multimedia theaters where you can view a 15-minute documentary film and slides about the tar pits; a life-like replica and the skeleton of the 9,000-year-old La Brea woman; an exhibit called "The Asphalt Is Sticky" that invites visitors to personally (though safely) experience the adhesive death trap; and the Paleontological Laboratory, where scientists are engaged in cleaning, identifying, and cataloging fossils. Over 100 pits, or excavations, have been made in Hancock Park since the turn of the century, but most have been filled in. Currently there are six pits (places where asphalt seeps to the surface to form sticky pools) scattered throughout Hancock Park, including the Observation Pit, and the Active Dig.

Both the museum and the Observation Pit are open from 10 a.m. to 5 p.m. Tuesday to Sunday (except on Thanksgiving, Christmas, and New Year's Day), with tours offered daily (call for schedule); the lab can be viewed Wednesday through Sunday only. Admission is $5 for adults, $3 for seniors 62 and older and students, $1.50 for children ages 5 to 12; those under 5 get in free. Admission is free for everyone the second Tuesday of each month. Joint admission to the Page Museum and Los Angeles County Museum of Art is $6.50 for adults, $3.75 for students and seniors, $1.50 for children. Tours of the tar pits depart from the Observation Pit at 1 p.m. Wednesday through Sunday. At the Rancho La Brea Project Viewing Station, during July and August, visitors may watch the excavation of fossils still in progress. Free parking is available off Curson in the Hancock Park lot.

---

3. More Museums

You will find even more museums scattered around the Los Angeles area, but these are centrally located. For a complete listing of museums covered in this book, see the "Sights and Attractions" section of the index.

MUSEUM OF CONTEMPORARY ART (MOCA)

Thousands upon thousands of words have appeared in publications from New York to Los Angeles and San Francisco to San Diego, expounding a variety of views about the city's new **Museum of Contemporary Art (MOCA),** but of all the verbiage the most important might well be "don't miss visiting MOCA." The museum formally opened in December 1986 at 250 S. Grand Ave. (tel. 213/621-2766). It is the only Los Angeles institution devoted exclusively to exhibiting art from 1940 through to the present. Whatever may be on exhibit at the time you're in Los Angeles, and whether or not contemporary art suits your fancy, a visit to this magnificent jewel in its handsome setting of skyscrapers is worth your time. MOCA is at the heart of California Plaza on Bunker Hill in the downtown L.A. business district.

MOCA is the creation of Tokyo architect Arata Isozaki—his first in the United States. The physical constraints of the new museum were considerable—MOCA had to be built above a parking garage, yet the height of the museum was not allowed to compete or interfere with adjoining structures developed by the partnership that underwrote the cost of the 98,000 square foot building. Because MOCA would eventually be dwarfed by the surrounding buildings, Isozaki intended it to attract attention with its materials and shapes.

You will first see a warm red sandstone exterior. The blocks were quarried by hand in India and refined in Japan. There is a great deal to marvel at—the enormous barrel vault of concrete poured in-place, the copper roofs that in time will take on a greenish patina, dark green aluminum panels cross-hatched with joints painted bright pink, pyramid skylights, and magnificent outdoor spaces. When you stroll up the stairs, past the ticket booth and sales office, to your right and left there are long rectangular reflecting ponds with benches and trees to either side—perfect for quiet relaxation.

When you pass the ticket booth, rather than going up the stairs, go to your right and down a gently curving slope and you will arrive at a handsome courtyard and the entrance to the galleries. The courtyard with its white umbrellas, tables, and chairs serves as a lovely uncluttered café area.

MOCA's Ahmanson Auditorium is the site for intimately

scaled performances and film and video programs scheduled throughout the year. The programs are intended to further development in these forms as they relate to MOCA's commitment to contemporary art. For information and tickets, call the MOCA Box Office (tel.213/626-6828).

The café I mentioned before is the "il Panino," after the popular Italian paninoteca (sandwich bar). The café serves a marvelous selection of sandwiches, soups, pasta salads, fruit salads, vegetable salads, desserts, and beverages including beer, wine, soft drinks, and coffee, tea, espresso, or cappuccino. And there is nothing commonplace about any of the sandwiches from the Norvegese—with smoked salmon and Mascarpone cheese, garnished with capers, onion, tomato, and dressing; to the Milano—with sliced turkey breast, goat cheese, avocado, and sun-dried tomato, served on Italian Ciabatta bread with dressing (each about $6.75).

The museum is open 11 a.m. to 6 p.m. on Tuesday, Wednesday, Friday, Saturday, and Sunday; to 8 p.m. Thursday. Admission is $4, students and seniors $2, children under 12 free. The museum's store, featuring changing displays of artist-designed objects, exhibition posters, catalogues, art books, contemporary jewelry, etc., is open during regular museum hours.

Parking other than metered is now available one block north of MOCA for visitors to the museum. For $4 and a MOCA validation, you can park at the 5-Star lot at First and Hope streets for four hours weekdays from 10 a.m. to 6 p.m.

WELLS FARGO HISTORY MUSEUM

In the Wells Fargo Center, at 333 S. Grand Ave., near 4th Street (tel. 213/253-7166), is the Wells Fargo History Museum. The museum highlights the history of Wells Fargo and its impact on California and the American West. It's a delightful place, well lit and pleasantly laid out. Among the exhibits are an authentic 19th-century Concord stagecoach; a coach under construction (you can sit inside and listen to taped excerpts from the diary of a young Englishman who made the arduous trip to California by coach); the tools used by coachmakers; the Challenge nugget—a two-pound gold lump of 76% purity found in 1975 (!); mining entrepreneur and Wells Fargo agent Sam Dorsey's gold collection; and a fascinating selection of mining and Wells Fargo artifacts. Hundreds of historical items and over 50 colorful exhibits bring the Old West to life.

The Wells Fargo Museum is open Monday to Friday, from 9 a.m. to 5 p.m.; closed on bank holidays. Admission is free.

LOS ANGELES CHILDREN'S MUSEUM

Situated above the Los Angeles Mall, 310 N. Main St. (tel. 213/687-8800), this museum is a place where children learn by doing. The entire building is full of touch-me exhibits geared especially to youngsters. Here they can create everything from Mylar rockets to finger puppets in The Art Studio. There's a City Street where they can sit on a policeman's motorcycle, play at driving a bus, or pretend to be firemen. They can become "stars" in the recording or TV studio; learn about health in a doctor's office and a dentist's office and about x rays in an emergency room; see their shadows frozen on walls in the Shadow Box; and play with giant foam-filled Velcro–edged building blocks in Sticky City.

In addition to the regular exhibits, there are all kinds of special activities and workshops from cultural celebrations to decorating T-shirts and making musical instruments. There is a 99-seat theater for children where live performances or special productions are scheduled every weekend. Call the museum for upcoming events.

The museum is open on Saturday and Sunday from 10 a.m. to 5 p.m., on Wednesday and Thursday from 2 to 4 p.m. Summer hours are 11:30 a.m. to 5 p.m. Monday through Friday and from 10 a.m. to 5 p.m. on Saturday and Sunday. Admission is $4.50, children under 2 years are admitted free.

NATURAL HISTORY MUSEUM

In **Exposition Park,** the county-administered Natural History Museum, the largest of its kind in the West, shelters seemingly countless exhibits.

The many halls and galleries chronicle people and their environment from 300 million years before they first appeared to the present day. Exhibits include brilliant examples of work by ancient Maya, Aztec, Inca, and pre–Inca potters, sculptors, and goldsmiths. Animals are shown in their natural habitats; there are halls detailing American history from 1660 to 1914, mineral halls, bird halls—even a few dinosaurs on hand. In the Cenozoic Hall you can see mammal fossils from 65 million years ago; also shown here is the complete evolution of the horse from a fox-terrier-sized animal to today's stallion. Other permanent displays include the world's rarest shark, Megamouth; a walk-through vault containing priceless gems; and an extraordinary collection of Los Angeles–built automobiles. There's much more, all of it fascinating.

At 900 Exposition Blvd. (tel. 213/744-3466), the Natural History Museum is open from 10 a.m. to 5 p.m. daily, except Monday. Admission is $4 for adults; $2 for seniors, those 12 to 17, and college students with ID; $1 for kids 5 to 12; those under 5 admitted free. Admission is free the first Tuesday of every month. Exposition Park, across from the campus of the University of Southern California, is reached via the Harbor Freeway (Hwy. 11); get off at the ramp leading to Exposition Boulevard.

WATTS TOWERS

If you had met Simon Rodia, you might have taken him for a simple immigrant. Only he wasn't so simple. A tilesetter who originally came from one of the poorest districts of Rome and grew up in Watts, he set out late in life to leave something behind in his adopted country ("because I was raised here, you understand?"). Perhaps unknowingly, he left his own memorial.

As a result, the Watts Towers stand as a unique personal statement of an eccentric man who pieced together articles of junk. A rugged individualist who ignored the jeers and scorn of his neighbors ("some of the people think I was crazy"), Mr. Rodia scavenged the city for flotsam and jetsam, bits and pieces of iron and tin, old bottles (especially green ones), tin and stone, seashells (over 70,000 of them), and colored tiles.

The towers took him 33 years to build ("I no have anybody help me out"). With the instinctive skill of the artist—and without elaborate blueprints—he made his towers soar, holding them together by rods of steel, mixing lime with water, then applying his own mortar to his network of mesh screens and sieves. Two towers soar ten stories high, nearly 100 feet. The others average 40 feet.

The task completed in 1954, Mr. Rodia suddenly and mysteriously left Watts, deeding his life-work to a neighbor. Because he was no longer there to guard his achievement in the years following, the towers fell into disrepair, the helpless victims of vandals, who cracked many of the seashells and some of the bottles—just for sport. Tracked down in 1959 in Martinez, California, Mr. Rodia seemed not to care—his spiritual link with the towers apparently was severed after their creation. He died in 1965 at the age of 86.

As it turned out, the greatest danger to the towers was not from the vandals, but from the municipal building department, which ordered that the towers be leveled as "hazardous to the general public." The owners did not comply. A hearing was called.

The issue became a *cause célèbre*. The towers that nobody had seemed interested in sparked massive support, the controversy spewing into a public hearing. Directors of museums and news-hungry magazine reporters "discovered" the spires, fanning them into nationwide attention. A decision was made to subject the steepest tower to the "pull test" to determine if it could withstand the pressure. In front of television cameras and newspaper reporters, the crucial experiment was carried out. The tower didn't budge, except for a stray shell.

Simon Rodia's dream was to live.

These days the towers are state property, restored and constantly maintained as a cultural treasure. At this writing, only group tours are conducted weekdays; however, you can always call to join a group touring the towers. On Saturday, from about 10 a.m. to 3 p.m., the staff at the art center will conduct tours through the towers for individuals. It's $2 per person. The adjoining art center is open Tuesday through Saturday from 7 a.m. to 4 p.m.

The towers are at 1765 E. 107th St. To reach them, take the Harbor Freeway (Hwy. 11) toward San Pedro, getting off and turning left onto Century Boulevard. Go right on Central, left on 108th Street, then left onto Willowbrook to 107th Street. For further information, call 213/569-8181.

---

4. Hollywood

For a city that's not a city (but actually a part of Los Angeles), Hollywood has been chronicled to death, though it celebrated its 100th birthday in 1987.

The legend of Hollywood as the movie capital of the world still persists, though many of its former studios have moved into the nearby San Fernando Valley. It's been a long time since the country waited with bated breath for the urgent bulletins of "Louella Parsons from Hollywood," announcing who's splitting up, who's expecting, etc.

But Hollywood seems unaware of its own demise. At the least the **HOLLYWOOD** sign is still on the hill and its price keeps going up. According to *The Los Angeles Times Magazine,* the cost of the original sign in 1922 was $21,000; the cost of building a new one in 1978 was $250,000. And the film industry itself seems to feel immune to the aging process—salaries are forever upscale. In 1988, Hollywood employees earned a total of almost $6.5 billion.

With its ordinary, everyday architecture, **Hollywood Boulevard** may remind one of Main Street, U.S.A. But look again. The stores may be pedestrian in design, but not in the merchandise offered. Hollywood Boulevard has also been labeled "the Times Square of the West." In the era of the silent screen, stars arrived in ermine and tails at the premieres at Grauman's (now Mann's) Chinese Theatre, after which they danced at garden court apartments. Today you'll find more bums, pimps, and prostitutes than stars.

However, look below your feet on Hollywood Boulevard. You'll be strolling along the **Walk of Fame** begun in 1958. Along the boulevard, bronze medallions with the names of over 1,800 stars and leading character actors dating from the days of the nickelodeon to the present TV age have been inserted at a cost of about $3,500 each.

Under the name of each personality is the symbol of his or her medium—be it film, radio, music, or television. In star-struck Hollywood, the walk is amazingly democratic and fair. That is, it honors not only the legends—Chaplin, Pickford, Crawford, Davis—but such beloved character actresses as Zazu Pitts, leading ladies of yesterday (Kay Francis, Una Merkel), even personalities totally unknown to today's generation, such as Betty Blythe. The latter's *The Queen of Sheba* was as big, for a while, as Valentino's *The Sheik*.

The corner of **Hollywood and Vine** is legendary—its fame larger than it deserves. Architecturally dull, it was known for the stars who crossed the intersection—all the big names in Hollywood. When Greta Garbo walked down the street in trousers, and was widely photographed, the pictures shocked women all over America. After recovering from their horror and the headlines— "Garbo Wears Pants"—women rushed to their astonished dressmakers (or, in some cases, their husbands' tailors) to have the slacks duplicated.

THE HOLLYWOOD WAX MUSEUM

One block east of the world-famous Mann's Chinese Theatre, Spoony Singh's Hollywood Wax Museum, 6767 Hollywood Blvd., near Highland Avenue (tel. 213/462-8860), perpetuates the movie-world legend. Spoony himself is a turbaned and bearded Indian Sikh. When he bought the museum about 20 years ago it was a mess: Shirley Temple's head had shrunk to the size of a tennis ball and Mickey Rooney's arms had fallen off. Today Spoony's 185 wax figures are in perfect shape, and his only problem was that guests continually stole Raquel Welch's bras (he finally let her go braless).

The most publicized figures are the tableaux of John F. Kennedy at the lectern and Marilyn Monroe in her famous dress-blowing scene from *The Seven-Year Itch.* A tableau of Leonardo da Vinci's *Last Supper,* as well as scenes depicting Queen Victoria and Martin Luther King Jr., are on display.

However, most of the wax figures are movie stars or celebrities from the entertainment world. Contemporary figures include Jane Fonda, Sylvester Stallone, Michael Jackson, Bruce Springsteen, Goldie Hawn, and Cyndi Lauper. Charlie Chaplin, W. C. Fields, and Mae West represent the stars of yesteryear.

In the Chamber of Horrors—evocative of Madame Tussaud's in London—you'll see the coffin used in *The Raven,* as well as a scene from Vincent Price's old hit, *The House of Wax.*

An added attraction is the **Movie Awards Theatre,** presenting a film that spans more than four decades of Academy Award winners and presentations. The sound track is composed of a medley of songs that won as the best of their respective years. Flashing before you is every movie from *Coquette* to *Chariots of Fire.*

The museum is open daily from 10 a.m. to midnight, on Friday and Saturday till 2 a.m. The adult admission is $7, children 6 to 12 $4, seniors $5, and kids under 6 get in free.

MANN'S CHINESE THEATRE, THE HOLLYWOOD BOWL, AND MULHOLLAND DRIVE

On Hollywood Boulevard (at no. 6925), **Mann's** (formerly Grauman's) **Chinese Theatre** was showman Sid Grauman's masterpiece. For the façade, he actually imported pillars of a Chinese temple, placing them in the forecourt. The inclusion of prints was accidental. Actress Norma Talmadge (before your time) stepped into still-wet cement—thus beginning the forecourt of the stars. A proper enclosure was created for the signatures and hand-and footprints of the stars. There are more than 170 prints at this time.

Some personalities went beyond a simple imprint. John Barrymore made an impression of his profile, Betty Grable of her shapely leg, William S. Hart of his gun, and Gene Autry of the hoofprints of Champ, his horse. Steven Spielberg and George Lucas recently left sneaker prints, Lucas's creations R2-D2 and C3PO left unique tracks of their own. Countless thousands of visitors match their feet and hands with those imbedded in the cement. You may find the hands or hands and feet of your favorites: Elizabeth Taylor, Charles Boyer, Barbara Stanwyck, Robert Taylor, Gary Cooper, Bing Crosby, Pola Negri, Loretta Young, Paul Newman, Tyrone Power, Ginger Rogers, Lana Turner, Bette Davis, Marie Dressler, Wallace Beery, Constance and Norma Talmadge, Humphrey Bogart, and many, many others.

Across the street and down a bit is **Mann's Egyptian Theatre,** a mock palace of ancient Thebes with a long forecourt, planted with semitropical trees and flowers, the setting for many a spectacular movie premiere, complete with klieg lights and appropriate bally-hoo. In Hollywood's great days, robed Egyptian guards (extras from the studios) paced the upper ramparts. Every usherette—in flowing robes and imitation jewelry—was a potential Cleopatra.

If you're a truly dedicated film buff, you can continue your experience with legendary Hollywood by paying a call at the **Hollywood Memorial Park Cemetery,** at 6000 Santa Monica Blvd., between Van Ness and Gower Streets (tel. 213/469-1181). This is where the mysterious lady in black annually (until her recent demise) paid homage at the crypt of Valentino on the anniversary of his death.

Peter Lorre is buried here, as is Douglas Fairbanks Sr., who captured "America's sweetheart," but didn't hold her. Clifton Webb, Adolph Menjou, Nelson Eddy, Eleanor Powell, Paul Muni, Joan Hackett, Norma Talmadge, Tyrone Power, Marion Davies, and the notorious Bugsy Siegel are also buried here. Director John Huston is interred here. Hours are 8 a.m. to 5 p.m.

Nestled in the foothills is the **Hollywood Bowl** at 2301 N. Highland Ave., summer home of the Los Angeles Philharmonic Orchestra since 1922. The most popular concerts each season are the Fourth of July Fireworks Family Picnic Concert and the two-day Tchaikovsky Spectacular with cannon shots, fireworks, and a military band. Other presentations include numerous opera and pop concerts, the traditional Easter Sunrise Service, and the "Open House at the Bowl" children's festival. The Los Angeles Philharmonic season runs from July through September, with ticket prices ranging from $12 to $60. Information on programs, artists, ticket availability, and RTD bus service to the Bowl is available by calling 213/850-2000.

Reached via Cahuenga Pass, **Mulholland Drive** commences in the Hollywood Hills, a winding scenic mountaintop highway that wends its way through Topanga Canyon, emerging near Malibu Beach. Mulholland Drive—in the stretch across the Santa Monica mountains—provides the most breathtaking view of the entire Los Angeles area, as well as the San Fernando Valley. From these heights, you can see for yourself the validity of the California wish fulfillment of a swimming pool for every home—well, almost.

In the northern hilly portion of Hollywood you'll find **Hollywoodland,** with a dam and lake surrounded by hillside homes (reached by Beachwood Drive, off Franklin Avenue). It's also the location of the famous "Hollywood" sign where a then-unknown Dolly Parton fantasized about a "Dollywood." Incidentally, the sign originally read "Hollywoodland."

---

5. Griffith Park, the Zoo, and Planetarium

Griffith Park, in Hollywood terminology, is a "spec." You've sat through many a western or war movie that purported to be somewhere else in the world, but was in reality the rugged terrain of what is the second-largest city-owned park in the world (4,253 acres). It has something for everybody!

The park straddles the foothills of the Santa Monica mountain chain, peaking at Mount Hollywood. Although the hills are covered with shrubbery, the lower parts—especially the ravines—are verdant and oak-studded parklands. Its position is north of Hollywood and the Los Feliz residential section. On the San Fernando Valley and Glendale peripheries, the Los Angeles River forms the border.

There are at least four major entrances to the park. The nearest to Hollywood is at the northern tip of Western Boulevard (along Ferndell). A second is at the northern extremity of Vermont Avenue, leading into that part of the park containing the Greek Theatre, the Observatory, bird sanctuary, and Mount Hollywood. Along the Los Angeles River, at the junction of Los Feliz Boulevard and Riverside Drive (also the Golden State Freeway), is an entrance leading to the Los Angeles municipal golf course, the zoo, and the Gene Autry Western Heritage Museum. The junctions of the Ventura and Golden State Freeways provide yet another entrance, adjacent to the zoo and "Travel Town." You'll be glad to know there's a picnic area near the junction of the Golden State and Ventura Freeways. There's a small fee to drive a vehicle into the park, which, however, includes parking.

The **Los Angeles Zoo,** 5333 Zoo Drive (tel. 213/666-4650), in keeping with the character of the film colony, bills its offerings as "a cast of thousands." In wildlife, the 115-acre zoo is virtually unbeatable. In fact, the sign "Endangered Species" is in front of more than 70 species in danger of extinction because of expanding human population, needless slaughter, and destruction of natural habitats. The protection of endangered animals has firmly established the Los Angeles Zoo as a major station in a network of wildlife conservation.

Animals are exhibited by origin in five continental areas: Africa, Eurasia, Australia, and North and South America. In addition, there is an Aviary with a large walk-through flight cage, an Aquatic section, a Reptile House and elephant shows. And there's also a new children's zoo with a number of fascinating exhibits creatively designed to involve adults and children.

The original children's zoo, built in 1963, was demolished in 1988. In its place arose **Adventure Island,** a fascinating place with all sorts of surprises in a zoo that wasn't intended to look like a zoo. Four distinct habitats were created to blend into one another in a space of about 2½ acres. There is the world of the mountain, the meadow, desert, and shoreline. Adventure Island houses an aviary, tide pool, petting zoo, animal nursery, and an outdoor theater for animal performances. There's also a marvelous cave built into a mountain. A lifelike Betty White (the actress and animal lover) appears in the cave, in miniature, to explain why and how skunks create their very unpleasant smell. In the Little House Under the Prairie, also inside the cave, you will see a prairie dog burrow and its "rooms." It's doubtful that you would be interested in petting tarantulas but it is nice to know that even they have air conditioning —it's essential to their survival since life in a restricted space is stressful to them.

Children can pose in life-size fantasies at "photo spots"

throughout Adventure Island, with a giant vulture (of course it isn't live, Henry), or a snake, or even seeming to hang upside down like a bat. All in all Adventure Island is fun and well worth your time.

Admission to the zoo is $6, $5 for seniors, $2.50 for children 2 to 12, free for children under 2. Facilities include picnic areas, snack stands, souvenir shops, and stroller and wheelchair rentals. Free parking. The zoo is open every day but Christmas, from 10 a.m. to 5 p.m. (till 6 p.m. in summer).

Crowning the hill in the park is the **Griffith Observatory and Planetarium** (entrance on Vermont Avenue), where the "great Zeiss projector" flashes about five shows a year across the 75-foot dome. You can see all the stars visible to the naked eye, take "a trip to the moon," or else go to Jupiter and Saturn. Still other projectors simulate the effects of the Northern Lights, as well as sunrise and sunset. One-hour shows are given daily, except Monday (every day in summer; for show times, telephone 213/664-1191; for other information call 664-1181). The price of admission is $4 for adults, $3 for children 5 to 15. Those under 5 are not admitted except to the first show on Saturday.

At night the Griffith Observatory and Laser Images, Inc., present *Laserium* light-show concerts under the planetarium stars. Powerful lasers produce dramatic effects covering the entire sky. Shows are presented Tuesday through Sunday. Call 818/997-3624 for show times. Tickets are $6 for adults, $5 for kids 5 to 12.

The loveliest section of the park is **Ferndell,** where New Zealand horticulturists planted ferns from around the world—creating a lush setting often used as a background for high-fashion photography. Amid sycamore and oak, you can bring your picnic lunch, and dine at tables placed there by the Recreation and Parks Department.

The **Greek Theatre** is especially popular (see Chapter VIII).

Travel Town Transportation Museum (tel. 213/662-5874), is a big attraction for children, who are allowed to climb up into the cab of a locomotive and view old retired rail cars, including an old Los Angeles tram and the Stockton Terminal and Eastern Railroad Engine No. 1, which saw more than 85 years of active duty (believed to be a record for a railroad engine). There is an outdoor display of railroad memorabilia dating back to the 1860s. Within the museum are antique fire engines, old carriages, and vintage cars. Admission is free. Travel Town is open November 1 to April 30 from 10 a.m. to 4 p.m. weekdays, to 5 p.m. on weekends and holidays (to 5 p.m. and 6 p.m. respectively for the balance of the year). There's a miniature train ride on weekdays from 10 a.m. to 4 p.m., to 5 p.m. on weekends (adults pay $3; children 2 to 13 $2, under 2 it's free).

And then there's an exciting new addition to Griffith Park: the **Gene Autry Western Heritage Museum,** 4700 Zoo Drive, Los Angeles, CA 90027 (tel. 213/667-2000). Don't miss it, with or without the kids.

The exterior of the museum complex is done in a contemporary California Mission style with plaza designs of the early West. Enter under a Hollywood–size arch and you are in a courtyard facing a life-size bronze of Gene Autry (once called "the singing cowboy") and his horse, Champion. Off the courtyard are entrances to the museum and the theater.

The entrance to the museum has an attractive exposed beam face with much glass paneling. Head for the information center, where you can rent a recorded Acoustaguide tour ($3) narrated by Willie Nelson.

The museum, opened in November 1988, is a remarkable repository of the history of the American West—undoubtedly one of the most comprehensive in the world. Its holdings contain over 16,000 artifacts and art pieces including 100 of Gene Autry's personal treasures. There are some superb bronze sculptures by Frederic Remington, a great artist of the West, including *The Bronc Buster* (1895) and *The Cheyenne* (1901), both donated by Mr. and Mrs. Autry. The museum's mission is both cultural and educational, done with artifacts that relate to the everyday lives and occupations of people who helped settle the West. The museum also depicts the West of romance and imagination as created by artists, authors, filmmakers, TV and radio. The exhibits were designed by Walt Disney Imagineering, the creative design subsidiary of the firm that planned the Disney theme park attractions and the exhibits at EPCOT Center.

The museum's many collections include firearms, common tools, magnificent saddles, stagecoaches (including one that the kiddies can pile into), clothing, toys, games, and posters. Some exhibits offer insights into the various philosophical motives of the early settlers, such as the desire of one group of Spanish explorers who "came to serve God and to get rich."

One of the most intriguing displays spotlights the women of the Wild West. The most famous of the female sharpshooters was pistol-packing Annie Oakley, who learned to shoot as a child on an Ohio farm. At 15 she beat Frank Butler, a professional marksman, in a local shooting match; she later married him. By mid-1890, these women began to participate in rodeos and exhibitions as bronc riders, trick riders, ropers, and bulldoggers.

Toward the end of your visit, you leave reality behind for the fascinating world of show business, beginning with items from Buffalo Bill's Wild West Show, movie clips from the silent days, contemporary films, and memorabilia from TV western series. There's a Hollywood–type set with viewer-activated videos, including one on the stuntmen who contributed to the drama and danger that made westerns so popular.

Now, about the museum shop. That, in itself, is worth a tour that could easily take an hour. The temptations include cowboy hats, Wild West posters, shirts, bolo ties, belts, and turquoise jewelry.

Although the Gene Autry Western Heritage Museum is just across from the zoo entrance, don't try to do both in one day. There won't be time and you'll miss out on much of the fun. When pangs of hunger set in, the **Golden Spur Café** just off the courtyard has a good selection of food (cafeteria-style). There are sandwiches including hot dogs ($2 to $3), soup ($2), salads ($3 to $4.50), desserts, and nonalcoholic beverages. The café also serves a light breakfast of biscuits, fruit, and fruit salad from 9:30 to 11 a.m. and remains open until 4:30 p.m.. There's space for dining inside or on a pleasant outdoor patio within an attractive open rotunda.

Admission to the museum is $5; $3.75 for seniors 60 and over, students 13 to 18, and college students with ID; $2.50 for children 2 to 12; under 2, free. The museum is open Tuesday through Sunday from 10 a.m. to 5 p.m.; closed on Monday, Thanksgiving, Christmas, and New Year's Day.

6. Beverly Hills

Beverly Hills is, as everybody knows, the adopted hometown of many a motion-picture and TV star—George Burns, Warren Beatty, James Stewart, Kirk Douglas, Harrison Ford, Jacqueline Bisset, Frank Sinatra, and Jack Nicholson, just to name a few. Its first mayor was the homespun philosopher/comedian/star Will Rogers.

If you'd like to get a close look at how the other half strives to live, Beverly Hills is the place. For a population of some 33,000 and an inestimable number of visitors, *The Los Angeles Times* points out that Beverly Hills has (give or take a few) 88 jewelry stores, over 100 restaurants, 60 financial institutions, and 15 limo services. In 1854 you could have purchased land here for about 25 cents per acre. I won't even mention the prices of today's regal real estate. And speaking of real estate, as they say in the world of big bucks—location is everything. The right zip code is as crucially important in Beverly Hills as it is in San Diego and many other towns. *The* zip code to have in Beverly Hills is 90201, in San Diego it's 92037 (La Jolla). Though parts of 90201 are not in Beverly Hills, the property values are right up there.

Although it contains many commercial establishments, the term "residential city" is apt. The municipality is completely encircled by Los Angeles. Three major boulevards—Wilshire, Olympic, and Santa Monica—traverse its southern border. Approximately two-thirds of Beverly Hills is in the flatlands, the other third in the foothills of the Santa Monica mountain range.

When the city incorporated at the outbreak of World War I, it contained only 675 registered voters. However, during the '20s, it earned the appellation of "boom town," so fantastically did its population soar. Beverly Hills currently has 33,000 residents, and proudly boasts its own city hall, police force (as Eddie Murphy fans already know), and mayor. It even has a **Chamber of Commerce & Visitors Bureau** at 239 S. Beverly Dr., between Charleville Boulevard and Gregory Way (tel. 213/271-8174 or 271-8126, toll free 800/345-2210), open weekdays from 8:30 a.m. to 5 p.m.

The business section of Beverly Hills lies between Wilshire and Santa Monica Boulevards, its prestigious hotels, restaurants, and upper-bracket department stores catering to the whims of decades of film personalities. It is the gathering place for a remarkable assemblage of Europe-based stores, many along Rodeo Drive. You'll probably see more stars in and around the shops on Rodeo Drive than anywhere else in town.

A drive through the glens, canyons, and hillsides of Beverly Hills may astonish you. Nowhere else in the world are you likely to find such an assemblage of luxury homes—each one a virtual candidate for inclusion in *House Beautiful*. You'll feel that each inhabitant should be a film star, whether she or he is or not. It's a cotton wool world, cut off from the rest of Los Angeles. Where else would you find a city which would refinish and redecorate a "convenience station" at the bus stop where household employees wait?

The most celebrated of all Beverly Hills residences is **Pickfair,** crowning the ridge at 1143 Summit Drive; unfortunately it's not open to public view. Set on 14 acres, Pickfair became the home of Douglas Fairbanks Sr. and Mary Pickford, beginning the trend in which Beverly Hills became the private enclave of movie stars, producers, directors, and your everyday multi-millionaires.

Beverly Hills is a part of town to drive around in, oohing and aahing and probably fantasizing that you too live here. Stop at the Polo Lounge in the Beverly Hills Hotel for a drink, lunch at La Scala & Boutique, dine at one of its posh eateries like the Bistro or Jimmy's, buy a little something at Giorgio, and absorb the glamour.

TOURS

The **Beverly Hills Chamber of Commerce & Visitors Bureau,** 239 S. Beverly Dr., Beverly Hills, CA 90212 (tel. 213/271-8174, or toll free 800/345-2210), now offers a **Trolley Tour** at no charge. The trolley's unique charm and the knowledgeable guides allow passengers to see Beverly Hills in style. The 30-minute tour leaves from the corner of Rodeo Drive and Dayton Way (you'll see a trolley sign there), and covers the posh downtown area as well as the exclusive residential neighborhoods. Tours are conducted Tuesday through Saturday from 10 a.m. to 6 p.m.

For a personalized look at Beverly Hills, you can book the Visitors Bureau's Ambassadear tour. The cost is $9 for members, $11 for nonmembers; and there's a four-hour minimum.

7. Toluca Lake/Burbank

Ever wonder where studios go when they leave Hollywood? Where motion-picture and TV stars live when they don't own homes in Malibu or Beverly Hills? In large part, they move to **Toluca Lake,** at the northern base of the Hollywood Hills. From Hollywood, it is easily reached via the Cahuenga Pass, Barham Boulevard, or Lankershim Boulevard—or from other points by way of the Golden State, Hollywood, or Ventura Freeways, which feed into the San Fernando Valley.

In the words of one resident, its boundaries are "Phantom-like." Taking its name from two natural, artesian-fed lakes, Toluca Lake as early as the 1920s started picking up the overflow from Hollywood. Today it encompasses a small, compact, and well-developed area, about a third of which lies within the city limits of **Burbank,** the remainder in Los Angeles proper.

Within its boundaries of hills and streets (Verdugo Road to the north, Buena Vista to the east, Forest Lawn and the Hollywood Hills to the south, Lankershim Boulevard to the west), the secluded community houses such film studios as Universal, Warner Brothers, Walt Disney, Columbia, and Cathedral Films, as well as NBC.

The list of former residents (many of whom have now retired, died, or moved on) is impressive: Bing Crosby, Oliver Hardy, Tennessee Ernie Ford, Richard Arlen, W. C. Fields, Helen Morgan, Frank Sinatra, Ruby Keeler, Dick Powell, Bette Davis, Mary Astor, even Amelia Earhart.

Not much more than 100 years old, Burbank is a city with pride in its history. In 1871, Dr. David Burbank, a New England dentist, purchased the Rancho La Providencia Scott Tract and raised sheep. The Providencia Land Water and Development Company built the Burbank Villa Hotel in 1887 and so began the enterprising city of Burbank. Lockheed Aircraft and Moreland Truck got their starts here.

Burbank now has a public record of its heritage—the **Gordon R. Howard Museum Complex,** 1015 W. Olive Ave. (tel. 818/841-6333), run by the Burbank Historical Society. The museum is open on Sunday from 1 to 4 p.m., other days by appointment.

The museum houses an eclectic collection of Burbank memorabilia. There are exhibits on Lockheed, Moreland, and Disney; artifacts and dioramas of 19th-century Burbank life; and, in a little garden near the museum buildings, one of the model houses built in the town around the turn of the century to lure residents to the Valley. (It's been completely restored and furnished by the Historical Society.) Also on display are a number of the jewels of Gordon Howard's collection of antique motor vehicles, including a 1922 fire engine, a 1937 Mercedes, a 1937 Rolls-Royce, a 1939 Daimler, and the 1922 Moreland bus used in the filming of *Some Like It Hot.*

It's a charming museum, well worth a visit. While there is no charge for admission, the museum appreciates a donation—usually $1.

From "Beautiful Downtown Burbank" to the backstage movie-lot tours at **Universal City,** there is much to see and explore.

8. Touring the Studios

Universal as well as NBC Television invites the public to tour their "cities within cities." Both offer a good look behind the scenes. Taking in the Burbank studios of Warner Bros. and Columbia Pictures can also be interesting.

UNIVERSAL STUDIOS HOLLYWOOD

Welcoming about five million visitors yearly to the world of make-believe, **Universal Studios Hollywood** has come a long way since its World War I beginnings as a chicken ranch. The largest stu- rugged mountain terrain and valley (entrance at 100 Universal City Plaza, at the junction of the Hollywood Freeway and Lankershim Boulevard; tel. 818/508-9600).

Many great names in the history of the cinema are linked to Universal. The founder, Carl Laemmle, hired Erich von Stroheim as a director, and he proceeded to make a number of movies that shocked post–World War I audiences with their candor. However, he was dismissed as a "spendthrift." In another era, the studio's sag- ging coffers were greatly enhanced by Deanna Durbin, only 15 in 1937 when she appeared in *One Hundred Men and a Girl.*

After World War II, and into the '50s, Universal lured audi- ences back to movie theaters with such pedestrian vehicles as the *Ma and Pa Kettle* series (with Marjorie Main and Percy Kilbride) and the *Francis* flicks (the talking mule teamed with his sidekick, Donald O'Connor), plus a rising set of young leading men such as Tony Curtis and Rock Hudson.

And then there was the box office winner *Jaws,* the blockbuster *E.T., The Thing, Conan the Barbarian, Twins,* and *Parenthood*—all Universal films.

The guided portion of the tour—aboard one of the brightly colored trams—lasts about 2 hours and takes you through the en- tire studio. Allow the rest of your day to see the five live action shows in the Entertainment Center (see below).

During the tour you'll learn much behind-the-scenes informa- tion. One of the most interesting aspects of the tour is a guided trip through "movie worlds"—a European street rebuilt and aged at a cost of $2 million; Sherlock Holmes' Baker Street; the streets of Par- is; Animal House; Six Points Texas, a western town with six intersecting streets; Colonial Street (Smalltown, U.S.A.), and New York Street, which has over the years been patrolled by Baretta, Kojak, and Columbo. More exciting, though, are the many perils encountered by the luckless tram: a flash flood, the parting of the Red Sea, a collapsing bridge, an encounter with King Kong, an al- pine avalanche, an attack by the shark from *Jaws,* and a raging laser battle with Cylon robots!

Universal's latest addition to the big scare is "Earthquake— The Big One." This is a re-creation of a monster earthquake (signifi- cantly greater than the 1989 quake in San Francisco)—an 8.3 that tears the ground right out from under you. It's an amazing, excit- ing, terrifying natural disaster. Actually, Universal Studios Hollywood is giving Disneyland competition.

Those over 12 pay $21; seniors, $16; children 3 to 11, $16.50; children under 3 admitted free. In summer, and on holidays year round, there are continuous tours daily from 9 a.m. to 5 p.m. The rest of the year tours are given weekdays from 10 a.m. to 3:30 p.m., and 9:30 a.m. to 3:30 p.m. weekends. Never on Thanksgiving and Christmas, however. There are 50 acres of parking next to Universal ($4).

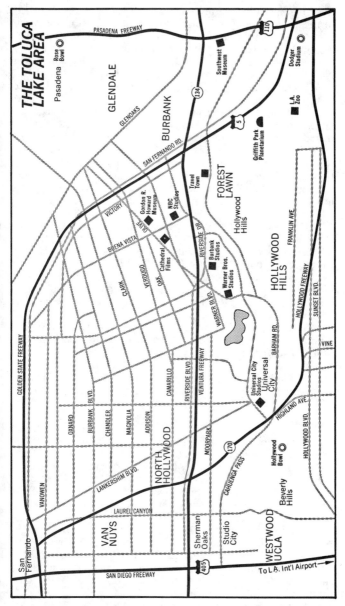

At a cost of millions of dollars, Universal City erected a **Visitors Entertainment Center,** where the tram will deposit you. Before or after your tour, you can spend as much time as you like, perhaps taking in the motion picture museum in the Cinema Pavilion, or going to any of five live-action shows, where you get to perform as a "guest star" in the Star Trek Adventure. You can also watch some amazing animals in action. And of course there's a once-is-enough encounter with a 30-foot-tall King Kong. You're carried into a dark sound stage and suddenly you're on an elevated train in New York, listening to newscasters warning about King Kong; then sirens, screams, and finally, King Kong—raging, tearing, just three feet away.

Three new attractions were added in 1990. Steven Spielberg's fantasy adventure *An American Tail* features all the stars of the animated film classic in the magical world of Fievel and his friends, including Dom DeLuise's voice as Tiger the Cat. Guests can play with the stars of the show in a re-created set adjacent to the production stage. There children slide on a banana peel, explore the inside of a bird cage, climb through a giant slice of Swiss cheese, cross a hot-dog bridge, and explore more than 40 larger-than-life cinematic effects.

The "Back To The Future Special Effects Stage" re-creates actual scenes depicting the ride on an outer space freeway to the futuristic Hill Valley and the climactic electrifying courthouse clock tower scenes from *Back To The Future I* and *II.*

"The Riot Act" goes beyond a traditional stunt show to never-before-seen live movie stunts, including blowing up a building, a dramatic high fall through floor planks, and the highest motion-pole balance ever attempted.

As the day stretches out, you may want to patronize one of the dining areas. There is **Victoria Station,** a complete restaurant; **Famous Amos;** and just outside the tour center is **Tony Roma's.** .

You can see a TV show taped at Universal too! Call 818/508-9600 for information and tickets, or write in advance to Universal Studios, 100 Universal City Plaza, Universal City, CA 91608.

NBC TELEVISION

Good-naturedly spoofed for its grand size by Johnny Carson, who calls it home for his "Tonight" show, NBC-TV's Burbank facilities are the largest color studios in the United States. For a behind-the-camera preview of this complex, you can get to the studios, 3000 W. Alameda Ave., Burbank, CA. 91523 (tel. 818/840-3537), in about five minutes from either the Ventura, Golden State, or Hollywood Freeway.

You are conducted through the studio by a knowledgeable NBC page. "Classic Concentration," "Scrabble," and "Saved by the Bell" are taped here. It's not guaranteed that you'll actually meet a star, though it sometimes happens (few actors can resist an admiring audience). Many big-name TV personalities, notably Bob Hope and Johnny Carson, also tape their shows here.

Aside from the limited glamour aspects, the tour is most informative, including looks at the scenery shop, the wardrobe department, set construction, special effects (where you can see yourself fly like Superman), the sound-effects center, and the rehearsal halls. NBC is the only major network to invite you behind the scenes of TV production, plus put you on camera in their mini-studio.

Continuous 1¼-hour tours are conducted weekdays from 8:30 a.m. to 4 p.m., on Saturday from 10 a.m. to 4 p.m., and on Sunday to 2 p.m. The charge is $9, $8 for seniors, $6 for children ages 5 to 14, and free for children under 5.

If you want to see one of the numerous shows taped at the NBC studios (including "The Tonight Show"), you may write to the address above. Be sure to include a self-addressed, stamped envelope, the name and date of the show you want to see, and the number of tickets you will need. The studio does not send out tickets, because show times and dates change, and in some cases tapings get cancelled. But you'll receive a "guest letter," which you can exchange for tickets when you arrive. The ticket counter is open weekdays from 8 a.m. to 5 p.m., and on weekends from 9:30 a.m. to 4 p.m. (*Note:* Tickets for "The Tonight Show" are available only on the day of the show; tickets for other shows can usually be picked up in advance. Minimum age limits for taping vary from 8 to 18; it's 16 for "The Tonight Show.")

THE BURBANK STUDIOS

Home of **Warner Bros.** and **Columbia Pictures,** the Burbank Studios, 4000 Warner Blvd. (tel. 818/954-1744), offer the most comprehensive and least Disney-esque of studio tours. They call it the VIP tour, because it's created not for mass audiences but for small groups—no more than 12 persons. It was, in fact, originally designed to introduce visiting VIPs to the workings of the studio and was later made available to film buffs.

The tours are very flexible, taking in whatever is being filmed at the time. Perhaps an orchestra is scoring a film or TV program—you'll get to see how it's done. Whenever possible, guests visit working sets to watch actors filming actual productions such as "Designing Women," "Murphy Brown," and "Night Court." You'll also tour set environments from jungles to Arctic tundra, from the Wild West to slum tenements. The wardrobe department and the mills where sets are made are also possible stops. It all depends on what's going on the day of your tour.

Because you're seeing the people at work, who mustn't be disturbed, there are only two tours a day (more during the summer); weekdays at 10 a.m. and 2 p.m., and children under 10 are not admitted. Admission is $24 per person, and you must make reservations at least one week in advance.

9. Glendale and Forest Lawn

A small residential and industrial community, lying roughly between Griffith Park and Pasadena, **Glendale** is the home of a number of ultra-conservative citizens, often satirized on television or made the butt of many a tired joke. Ironically, within the boundaries of the former "ranch" is one of the world's most unconventional and controversial cemeteries, **Forest Lawn.**

The "sacred gardens" are in the hills, about half a block off San Fernando Road, just three short blocks south of Glendale Boulevard. To reach Glendale and Forest Lawn from Hollywood, drive east on Los Feliz Boulevard, crossing over Riverside Drive and Los Angeles Drive. This portion of Los Feliz Boulevard is visited chiefly for its famed "Antique Row." Turn right on San Fernando Road, and the entrance to Forest Lawn will be three blocks on your left.

FOREST LAWN

This is a cemetery extraordinaire! Actually, there is a quintet of Forest Lawns (others at Cypress, Hollywood Hills, Long Beach, and Covina Hills), but the best-known one is at 1712 S. Glendale Ave., at Los Feliz Road (tel. 213/254-3131). The admission-free gardens may be visited from 9 a.m. to 5 p.m. Pick up a map at the Information Booth (at the entrance) when you arrive—it lists major points of interest. When you go to see the displays which have timed showings, be sure to arrive ten minutes early. The gates close promptly.

In the introduction of Adela Rogers St. John's *First Step Up Toward Heaven* (the biography of the founder, Hubert Eaton) appeared this description of Forest Lawn: "Imagine the greenest, most enchanting park you ever saw in your life. Imagine hearing the singing birds in the tops of the towering trees, or letting your gaze sweep over vistas of sparkling lawns, with shaded arborways, and garden retreats, and beautiful noble statuary. It sounds unreal— perhaps —an unearthly park-paradise."

Evelyn Waugh in his satirical *The Loved One*, some 40 years ago, saw Forest Lawn differently. In his fictional "Whispering Glades," he depicted an ominous graveyard with "mortuary hostesses," "Before Need" reservations, coffins like "The Egypt of the Pharoahs," and "slumber rooms" where corpses lie in repose.

Of particular interest is the *Last Supper* window—based on Leonardo da Vinci's painting and displayed in the "Memorial Court of Honor" in the Great Mausoleum. The panels open daily every half hour from 9:30 a.m. to 4 p.m., revealing the work of Signorina Rosa Moretti, the last member of a Perugia, Italy, family known for its secret process of making stained glass.

Thousands of Southern Californians are entombed in the Great Mausoleum, including such celebrities as Jean Harlow, W.C. Fields, Carole Lombard, and Clark Gable. On the art terraces and in the corridors are displayed reproductions of statuary, such as Michelangelo's *Twilight* and *Dawn*, as well as Donatello's *St. George.*

The big draw on the hill—next to the Forest Lawn Museum— is a special theater with the world's largest single curtain (210 feet long, 65 feet high), for the multimedia presentation (a veritable sound-and-light show) of two paintings. One is *The Crucifixion,* the largest permanently mounted religious painting in the United States, perhaps the world. Paderewski dreamed it, and Jan Styka painted it. The other is *The Resurrection,* completed by Robert Clark in 1965. The paintings are shown every hour from 10 a.m. to 4 p.m. After viewing them, you can explore the museum, with its reproductions of Ghiberti's *Paradise Doors* and the recently discovered *Sotterraneo* by Michelangelo.

Other attractions include the Court of David, with its reproduction of Michelangelo's famous sculpted masterpiece. Interesting churches include the Church of the Recessional, modeled after a 10th-century building in Sussex, England, and dedicated to the poetry of Rudyard Kipling (see his family album and literary mementos in an adjoining wing), and the Wee Kirk o' the Heather, based on a church built early in the 14th century in Glencairn, Scotland. A stained-glass window depicts the story of Annie Laurie, a 17th-century heroine who "reluctantly married someone else," though "her heart remained faithful to Douglas, love of her youth."

Forest Lawn also serves the living. It is estimated that wedding chimes have rung for over 60,000 persons. The memorial churches are also the setting for numerous christenings, church services, ordinations of ministers, and other ecclesiastical functions.

In other words, Forest Lawn gets the business from birth to death.

---

10. Highland Park

For an introduction to the spirit of the great Southwest, head for Highland Park, where the following little-known attraction awaits you. You can take the Pasadena Freeway (Hwy. 110), exiting at Avenue 43.

THE SOUTHWEST MUSEUM

Crowning the crest of a steep hill, overlooking Arroyo Seco, is the Southwest Museum, Los Angeles' oldest art treasury. The museum was founded in 1907 by amateur historian and Indian expert Charles F. Lummis, utilizing private funds. It contains one of the finest collections of Native American and southwestern Hispanic art and artifacts in the United States. Located at 234 Museum Dr., at Marmion Way (tel. 213/221-2163, recording; or 221-2164), it can be approached either via a winding drive or else through a tunnel at the foot of the hill, which opens onto an elevator which will carry you to the top.

Inside the two-story structure, in a panoramic exhibition, is the Indian world of the Americas, complete with a Cheyenne summer tepee, rare paintings, weapons, moccasins, and other artifacts of Plains Indian life. A two-level hall presents the culture of the native peoples of southeast Alaska, Canada's west coast, and the northern United States. There is a major exhibition covering 10,000 years of history of the people of the Southwest and featuring art and artifacts of native people in Arizona, New Mexico, Colorado, and Utah. The

California Hall offers insights into the lifestyle of the first Californians.

A new study-storage area in the Caroline Boeing Poole Memorial Wing provides a changing display of over 400 examples of North American Indian basketry from the museum's collection of over 11,000 baskets.

Lummis, who was the director of the Los Angeles Library, collected a great many rare and valuable books on the Southwest, which he turned over to the museum, along with his extensive archeological collection.

The museum also contains a portrait of Gen. John Charles Frémont, the famous 19th-century explorer and politician, and his well-known wife, Jessie Benton, daughter of a Missouri senator. Frémont is remembered chiefly for his career as an explorer ("From the ashes of his campfires have sprung cities"). He explored the country west of the Mississippi all the way to the Pacific, and is credited with trail-blazing efforts by the forty-niners.

The museum has an exceptionally interesting and changing calendar of events and exhibitions throughout the year such as the Native American Film Festival, which features documentaries and short films; lectures on the sacred art of the Huichols; and presentations of Mexican song, dance, costumes, and masks, to name just a few.

The Southwest Museum has undergone significant changes over the past six years and if you've never visited it before, or haven't been there recently, you'll find it fascinating and well worth your time. The museum is open Tuesday through Sunday from 11 a.m. to 5 p.m. Adults pay $4.50; seniors and students $2.25; and young people 7 to 18 $1; under 7, it's free.

You can also visit **El Alisal,** the rugged home of Charles F. Lummis, founder of the museum, at nearby 200 E. Avenue 43 (tel. 213/222-0546). Lummis built this two-story "castle" himself, using rocks from a nearby arroyo and telephone poles purchased from the Santa Fe Railroad. His home became a cultural center for many famous personages in the literary, theatrical, political, and art worlds. Himself an author, editor (he coined the slogan "See America First"), archeologist, and librarian, Lummis was equally at home with Will Rogers, Teddy Roosevelt, singer Mary Garden, and Madame Schumann-Heink, and writers such as Blasco Ibáñez.

One of the particularly interesting aspects of El Alisal is its new and most attractive water-conserving garden. The primary plants are those which thrive in a Mediterranean climate. The experimental section, the yarrow meadow, is a substitute for a water-consuming lawn. The house is open free to the public Wednesday to Sunday from 1 to 4 p.m.

Yet a third attraction in the area is the **Casa de Adobe,** at 4605 N. Figueroa St. (tel. 213/225-8653), a recreation of an early 19th-century Mexican California rancho. Latino art and artifacts are on exhibit from the Southwest Museum permanent collection, along with Spanish Colonial–period furnishings. It's open Tuesday to Saturday from 11 a.m. to 5 p.m., on Sunday from 1 p.m. Admission is free (donations are accepted).

11. Six Flags Magic Mountain

On a 260-acre site of green rolling hills at Valencia, 25 miles north of Hollywood, is one of the best family fun parks in the West. Opened in the spring of 1971, with its ponds, lakes, and waterfalls, as well as thousands of trees and flowering plants, the "mountain" is an attractive garden. But the emphasis is on the 100 or so rides and attractions, some of the former costing millions of dollars to construct.

There's the Condor, which twirls you (and your stomach) at the top of a 112-foot pole. Or you can look forward to an incredible Tidal Wave, where you plunge 50 feet into a 20-foot wall of wild water—guaranteed to be a hair-raising experience. Then there's the Z-Force, which will leave you hanging upside down from a swinging gondola so that a sheer drop of four stories seems certain. Or the thrill you've always wanted just may be Roaring Rapids, which takes passengers on a raft ride down a whitewater river complete with a waterfall, whirlpools, and stair step rapids. Yes, you'll get wet!

If that's not enough excitement, Freefall, another great thrill ride, drops riders 98 feet in a gondola at speeds up to 55 mph giving the sensation of free fall experienced by skydivers. Of course, everyone also wants to ride the Log Jammer, hollowed-out fiberglass logs that careen through the mountain in a log flume water course, ending with a 47-foot plunge into a lake. Rivaling this attraction is the Jet Stream ride. The Sky Tower, on the other hand, takes you to the top of a 384-foot structure, about equal to the height of a 38-story building. From the observation decks, a panoramic view unfolds. Colossus, the world's largest double-track wooden roller coaster, travels at 60 mph and offers two terrifying 100-foot drops. And if you want more thrills you can ride the Revolution, with its 360° loop, or the Buccaneer, a pendulum-shaped giant pirate ship that swings to and fro in a 70° arc. Aha! but wait until you try Ninja, the black belt of roller coasters. It's the first and only suspended coaster on the West Coast which propels passengers from an overhead track through trees and along hills at angles of up to 110° and speeds of 50 mph.

But the screamer of them all is the **Viper,** described by Magic Mountain as pound-for-pound the most frightening roller coaster on earth. You're tossed into a loop, a corkscrew, and a 70 mph 18-story drop from 188 feet above the ground and spiraled completely upside down seven times. It's the ultimate fear machine with its 55-degree drop—the longest dive of any steel looping coaster—then through three consecutive vertical loops, into a head-over-toes double loop, then upside down twice more. It's 2½ minutes of top-of-the-lungs screaming. I suggest that if you haven't already eaten, wait until after the ride.

Other somewhat less hysterical rides include the Metro, a monorail; the Grand Carousel, originally built in 1912 and restored at great cost; Spin Out, in which centrifugal force keeps whirling passengers stuck to the walls when the floor drops out from under them; the Sand Blasters, dune buggies propelled by exhaust-free electric motors; the Gold Rusher, another "white knuckler" featuring a runaway mine train; Grand Prix, sports cars racing around a fully landscaped track; the Funicular, a cable railroad imported from Europe; the Bobsled; and the Steam Train, a narrow-gauge steam replica of a turn-of-the-century passenger train.

Bugs Bunny's World features 13 pint-sized rides, everything from a roller coaster to Red Baron airplanes. In the one-acre **Animal Farm,** children are invited to pet and feed the animals in their natural environment.

Then there's the **Aqua Theatre,** where daily entertainment consists of dolphin shows and champion high divers.

In **Spillikin Handcrafters Junction,** an authentic 1800s crafts village, visitors can watch woodcarvers, glassblowers, weavers, blacksmiths, and other artisans at work. And in addition to all the above there are clowns, strolling musicians, magicians, animal shows, and much, much more.

Although there are many snackbars and cafeterias, the best food is at the **Four Winds,** a restaurant on Samurai Summit. Amusement-park fare from fried chicken to cotton candy is also available.

The major entertainment center is the 3,400-seat **Showcase Theatre,** which draws name performers.

You get everything—rides, amusements, special attractions; the showcase entertainment—for just one admission price: $23 for adults, $12 for children under 48 inches, seniors over 55 pay $12, and kids 2 and under enter free. The park is open in summer from 10 a.m. to midnight daily. Off-season hours (weekends and holidays only) vary, so it's best to call ahead (tel. 805/255-4111 or 818/367-5965) for information. Parking is $5.

The amusement park is reached from U.S. 101 in Ventura by taking Calif. 126 through Fillmore to Castaic Junction, then turning south for about one mile at the junction of 126 and Interstate 5. From either direction, the park is two minutes west of the Golden State Freeway (Interstate 5) at the Magic Mountain Parkway exit.

---

12. William S. Hart Park

He was the prototype of the cowboy hero, the western good guy who loved his horse more than his girl. Before he died on June 23, 1946, at the age of 81, Bill Hart expressed a hope that has since been fulfilled: "While I was making pictures, the people gave me their nickels, dimes, and quarters. When I am gone, I want them to have my home."

Purchased in 1920, his Horseshoe Ranch is now the William S. Hart County Park, whose entrance is at the junction of Newhall Avenue and San Fernando Road, at 24151 Newhall Ave., Newhall (tel. 805/254-4584, Wednesday to Friday 9:30 a.m. to 3:30 p.m. or 805/259-0855 daily). To reach the ranch, drive north on Golden State Freeway (Interstate 5) to Hwy. 14, then north on Hwy. 14 to San Fernando Road, go west to Newhall Avenue.

The park is stocked with farm animals, including a small, rare buffalo herd. Walt Disney provided the nucleus of the herd in 1962. Visitors are allowed to take along a picnic lunch, enjoying it at designated spots on the 265-acre site.

At the entrance to the park, a shuttle (operating weekends only) will take you to the museum, housed in the old Hart home, which he called "La Loma de Los Vintos." The museum is open from mid-October to mid-June from 10 a.m. to 12:30 p.m. Wednesday to Friday and 11 a.m. to 3:30 p.m. on Saturday and Sunday; mid-June to mid-October from 11 a.m. to 3:30 p.m. Wednesday to Sunday, the park is open daily from 9:30 a.m. to sunset, except on Christmas, New Year's Day, and Thanksgiving. Built in the Spanish-Mexican style, the house contains 14 rooms, filled not only with mementos of Hart's career, but with genuine relics of the Old West. The furnishings are pretty much as Hart left them. The museum also owns 18 paintings and five bronze statues by Charles M. Russell, a close friend of the cowboy hero.

As Hart stipulated in his will, no one is charged admission.

13. The Spanish Missions

On July 16, 1769, a Franciscan padre, Junípero Serra (soon to be canonized), established the first in a string of missions that were to stretch along **El Camino Real** (the Royal Road). Eventually, the missions were to total 21, reaching from San Diego to Sonoma.

Tolerated by the Spanish king, the mission chain formed in a colonization bulwark against possible Russian aggrandizements in the north. The missions each functioned much like a commune, with the padres and Indians creating their own centers of agriculture and industry. They raised cattle, sheep, and goats, planted citrus groves and olive trees, made soap, blankets, wine, even ironware. The Indians were taught methods of irrigation and many of the communities prospered. Four of the most visited missions include the following:

SAN JUAN CAPISTRANO

About 56 miles south of L.A. is the historic town of **San Juan Capistrano,** known for the swallows that return there each year thanks to a song, "When the Swallows Come Back to Capistrano," written over 50 years ago. Though the swallows are getting scarcer (a trend that many residents welcome), they still return to the mission on St. Joseph's Day, March 19. On October 23, the Day of San Juan, the swallows punctually leave for their home to the south, probably somewhere in South America.

The mission dates from 1775. A museum was added 10 years ago and is a repository of fascinating artifacts and murals depicting the mission era. The mission's great feature is the Serra Chapel, the oldest building in California still in use. The ruins of the Old Stone Church, the restored metal working furnaces, and the original adobe walls contribute to the site's historic charm. The mission may be visited from 7:30 a.m. till 5 p.m., and it charges $2 per person (children under 12, $1). For information call 714/493-1424 for a recording, 493-1111 for a human.

MISSION SAN FERNANDO

In 1797, Padre Fermin Lasuen founded a mission, 17th in the eventual chain of 21, in what was to be called the San Fernando Valley. At 15151 San Fernando Mission Blvd., Mission Hills, near the junction of the Golden State (I-5) and San Diego (Hwy. 405) freeways, the mission reached its apex in the same year—1812—that an earthquake struck.

On the grounds you can explore a *convento*, with rooms like narrow quadrangles. Completed in 1806, with an arcade of 21 classic arches and adobe walls four feet thick, it was here that many of the wayfarers along El Camino Real were sheltered for the night— or as long as they wanted to stay. It also served as sleeping quarters for the padres, and contained a dining room and kitchen, as well as a vat and wine cellar.

The mission chapel (of which the present structure is an exact replica, the original having been irreparably damaged in the 1971 earthquake), its walls seemingly jutting outward, was originally completed in 1806 and is graced with primitive Indian wall paintings in cobalt blue. The adjoining cemetery, with its tiny brook and semitropical vegetation, is the most serene spot (half a dozen padres were buried there, along with hundreds of Shoshone Indians). There's also a gift shop on the premises. In the museum is an exceptional altar, dating from the early 17th century, with intricate handcarved wooden vines and gold leaf. You can walk through the peaceful grounds from 9 a.m. to 4:30 p.m. daily for a $2 admission for adults, $1 for children 7 to 15. For information call 818/361-0186.

MISSION SAN GABRIEL ARCANGEL

Due to the earthquakes of October 1 and 4, 1987, it has been necessary to close the church, museum, and winery. Precisely when the mission will be able to open depends on how long it will take to raise the $3 million needed to repair and restore the buildings. The remainder of the grounds are still open to visitors. Formerly one of the best preserved of the missions built under the leadership of Padre Junípero Serra, San Gabriel traces its origins back to 1771, when it was founded fourth in the 21-link chain. It's a completely self-contained compound, with a famous set of bells, soap vats, an old kitchen, and aqueduct, a cemetery, a winery, a tannery, and a mission church. Because of its strategic location, it was visited by numerous wayfarers en route to and from Mexico.

Construction on the church—distinguished by its buttresses —was begun in 1790. Erected to withstand the ravages of time, the walls are about five feet thick. In the sanctuary was a revered 17th-century painting, an oval-faced and sad-eyed *Our Lady of Sorrows*— said to have subdued hostile Indians with its serenity. It has been stolen. The glittering polychrome statues surrounding the altar were handcarved, and in the copper font the first Indian was baptized in 1771.

In the museum are some "aboriginal" Indian paintings depicting the Stations of the Cross—painted on sailcloth, with colors made from crushing the petals of desert flowers. The childlike primitives tell their story crudely but vividly.

The mission is open daily, except Christmas, Thanksgiving, and Easter, from 9:30 a.m. to 4 p.m. You can buy a gift at the curio shop. It's located at 537 West Mission Dr., San Gabriel, about one mile south of the Huntington Museum at San Marino (tel. 818/282-5191). There is no admission fee, but donations are accepted.

MISSION SANTA BARBARA

On the edge of Mission Canyon, this old mission lent its name to the seaside resort and residential city 98 miles northwest of Los Angeles. (You might plan an overnight stay in Santa Barbara, as it's rather a long trip for one day. See Chapter X for places to stay and dine.) Founded shortly before Christmas in 1786, the "Queen of the Missions" was built in the neoclassical style. Today it is the headquarters of the Pacific coast district of the Franciscans. It contains a trio of quadrangles in the original style, plus a façade of splayed Moorish windows. Perhaps its most idyllic spot is the cloister garden, with a circular lily pond, the twin towers along the front reflected in the background.

A church that stood on this spot was gutted in an earthquake that hit in 1812. The reconstruction began in 1815, lasting for five years. The mission was again damaged by an earthquake in 1925. Some $375,000 needed for its restoration poured in, mainly through public contributions. However, because of a defect in the building materials, a quarter of a century later the façade and towers were torn down and rebuilt, and reblessed once again in 1953.

At the dawn of the 19th century the number of Indians living at the mission totaled around 2,000. Under the direction of the padres, the Indians raised livestock and cultivated the fields. It was the stated goal of each mission to be self-sustaining, making and providing the clothing of its members as well as their foodstuff. Trades such as saddle-making and blacksmithing were also learned.

The mission, at Laguna and Los Olivos streets, is open daily from 9 a.m. to 5 p.m., and requests a donation of $1 for adults (children under 16 admitted free).

---

14. Pasadena Area

The grande dame of the Greater Los Angeles area, **Pasadena** is a residential city 11 miles northwest of the downtown district, hugging the foothills of the Sierra Madre mountain range in the San Gabriel Valley. It has street after street of large estates, surrounded by semitropical gardens—a haven for "old money."

Of course, it is known chiefly for its **Rose Bowl,** with its New Year's football game (where the champions of the East meet those of the West), and its annual **Tournament of Roses** parade. Since its beginnings in 1890—with "flower-bedecked buggies and surreys"

—the parade has included such "grand marshals" as Bob Hope and Mary Pickford, even Richard Nixon and Shirley Temple. Since the early 1950s both the parade and play-off game have enjoyed a nationwide audience.

If you're not around for the Tournament of Roses, and you're not in the mood for culture, there's always bargain hunting at one of the country's largest flea markets. The second Sunday of each month there's a **flea market** at the Rose Bowl with 1,500 vendors and homespun entertainment. Be sure to make a note of where you parked your car.

Just south of Pasadena is another primarily residential community, **San Marino,** visited chiefly because of its world-famed **Huntington Library and Museum,** and the nearby **Descanso Gardens** and **San Gabriel Mission.**

From these hill-hugging communities, you can reach the Los Angeles National Forest mountain resorts, such as **Big Bear, Mount Wilson,** and **Mount Baldy.**

HUNTINGTON LIBRARY, ART COLLECTIONS, AND BOTANICAL GARDENS

At 1151 Oxford Rd., in San Marino (tel. 818/405-2100, or 405-2141), stands the fulfillment of a dream of its creator, Henry E. Huntington (1850–1927). About 12 miles from downtown Los Angeles, the 207-acre estate of the pioneer industrialist—complete with gardens and mansion—has been converted into an educational and cultural center for scholars, art devotees, and the general public. Mr. Huntington's thirst for original manuscripts, rare books, great paintings, and skillfully planned gardens led to the formation of what may be considered one of the greatest attractions in Southern California.

His home is now an art gallery, housing paintings, tapestries, furniture, and other decorative arts, chiefly English and French works of the 18th century. In the art gallery, the most celebrated painting is Gainsborough's *The Blue Boy.* Another famous portrait is that of the youthful aunt of Elizabeth Barrett Browning, *Pinkie,* by Sir Thomas Lawrence. Equally well known are Sir Joshua Reynold's *Sarah Siddons as the Tragic Muse;* Rembrandt's *Lady with the Plume,* and Romney's *Lady Hamilton in a Straw Hat.* You'll also find a collection of Beauvais and Gobelin tapestries.

The Virginia Steele Scott Gallery for American art opened in 1984. Paintings range in date over a 200-year span from the 1730s to the 1930s. Some of the better known works are Gilbert Stuart's portrait of George Washington, John Singleton Copley's *Sarah Jackson,* George Caleb Bingham's *In a Quandary,* Mary Cassatt's *Breakfast in Bed,* and Frederic Church's *Chimborazo.*

The Library Exhibition Hall contains a few dozen of the great treasures drawn from its remarkable collection of English and American first editions, letters, and manuscripts. They include one of the copies of the Gutenberg Bible printed in the 1450s in Mainz, a 1410 copy of Chaucer's *Canterbury Tales,* a First Folio of Shakespeare's plays, and Benjamin Franklin's *Autobiography* in his own handwriting. There are more than 300,000 rare books and over two million manuscripts ranging from the 11th century to the present.

Of special interest are the Botanical Gardens, with greenery, rare shrubs, and trees, studded with 17th-century statuary from Padua and surrounded by azaleas and camellias. You can also stroll through, among others, a Desert Garden, with extensive cacti in all shapes; a Camellia Garden with 1,500 varieties; and a Japanese Garden, with curving pathways, dwarf maples, an arched drum bridge, reflection pools; a Japanese house; a Zen Garden, and a bonsai court.

The admission-free museum and grounds are open Tuesday through Sunday from 1 to 4:30 p.m. (closed on major holidays). A donation of $2 per adult is suggested. *Note:* Sunday visitors must make reservations in advance if they are residents of Los Angeles County. Those who are not residents of the county, or those who are but are accompanied by out-of-town guests, do not need reservations.

NORTON SIMON MUSEUM OF ART

One of the most important museums in California is at Colorado Boulevard at Orange Grove (tel. 818/449-3730). The museum sits among broad plazas, sculpture gardens, a reflection pool, and semitropical plantings.

Important areas covered here are old masters from the Italian, Dutch, Spanish, Flemish, and French Schools; Impressionist paintings; Franco-Flemish tapestries; and 20th-century painting and sculpture. Some highlights of the collections are works by Raphael, Rubens, Rembrandt, Rousseau, Courbet, Matisse, Picasso, Corot, Monet, and van Gogh. A superb collection of Southeast Asian and Indian sculpture is also featured.

The museum is open Thursday through Sunday from noon to 6 p.m. Adults pay $5; senior citizens over 62 and students, $2.50; children under 12 are admitted free with an adult. The bookshop closes at 5:30 p.m.

DESCANSO GARDENS

Here you'll see one of the largest collections of camellias in the world, more than 100,000 plants. The rose varieties are spectacular as well, including some from Damascus dating from the time of Christ. You can also admire lilacs, azaleas, orchids, and daffodils, plus many species of native flora—all planted in or around a mature Southern California oak forest. A stream and many paths run through the oaks, and a chaparral nature trail is provided for those who wish to observe native vegetation. Other features of the gardens are monthly art exhibitions in the Hospitality House; a Japanese Teahouse serving tea and cookies Tuesday through Sunday from 11 a.m. to 4 p.m.; lunches served daily at the Cafe Court; docent-guided walking tours on Sundays at 1 p.m.; a gift shop; guided tram tours ($2) Tuesday through Friday at 1, 2, and 3 p.m., and at 11 a.m. on Saturday and Sunday.

The gardens are at 1418 Descanso Dr., La Canada, at the junction of the Glendale and Foothill Freeways, and are open daily from 9 a.m. to 4:30 p.m. For additional information, telephone

818/790-5571. Admission is $4 for adults, $2 for seniors, and $1 for children 5 to 12. Persons under 18 must be accompanied by adults. Picnicking is allowed only in specified areas. The gardens are run by the Los Angeles County Department of Arboreta and Botanic Gardens. Parking is free.

15. Organized Tours

The quickest, easiest, and most efficient way to explore the sights of Southern California is by an organized sightseeing tour. A number of companies offer such tours, the most outstanding of which is **Gray Line Tours Company,** 6541 Hollywood Blvd., Los Angeles (tel. 213/481-2121 for information). In air-conditioned coaches, with commentaries by guides, the tours include such sights as Disneyland, the movie studios, the homes of the stars in Beverly Hills, Farmers Market, the Movieland Wax Museum, Six Flags Magic Mountain, Universal Studios, Hollywood, Sunset Strip, Knott's Berry Farm, the *Queen Mary* and *Spruce Goose,* Catalina Island (check for cruise availability), the San Diego Zoo, Sea World of San Diego, and Tijuana, Mexico. All fares include admission to attractions.

Don't forget the tours run by the **Beverly Hills Chamber of Commerce & Visitors Bureau** described in Section 6 and the tours of the studios in Section 8, both in this chapter.

16. Sports

While sports buffs in less favorable climates are moving indoors after Labor Day, the Los Angeles fans can attend outdoor events almost all year round in the warm California sunshine. Of course, there are indoor sports such as basketball, but Angelenos can enjoy an afternoon at the racetrack in January while most of the country is shoveling a path through the snow. Most of the sporting events are held on the outskirts of the city or in nearby communities, where you'll find huge parking lots for that Los Angeles necessity, the automobile.

HORSERACING

A day at the track in one of the famous racing parks near Los Angeles is a memorable event—whether you win or lose. More than just a betting window and an oval-shaped track, the race tracks in Southern California are among the most beautiful anywhere. Some have elaborate infields complete with ponds and decorative wildlife, tropical gardens, or picnic parks. Many have elegant restaurants, and one even has a fashionable shopping mall. Here are three of the most popular:

Set against a dramatic background of rugged mountains is **Santa Anita Park,** 285 W. Huntington Dr., near Colorado Place,

Arcadia (tel. 818/574-7223). The track, in operation since 1934, has its winter season from late December to late April. Gates open at 10:30 to 11 a.m. Races are generally held Wednesday through Sunday only. The Oak Tree Racing Association sponsors racing during October. During the season, visitors can watch the morning workouts (beginning at 7:30 a.m.), have breakfast, and even take a tour of the stables on weekends. Admission to the park is $3 for the grandstand and infield, $6.50 for the clubhouse. Children 17 and under are admitted free with a parent. Parking is $2 to $8, depending on location and convenience. Santa Anita is just 14 miles northeast of Los Angeles, directly accessible from the Foothill Freeway.

For an enjoyable day of racing, you can go to **Hollywood Park**, 1050 S. Prairie Ave., at Century Boulevard, in Inglewood (tel. 213/419-1500)—rarely will you find a more attractive 50-plus-year-old park. Just 11 miles southwest of downtown Los Angeles, and 3 miles east of LAX, the park is spread across 320 landscaped acres.

The thoroughbreds run from late April to mid-July and early November to late December. Post time is 1:30 p.m. Wednesday through Sunday. The admission charges are $3 for the grandstand (plus $3 for a reserved seat), $6.50 for the clubhouse (plus $3 to $4 if you want a reserved seat), and $7 for the Cary Grant Pavilion (plus $5 for a reserved seat). There is space for 30,000 cars in the parking lot; it's $2 for general parking, $4 for preferred parking, and $8 for valet parking. Numerous eateries and refreshment stands are scattered throughout the park, including two restaurants in the Cary Grant Pavilion, and five (count them) Häagen Dazs Ice Cream Shoppes. If you don't have a car, this track can be reached via the L.A. Metro RTD (call 213/626-4455 for information).

"Where the world's fastest horses race" is not just an idle claim made by **Los Alamitos**, 4961 Katella Ave., at Walker Street in Los Alamitos (tel. 213/431-1361, or 714/995-1234). From May through August the lightning-fast quarter horses race each evening, Tuesday through Saturday, at 7:30 p.m. There's also a winter season from early November to mid-January, and a harness-racing season from February to May. The park itself is luxuriously designed, with an infield featuring palm- and flower-lined ponds stocked with swans and other waterfowl. The glassed-in Turf Terrace offers racing fans an unobstructed view of the track while they dine. Admission is $2.50 for grandstand seats, $5 for entry to the clubhouse, and $2 additional for reserved seats. General parking is $2, $3.50 for preferred parking. Los Alamitos is just west of Disneyland on Katella Avenue.

THE GREAT WESTERN FORUM

The Great Western Forum, billed as "the world's most beautiful showplace for sports and entertainment," is located at 3900 W. Manchester Ave., at Prairie Avenue in Inglewood (tel. 213/673-1300, or 213/419-3100). This massive sports arena is home to the former NBA champions, the Los Angeles Lakers, and to exciting hockey with the Los Angeles Kings. The Forum stages championship boxing each month, and world-ranked tennis players—Ivan

Lendl, Martina Navratilova, John McEnroe—also play quite regularly at this stunning venue. Big-name concert stars, the Harlem Globetrotters, ice shows, and championship rodeos round out the roster of the Forum's events. Prices and ticket availability vary, so be sure to call ahead for information. You can obtain tickets at the box office or through Ticketmaster (see "Tickets" in Chapter III).

DODGER STADIUM

Remember when they were called the Brooklyn Bums? The present home for the Dodgers is not Ebbets Field but this modern stadium at 1000 Elysian Park Ave., at Stadium Way, near Sunset Boulevard, Los Angeles (tel. 213/224-1500 for information, 224-1400 for tickets, or call Ticketmaster or Teletron). It's considered one of the best baseball fields in the world, offering every one of the fans (the stadium seats 56,000) an unobstructed view because of its unique cantilever construction. The game season lasts from April through early October. Admission is $9 for box seats, $7 for reserved seats, and $5 for general admission ($3 for children under 12 if purchased at the box office 1½ hours before game time; otherwise it's $4). Parking in the 16,000-car lot costs $3 per vehicle.

THE L.A. MEMORIAL COLISEUM

Built for the 1932 Olympic Summer Games, and also the site of the 1984 Summer Games, this 92,000-seat stadium is considered one of the most impressive modern sports structures. At 3911 S. Figueroa St., at King Boulevard, it is the home of the NFL Los Angeles Raiders. Football season runs from September through December, and tickets for the Raiders' games may be purchased by calling 213/322-5901 (also Ticketmaster and Teletron). "Next door," across the massive parking lot, you'll find . . .

THE L.A. SPORTS ARENA

Located at 3939 S. Figueroa St., this is the home of the NBA Clippers. Tickets to these games, running from $9 to $18, can be purchased at the gate or by calling Ticketmaster (see "Tickets" in Chapter III).

ANAHEIM STADIUM

For information about this home of the California Angels and the Los Angeles Rams, see Chapter IX.

SHOPPING IN LOS ANGELES

In Southern California, you can combine a shopping expedition with a visit to a sightseeing attraction, which permits you not only to find widely varying merchandise, but to enjoy the atmosphere as well. From Disneyland to Olvera Street to the Ports O' Call Village to the Farmers Market, you can purchase exotic items from all over the world.

1. Olvera Street

In the Pueblo de Los Angeles, Olvera Street offers a quickie shopping trip to Mexico. Believed to be the city's oldest street, it is flanked with shops featuring merchandise imported from all regions of Mexico. The tile-paved Paseo has rows of stalls down its center, selling wares spread out in the fashion of an authentic Mexican market. A wide range of articles is handsomely displayed, and at times you can see the artisans at work. The candle-dipping shops are highly scented by herbs, spices, and perfumes used in the beeswax and tallow. At a glassblowing shop, you can buy trinkets for your what-not shelf (stemmed goblets, plates, and bowls). In addition, you'll find assorted baskets and straw hats, costume jewelry, pottery bowls, decorative tinware (candlesticks, picture frames), and hand-woven sandals known as *huaraches*. At a number of *puestos*, you can purchase select hand-woven scarves in primitive, vibrant colors. Shopping here is like participating in a musical pageant; strolling guitarists and singers entertain with the music of Old Mexico. A few such Olvera Street vendors are the **Olvera Candle Shop** at W-3 Olvera St. (tel. 213/628-7833); the **Casa de Sousa** at W-19 (tel. 213/626-7076) for ceramics; and the **Casa de Bernal** at W-23 (tel. 213/687-4568) for clothing.

2. New Chinatown

In shop after shop around the central plazas and lanes, you'll find goods imported from Asia. The district lies between North Broadway and North Hill Street. Each year newer buildings appear —all built in the classic manner, even the banks! Among the pagoda-style shops, **Jade Tree,** 957 Chungking Rd. (tel. 213/624-3521), is notable for prestigious merchandise from the Far East as well as mainland China (bronze Buddhas, chairs and tables, miniature boxes and chests, cloisonné, plus carved ivory, carved hardstone, snuff bottles, fine jewelry, and high-quality antiques including Chinese porcelains). The shop is open from 11:30 a.m. to 5 p.m. Tuesday through Thursday, till 9 p.m. on Friday and Saturday, and from 2 to 9 p.m. on Sunday.

Chong Hing Goldsmith Corp., 956 N. Hill St. (tel. 213/623-3645), is an owner-operated custom-jewelry shop. Ronald and Ellen Lee make their own exquisite jewelry, good-luck medallions, bracelets, and rings, and also sell a good selection of jade figures. They're open from 11 a.m. to 8:30 p.m. daily.

Sam Ward, 503 Chungking Court (tel. 213/625-8549), has an excellent selection of teas and a collection of chinaware dishes and teapots. Sam Ward is open from 9:30 a.m. to 5:30 p.m., weekdays only.

Finally, at **King's Gift Shop,** 504 Chungking Court (tel. 213/623-2002), opposite the fountain, you'll find a good collection of gifts. King's hours are noon to 6 p.m. daily.

For authentic Japanese products, you can visit Little Tokyo, near City Hall in downtown Los Angeles, where **Rafu Shoten,** 309 E. 1st St. (tel. 213/626-3970), presents a miniature Japanese department store selection. You can purchase kimonos for men and women, tasseled lanterns, urns, porcelain, figurines, incense burners, ivory figures, jade, and a large collection of Buddha figures. Rafu Shoten is open daily from 10 a.m. to 7 p.m.

3. Farmers Market

At Fairfax Avenue and 3rd Street, the original Farmers Market has, in addition to its food stalls and patio restaurants, more than

150 shops offering top-notch gift buys, ranging from Indian mocca-sins to trained parrots. Before you begin exploring, you may want to mount the stairs over Gate 1 in the main building to the **Farmers Market Office** (tel. 213/933-9211). There you can pick up a very useful map of the complex with a list of the stores and shops, and a copy of *The Farmers Market Newsletter.*

The following represents just a sampling of what is available. Go to the **Indian Dancer** (213/936-5662) for Native American ob-jects, jewelry, katchina dolls, and "findings"; **Walter Wright** (tel. 213/936-6316) for modern gold and silver jewelry with precious stones; the **Western Frontier Establishment** (tel. 213/934-0146) for a vast selection of moccasins and hand-tooled belts; the **Nordic Country** (tel. 213/857-2007) for gifts imported from the Scandi-navian countries, Finland, and Iceland; **Teddy's of Bearverly Hills** (tel. 213/936-6560) for the most unique collection of teddy bears "in the world"; the **Roos Linen Shop** (tel. 213/938-4343) for lin-en gifts from all over the world; **See Spot Run** (tel. 213/938-7768) for fun and creative rubber stamps and stamping accessories; **Littlejohn's English Toffee House** (tel. 213/936-5379) for a delectable selection of handmade candies (you are welcome to stop and watch whenever they are dipping); **The Bread Bin** (tel. 213/936-0785) where they have over 110 varieties of bread, some of which can be eaten as dessert—try the Hungarian cin-namon loaf.

Farmers Market is a great place to browse, shop, and snack on everything from ravioli to blintzes from the many food stalls.

4. Shopping Complexes

Shopping in Southern California is finding its own free form, as reflected by the widely diverse selection of complexes previewed be-low. These compounds of boutiques often spring up in the most unlikely places.

ARCO Plaza, 505 S. Flower St., Los Angeles, offers convenient shopping and elegant dining in a most unique subterranean mall. Take a handy escalator outside at the corners of 5th and 6th streets on Flower Street. Beneath the Atlantic Richfield/Bank of America Twin Towers, corridors lead to shops and restaurants. Stores and boutiques are on the second and third underground levels. You'll even find a Catholic chapel! You can enjoy steak and seafood at **O'Shaughnessy's.** There are art exhibits, fashion shows, education-al seminars, concerts—everything enhanced by a colorful background with flowers and plants. The **Greater Los Angeles Vis-itors and Convention Bureau** is within ARCO Plaza's precincts. And, of course, there are the shops selling everything from needle-point patterns to insurance.

The Broadway Plaza, 750 W. 7th St., is a two-level shopping mall between a duo of steel-and-glass towers, one housing a 32-sto-ry office building, the other the Hyatt Regency Hotel recommended earlier. In the complex is the **Broadway Depart-**

ment Store, one of the largest and most complete in Los Angeles, plus about 30 specialty shops selling everything from books to jewelry. The Hyatt House and Broadway store are bounded by 7th, 8th, Hope, and Flower streets. The glass-covered plaza itself is reached via many escalators. The Plaza has not only an indoor sidewalk café, but a gourmet restaurant attached to the hotel, several fast-food eateries, and a revolving rooftop restaurant called **Angel's Flight.** Daily pipe organ and banjo concerts entertain the shoppers, and there's parking for 2,000 cars.

Fisherman's Village, Fiji Way, Marina del Rey (tel. 213/823-5411), is the shopping, dining, and boating center at the Marina del Rey harbor. It hosts over 20 specialty shops, restaurants, and snack-food stops. Harbor cruises, boat rentals, and yacht charters are available at the village.

Lido Marina Village, 3420 Via Oporto, Newport Beach, CA 92663 (tel. 714/675-8662), is a smart waterfront shopping mall with an old-fashioned look. Chic shops open onto bricked walks, and rows of boutiques, art galleries, and restaurants front the yacht and sailboat wharf. Altogether, the village is a delightful spot where you can window-shop or purchase anything from a yacht to the delicious goods of the German Home Bakery.

Cannery Village, in Newport Beach, runs for about five square blocks along the wharf, which is now a complex of nearly 30 fascinating shops, boutiques, and restaurants. Old bungalows, houses, and stores have been given a new lease on life. Little marine factories have been divided into stalls where artisans, collectors, vendors, artists, dressmakers, and craftspeople make and sell unusual items. A good starting point is the **Cannery Restaurant** on the wharf, where you'll find many of the shops along 29th, 30th, and 31st Streets.

PORTS O' CALL IN SAN PEDRO

At the Ports O' Call and Whaler's Wharf in San Pedro you'll find one of the widest selections of gifts in Southern California—something to suit every taste. The setting combines the atmospheres of old California and a 19th-century New England whaling port, all of it overlooking the boat-filled harbor. To reach it, take the Harbor Freeway (Hwy. 11) to the Harbor Boulevard off-ramp and turn right.

In shops resembling the personally run stores of the late 19th century, you can select from such merchandise as American bottles (everything from the Kickapoo Indians' tapeworm secret to love-power jugs!); okra pickles; excellent reproductions of antique pewter; pepper mills; salad spoons and forks; Mexican wrought-iron fixtures and furniture; Iron Mountain stoneware; homemade candles; Hawaiian casuals; imports from India; Western and Native American souvenirs; Oriental articles in brass, teak, and lacquered wood; paintings; boutique clothing; gunpowder tea from Japan; even wigs. You name it!

There are also several eating places, including the **Ports O' Call Restaurant** featuring South Seas and seafood specialties.

For more information about the San Pedro area, see Chapter XI, Section 9.

5. Melrose Avenue

Melrose Avenue is another great spot for shopping. Between La Cienega and Robertson boulevards, there are more than 100 exquisite and tasteful little boutiques and antique shops, making it one of the finest antique centers this side of Portobello Road in London. What was once a residential street now has converted bungalows, where proprietors have incorporated their gardens and patios into the general scheme. Sturdy shoes are recommended.

Other interesting places to shop include **La Luz de Jesus,** at 7400 Melrose Ave., near Gardner (tel. 213/651-4875) above the Soap Plant, which exhibits the work of a number of artists as well as Oaxacan rugs and blankets, pottery, and a variety of religious items. A bit farther west, **Sonrisa,** at 8214 Melrose Ave. (213/651-1090), features the work of local Mexican artists, folk crafts, and country antiques. **Umbrello,** at 8607 Melrose Ave., near La Cienega (213/655-6447), has furniture, pottery, antiques, and antique reproductions.

6. Beverly Hills

The heart of American chic, Beverly Hills is one of the country's most prestigious shopping areas, and **North Rodeo Drive** one of its most distinctive addresses. The main shopping area is bounded by the triangle of **Wilshire** and **Santa Monica boulevards** and **Doheny Drive,** with other stores located in the outlying areas to the north and south. The choices include Cartier, Courrèges, an Elizabeth Arden Salon, Hermès of Paris, Saint-Laurent Rive Gauche, Battaglia, Ted Lapidus, Van Cleef & Arpels, Pierre Deux, Georgette Klinger, Gucci, and Tiffany's. For a complete rundown on Beverly Hills shopping, stop by the **Chamber of Commerce** at 239 S. Beverly Dr. and pick up their *Guide Through Beverly Hills.* It describes over 100 of the area's most important shops, hotels, restaurants, and points of interest.

7. Antiques Around Town

Aside from the special antiques shops I referred to in the Melrose area (above), here are some other sources to check out.

The Antique Guild, 8800 Venice Boulevard, near Culver City (tel. 213/838-3131), bills itself as "the world's largest antique outlet"—over three acres of antiques under one roof. Housed in the Old Helms Bakery Building, an L.A. landmark, the guild has more than 40,000 pieces from Europe on sale at all times—at reasonable prices. Because the guild is so large, they can buy in quantity and pass the benefit of volume buying on to the customers. Their buyers are constantly checking out and purchasing the entire contents of European castles, beer halls, estates, and mansions. With new shipments coming in every week, the merchandise is constantly changing, and it's fun to browse through the old armoires, chandeliers, stained glass, crystal, china, clocks, washstands, tables, mirrors, etc., even if you don't want to buy.

In addition to the huge selection of antiques and Old-World originals, the guild also has an Indoor Garden Center selling everything for the home garden; an Antique Jewelry Boutique; and Room Vignettes—period settings and eclectic mixes of the old and the contemporary. Should you get hungry, there's even an indoor sidewalk café called The Café for lunch and snacks.

Open weekdays from 10 a.m. to 9p.m., on Saturday to 6 p.m., the guild is easily reached by freeway from any point in Los Angeles.

But one of the most fascinating places of all is in North Hollywood—**Arte de Mexico,** at 5356 Riverton Ave. (tel. 818/769-5090), where you'll find seven warehouses full of carved furniture and wrought iron reportedly once sold only to moviemakers and restaurants.

Over in Pasadena is **The Folk Tree,** at 217 S. Fair Oaks Ave. (tel. 818/795-8733), where you'll find items from throughout Mexico. There are textiles, Oaxacan rugs, tinware, Tarahumara pots, housewares, and religious artifacts.

In Manhattan Beach look for **Los Munequitos,** at 1008 Manhattan Ave. (tel. 213/379-2777), where you'll find a wide variety of selectively chosen carved animals, tin mirrors, masks, pottery from Guanajuato, Oaxacan rugs, candlesticks, etc.

LOS ANGELES AFTER DARK

With the passage of Hollywood's heyday, nightlife in Los Angeles seems comparatively tame somehow. Once the antics of stars were splashed on the front pages of tabloids around the world—for example, Humphrey Bogart's drunken brawls on Sunset Strip. Readers were titillated to read that Franchot Tone had been arrested for "expectorating" in the face of Florabel Muir, New York *Daily News* columnist; that the king of the big prank, Jim Moran, had impersonated Saud El Saud of Saudi Arabia, giving out fake jewelry to near-hysterical waiters at a Hollywood nightclub; that Darryl Zanuck had "performed" on the trapeze at Ciro's; that Bogey and Baby and fellow rat-packers Frank Sinatra and Judy Garland were up to their well-publicized and wildly impractical jokes at the citadel of Michael ("The Prince") Romanoff.

Nowadays, it seems that many Angelenos frequent nightclubs rarely if at all. Essentially, Los Angeles is an informal town whose denizens prefer to entertain in their private homes. For many families, the emphasis is on the rear patio garden, with a barbecue pit placed conveniently near the oval-shaped swimming pool. Even motion picture stars like to take off their makeup and relax in the evening, unlike the past, when studios compelled them to dress up and go out with starlets or actor escorts they often detested.

Nevertheless, for gregarious young people in particular, there is a wide range of discos, folk-music enclaves, whatever. In summer, the hottest little spots are those along the Pacific strip between Santa Monica and Laguna Beach. Some of these clubs come and go seasonally with exasperating irregularity, but when functioning often feature first-rate entertainment—struggling young groups who may be the headliners of tomorrow.

The entertainment business—film, TV, records, theater—is still the most important industry in Los Angeles. In and around L.A. there are over 150 active theaters, large and small, with plays, revues, concerts. There are over 60 jazz clubs. And in addition to all this, the Pacific Amphitheater and the Universal Amphitheater feature name performers, as do the Greek Theatre, the Hollywood Bowl (mostly classical), The Forum located in Inglewood, and the Meadows Amphitheatre in Irvine.

If you'd like an idea of what's going on (the schedule of events can change weekly), buy the Sunday edition of *The Los Angeles Times*. The "Calendar" section is what you want to save: "Outtakes" updates the lowdown and "Movies" hypes the new faces in films and new films in production. There's a parental film guide, a handy list of family attractions, and a description of new movie openings and special programs (offbeat films) showing that week, plus all the museums, lectures, and exhibits you'd ever want to see. And if you have it in mind to make a side trip to Las Vegas, Laughlin, Reno, or Lake Tahoe, there are ads for many of the hotels, the headliners, and what's being offered that week in special rates. The "Calendar" also lists theaters, club acts, and what's opening or closing, including restaurants.

1. Sunset Strip

"The Strip" is the nickname of a 20-block stretch of Sunset Boulevard, linking the western boundaries of Hollywood with the eastern periphery of Beverly Hills. It is familiar to fans of the old TV series "77 Sunset Strip."

In the 1920s gambling clubs appeared on the Strip; the Crosby brothers constructed their own office building to house various enterprises there, and nightspots, such as Ciro's, soon cropped up. Supper clubs, high-rise apartment dwellings (the Sunset Towers, erected primarily for film-industry people), decorator showrooms, and boutiques joined the rush. William Haines, of silent-screen fame, turned decorator and opened a Greek Revival shop. And fans gathered outside expensive clubs to collect autographs of movie stars, many of whom weren't in any condition to sign anything.

Sunset Strip makes for a good stroll, certainly an interesting one for avid people-watchers. Starting at the site of the long-departed Schwab's Drugstore at Sunset and Laurel Canyon Boulevards, you can walk west, passing a number of rock clubs, head shops, nudie nightclubs, and glorified hamburger joints, and watch the action—what it lacks in class it makes up for in human interest, albeit a bit sleazy here and there.

But whether you watch the passing parade, or decide to join it, Sunset Strip is fascinating.

2. Live Music

The Lighthouse Café, 30 Pier Ave., Hermosa Beach (tel. 213/372-6911), makes a sensible and needed contribution to the nighttime scene in this beachfront town. The music varies from night to night, but it's among the oldest jazz establishments in L.A. You might hear reggae, rock, or rhythm and blues on any Saturday night. The stage is in the middle of the room surrounded by tables filled with people eating and drinking in a very casual atmosphere. Show times vary and there is seldom a cover charge. Special attractions, once a month, have a cover, depending on the artist appearing. Food is pizza, burgers, plus a choice of sandwiches ($4 to $5). Most drinks are $3; those under 21 are not admitted without a parent or guardian. There's a $5 minimum. The Lighthouse is open Monday to Friday from 6 p.m. to 1:30 a.m., on Saturday and Sunday from 10 a.m.

With one format or another, and under various monikers, **Gazzarri's on the Strip,** 9039 Sunset Blvd., near Doheny Drive (tel. 213/273-6606), has been going strong for many years. Several years ago it began presenting live rock 'n' roll bands for dancing, with a little disco between sets. Currently two bands play every evening. Gazzarri's is open from Wednesday to Saturday from 8 p.m. to 2 a.m. Admission varies from about $10 to $14 depending on the performers. The age group is early 20s, and dress is casual. No credit cards. There's a two-drink minimum for those over 21, and you must be at least 18 to get in.

3. Comedy

The Comedy Store, 8433 Sunset Blvd., one block east of La Cienega Boulevard, West Hollywood (tel. 213/656-6225), is the most important showcase for rising comedians in Los Angeles and probably in the entire United States. Owner Mitzi Shore has created a setting in which new comics can develop and established performers can work out the kinks in new material. It's always vastly entertaining.

There are three major parts to it. The **Mainroom,** which seats about 500, features an "open mike" (anyone can do three minutes of comedy) from 8:30 to 10 p.m. on Monday, followed by professional stand-ups from 10 p.m. to 1 a.m. Admission is free, but there's a two-drink minimum. Other nights there's a continuous show of comedians, each doing about 15-minute stints. The talent here is always first rate, ranging from people you've seen, or may see, on "The Tonight Show" and suchlike to really big names. Admission is for $10 Tuesday to Thursday and for $14 for the 9 p.m. and

11:30 p.m. shows on Friday and Saturday, with a two-drink minimum.

The original **Comedy Store,** open nightly with two shows on Saturday at 9 and 11 p.m., charges $12 for the early show, $14 for the late show, $9 on all other nights, and has a two-drink minimum. About 15 to 20 comedians perform. Monday night is amateur night, when anyone with enough guts can take the stage for three to five minutes; there's no cover, but there is a two-drink minimum.

Finally, there's the **Belly Room,** where on Thursday nights a singer is showcased starting at 9 p.m.; Friday through Wednesday is reserved for comediennes; there's a $3 cover and a two-drink minimum. Other nights you can enjoy music at the piano bar. There's no cover, but there is a one-drink minimum. Drinks are from $3.50 to $7.

Improvisation, 8162 Melrose Ave., at Crescent Heights Boulevard, West Hollywood (tel. 213/651-2583), offers something different each night.

The club's own television show, "Evening at the Improv," is now filmed at the Santa Monica location for national distribution. Although there used to be a fairly active music schedule, the Improv is mostly doing what it does best—showcasing comedy. Major stars often appear here—people like Jay Leno, Billy Crystal, and Robin Williams.

There is comedy nightly. Monday and Wednesday performances are at 8:30 and 11 p.m.; Tuesday, Thursday, and Sunday at 8 and 10:45 p.m.; Friday and Saturday at 7:30, 9:45, and 11:45 p.m. Sunday through Thursday, admission is $6.50 plus a two-drink minimum; Friday and Saturday, it's $8, $10, and $8 respectively for the three performances, plus the two-drink minimum.

The larger Improvisation is at 321 Santa Monica Blvd., near 4th Street, Santa Monica (tel. 213/394-8664). Show times are the same as those at the Melrose location, plus a Tuesday performance at 9 p.m., and the 8 p.m. Monday evening performance of the Bargain Basement Players. Admission prices are the same, as is the two-drink minimum.

Both locations have restaurants—Hell's Kitchen serving Italian entrees at the West Hollywood club, and Tex-Mex cuisine at the Santa Monica spot.

4. ABC Entertainment Center

At Century City, the **ABC Entertainment Center** has become one of the most important nighttime spots in Greater Los Angeles. Part of the Century City complex, it boasts the **Shubert Theater,** where you can see big-time musicals like *Cats* and *Les Misérables.* For musicals in the evening, the range is from $25 to $55 (cheaper for matinees). Call 800/233-3123 for ticket and show information.

The center has four movie theaters (telephone 213/553-5307 to find out what's showing).

Harry's American Bar and Grill (see the restaurant listings in Chapter V for details) is a faithful reproduction of its namesake along the Arno in Florence and serves the *cucina* of northern Italy. For reservations, telephone 213/277-2333). It's one of several restaurants here.

5. A Hotel Sampler

Bel-Air Hotel Bar, 701 Stone Canyon Rd., Bel-Air (tel. 213/472-1211), is one of the mellower places in Greater Los Angeles. If you want a quiet, romantic evening, drive out for drinks in the bar where a pianist and singer will often do one of your favorite songs. There's no cover, and drinks cost around $5.

L'Escoffier, 9876 Wilshire Blvd., at Santa Monica Boulevard, Beverly Hills (tel. 213/285-1333), is the Beverly Hilton's penthouse restaurant offering dining and dancing with a view. The award-winning Continental cuisine, the panorama of the city, and dancing to live music promise a memorable evening. Open Monday through Saturday from 6:30 p.m., L'Escoffier offers an à la carte menu with most entrees ranging from $24 to $32. The ultimate in dining is Le Diner Gastronomique, a seven-course meal for $62. You can dance until midnight, and you can have drinks only (average drink is $6) in lieu of dinner.

The Library, also at the Beverly Hills Hilton, is an incongruity, hidden behind an Edwardian entrance of stained glass just off the main lobby of this modern deluxe hotel. It's like a re-creation of a library in an English manor house and is done in delicate pastel tones. Ceiling-to-floor shelves contain actual books. Knights in armor stand guard at the back, surveying a crowd likely to include a sprinkling of celebrities. The average drink is $5.

6. Mexican Nights on Olvera Street

Casa La Golondrina, W-17 Olvera St., Los Angeles (tel. 213/628-4349), is the best place in Los Angeles for Mexican entertainment. On the city's oldest street, it is sheltered in the first brick building (circa 1850), the Pelanconi House. The café itself dates from 1924, when it was founded by Señora Consuelo Castillo de Bonzo. You get not only flamenco and Mexican singing, but authentic south-of-the-border meals as well. On nippy evenings, with luck you will be seated by the open fireplace, where you can listen to the strolling troubadours as they create a romantic and mellow mood. (For lunch, you can dine on the outside terrace.)

Fiesta night entertainment is presented on Friday and Saturday nights. There's no cover charge. You can just drop in for drinks and the show or dancing. Mexican beer goes for about $2.50; a margarita big enough to wade in (well almost) for $6.95 (keep the glass). Smaller sizes are $2.75 to $5.50.

At dinner you might begin with nachos ($4.50). As an entree, perhaps tostadas—a Mexican salad with guacamole, beef, red chili, and tortilla ($3.95)—or a combination plate of carnitas and an enchilada ($6.95). You can also get a full meal of two entrees (perhaps crabmeat enchiladas and chili relleno) with rice and beans for under $10. The café is open every day from 10 a.m. to 10 p.m. Monday to Wednesday there's an all-you-can-eat lunch buffet from 11 a.m. to 2 p.m.

After dining, you can enjoy a leisurely stroll along the brick-and-tiled "Walk of the Angels," with its colorful shops, restaurants, taco cafés, and flamboyantly garbed attendants. For a final snack, try some of the roasted nuts along "El Paseo." Instrumental groups outside add further zest.

---

7. Concerts—Classical, Rock, Pop, Etc.

Hollywood Palladium, 6215 Sunset Blvd., near Vine Street, Hollywood (tel. 213/962-7600). It's best to call first and check on who is appearing at this famous entertainment landmark. The offer-

---

Cocktails in a Japanese Palace

Yamashiro, 1999 N. Sycamore Ave., at Franklin Avenue, Hollywood (tel. 213/466-5125), is a stunning Japanese restaurant at the top of a winding road, set on the crest of a 300-foot hill amid acres of exquisite gardens. Originally a private estate built as an exact replica of one of the most beautiful palaces in the high mountains of Japan, it was constructed by hundreds of craftsmen brought over from the Orient. A 600-year-old-pagoda was imported and set beside a small lake.

During the golden age of Hollywood it served as a clubhouse for the "Club of the 400," but since 1960 it has been a restaurant and cocktail lounge. The dining areas are gorgeous, especially the inner garden that centers around a Japanese garden with a koi pond and fountain. For drinks, the setting is unbeatable. From the terrace, you can enjoy a panoramic view in the afternoon, the city at sunset, or the twinkling lights of Greater Los Angeles by night.

If you're a movie fan, you may already have been introduced to Yamashiro, as it was used for the background shots in Brando's *Sayonara,* as well as for such classic TV shows as "I Spy," "Route 66," and one of the "Perry Mason" episodes. The late Ian Fleming, creator of James Bond, recommended a visit here in his travel saga *Thrilling Cities.*

In addition to all regular drinks, Yamashiro serves hot sake and exotic cocktails like zombies and mai tais. You can also get appetizers with your drinks. Yamashiro is open for cocktails from 4:30 p.m. to 12:30 a.m. Sunday through Thursday, to 1 a.m. Friday and Saturday.

ings range from big bands like Ray Anthony and Tex Benecke, to groups like the Ramones, to vintage rockers like Chuck Berry. However, there might also be a Latin dance night, a fashion show, or an award show. Lawrence Welk used to do New Year's Eve here. The current musical focus is on rock, with groups like the Clash from England performing. Latin music is also popular. Prices vary with the attraction, but gone are the days when Frank Sinatra performed here.

The **Greek Theatre,** 2700 N. Vermont Ave., en route to the Observatory, Griffith Park (tel. 213/665-5857), patterned after the classic outdoor theaters of ancient Greece, is one of the most important showcases for stellar personalities appearing in the summer. In Hollywood's past, such entertainers were featured as Maurice Chevalier, Judy Garland, and Jack Benny.

Nowadays, you might see the Dance Theatre of Harlem, Barry Manilow, Ben Vereen, Tom Jones, Neil Diamond, or the Manhattan Transfer, to cite a few examples.

The season runs from late May to early October. For good seats at special shows, you pay an average of $20 to $50. The box office is open weekdays only from 10 a.m. to 6 p.m. Above all, be sure to bring a sweater or jacket—a necessity for outdoor evening concerts.

Hollywood Bowl, 2301 N. Highland Ave., at Odin Street, Hollywood (tel. 213/850-2000) draws music devotees in the summer. The Bowl was created in the early 1920s when a musician—hiking in the hills—was startled to discover its perfect natural acoustics. Launching into song, he heard his voice carried virtually to the ridges of the mountains. Music lovers banded together, financing tiers of seats to be dug, Greek fashion, out of the mountainside. A stage and shell were constructed, the future home of the Los Angeles Philharmonic Orchestra. Box seats were installed in the front, and since many were reserved for film stars, intermission time at the Bowl became an extra added attraction.

Nowadays, internationally known conductors and soloists join the Los Angeles Philharmonic in classical programs on Tuesday and Thursday nights. The Philharmonic's Friday and Saturday concerts are more pop oriented. The season also includes a jazz series, a Virtuoso series and a Sunday Sunset series. Presentations usually begin in early June, ending around mid-September. An added attraction is fireworks on July Fourth, at the season's last performance, and sometimes on weekends in between.

Tips from habitués: A part of the ritual is to order a picnic basket with a choice of hot and cold entrees, a weekly special, and a selection of wines and desserts from the Hollywood Bowl (call 213/851-3588 the day before), which you can pick up on Pepper Tree Lane on your way in and enjoy in the picnic grounds before the concert. If you're sitting in a box, you can have your picnic delivered to you there! It's cheaper, of course, to bring your own.

Music lovers can purchase tickets for seats high on the hill, enjoying the panorama of the Hollywood hills along with the performance.

Tickets for the classical concerts begin as low as $2 and go up to $18 for seats on the benches. However, for the box seats, you'll pay anywhere from $30 to $70. The box office opens in May, and stays open Monday to Saturday until July 3 from 10 a.m. to 6 p.m.; the rest of the season it's open to 9 p.m. and on Sunday from noon to 6 p.m. Parking space can be reserved for $9, subject to availability. At lots adjacent to the Bowl entrance, you can park free of charge and then take a shuttle. The round-trip bus ticket is $2.

The **Universal Amphitheater,** 100 Universal City Plaza, just off the Lankershim Boulevard exit of the Hollywood Freeway (U.S. 101), in Universal City (tel. 818/980-9421), was built in 1969 at a cost of $1 million. This 6,251-seat enclosed arena, overlooking the San Fernando Valley, is next to the Visitors Entertainment Center of Universal Studios Tours. No seat is more than 140 feet from center stage. Only top names perform in this acoustically perfect arena, and tickets are often sold out well before the concert date. Artists are usually scheduled for three to five days, and include such superstars as Frank Sinatra, Gladys Knight and the Pips, the Temptations, George Carlin, and Robin Williams. Tickets (generally priced between $20 and $50) are available in advance. Box office hours vary, so call the above number to find out when they are; then go early, as lines often form at dawn. Or you can charge your tickets by telephone (tel. 213/480-3232) and pay a fee per ticket for the privilege.

The **Dorothy Chandler Pavilion** at the Music Center, 135 N. Grand Ave., at 1st Street (tel. 213/972-7211), the home of the Los Angeles Philharmonic, the Joffrey Ballet, the Master Chorale and the Los Angeles Opera, is a 3,197-seat hall where concerts, recitals, opera, and dance performances are presented.

8. Theater

The **James A. Doolittle Theatre** (formerly the Huntington Hartford Theatre), 1615 N. Vine St. (tel. 213/462-6666 for current information), is near Hollywood Boulevard. Dramatic plays are presented—some with top touring companies, others produced in Hollywood with stars from the screen, TV, and Broadway. The theater offers more than 1,000 seats and is considered one of the most attractive and intimate in the country. Recent productions have included *Who's Afraid of Virginia Woolf,* Kate Mulgrew in *Hedda Gabler* and Michael Gross and Linda Purl in *The Real Thing.* Prices for seats generally range from $15 to $30.

Three theaters at the **Music Center,** 135 N. Grand Ave., at 1st Street (tel. 213/972-7211), including the Dorothy Chandler Pavilion discussed above, offer a wide range of theatrical productions.

The **Mark Taper Forum** (tel. 213/972-7373), generally features contemporary productions such as *Green Card, Rat in the Skull, The Immigrant,* and *Ghetto.* However, the territory they cover is varied and might also include such drama classics as *The Tempest* or *A Christmas Carol* in any given season.

Finally, there's the **Ahmanson Theatre,** which, in conjunction with the Mark Taper, is home base for the Center Theatre Group. The CTG presents four plays during a season lasting from mid-

October to early May. Recent offerings have included Christopher Reeve in *Summer and Smoke*, Daniel J. Travanti in *I Never Sang For My Father*, and the West Coast premiere of Neil Simon's *Broadway Bound*. A variety of international dance companies and concert attractions round out the season.

Prices generally range from $12 to $50, but there are reductions available for students and senior citizens for specified performances. Phone the Music Center number above for ticket information.

The **Wilshire Theatre,** 8440 Wilshire Blvd., near La Cienega Boulevard, Beverly Hills (tel. 213/939-1128), opened its doors in May 1980 with a production of *The Oldest Living Graduate*, starring Henry Fonda. Recent productions have ranged from musicals like *A Chorus Line* to *Aren't We All?* with Rex Harrison and Claudette Colbert. In-concert offerings have included Shirley MacLaine, Charles Aznavour, Spandau Ballet, and Eurythmics. There's a lobby bar, and parking for 1,200 cars. Tickets are in the $15 to $45 range.

Opened in 1930 as a luxury movie house, the **Pantages Theatre,** 6233 Hollywood Blvd., just down the block from Vine Street, is a Hollywood landmark with a glorious stage and screen history. Its opening show was a mixed bill: Marion Davies in *The Floradora Girl*, an edition of *Metronome News*, a Disney cartoon, music by the Greater Pantages Orchestra, and a stage piece called *The Rose Garden Idea*. You got your money's worth in 1930. The theater itself was as impressive as the show. Built at a cost of $1.25 million (the equivalent of $10 million today), the Pantages was incredibly deluxe and boasted the most elaborate sound system of its day. In 1949 Howard Hughes purchased the theater and moved into a second-floor office complete with desk and cot. For the next 10 years it was the setting for the presentation of the Academy Awards, including the first Oscar ceremony ever televised. In 1963 celebrity patrons attended a special screening of *Cleopatra* at $250 apiece here, the proceeds going to the construction fund for the new Music Center. In 1967 the Pantages was completely refurbished, after which it continued for nearly a decade as one of the West Coast's finest movie houses. Now tickets for its live theater productions range from $18 to $45, and are available through Teletron, 213/410-1062.

IX

ANAHEIM, DISNEYLAND, AND ENVIRONS

1. ANAHEIM AND DISNEYLAND
2. BUENA PARK
3. IRVINE

In and around Anaheim, you'll be immersed in a theater of involvement. Disneyland dramatizes everything from a simulated trip to the moon to pioneer America, and Knott's Berry Farm at Buena Park re-creates the Old West, complete with train robberies and panning for real gold. The Movieland Wax Museum re-creates the legendary scenes of motion pictures in tableaux with dummies. The sights of Orange County are many, ranging from alligator parks to simulated safaris. It's a lot of fun—and ideal for families.

1. Anaheim and Disneyland

Anaheim, 27 miles south of the Los Angeles City Hall, reached via the Santa Ana Freeway, provides the space needed for so large an entertainment center as Disneyland. Once the heart of an orange grove belt, it offers excellent motels, hotels, and restaurants, catering to the millions of tourists who visit the world-famed attraction annually.

If you're going by car, just get on the freeway heading south, and you'll be in Anaheim in about an hour. If you go by bus, take no. 460 from the RTD/Greyhound terminal in downtown Los Angeles at 6th and Los Angeles Streets. Fare is $2.50 each way.

The **Anaheim Convention Center,** 800 W. Katella Ave. (tel. 714/999-8900), is a 40-acre exhibit facility right next door to Disneyland. Something is always going on there, whether it's a rock festival in its 9,100-seat arena, a special art or antiques fair in one of the three 100,000-square-foot exhibition halls, or a sales conference in one of the 40 meeting rooms. There are even kitchen facilities, a cocktail lounge, and attractive grounds for wandering between sessions.

The **Anaheim Stadium,** 2000 State College Blvd. (tel. 714/937-6750), cost $50 million to build (including the 1980 27,000-seat expansion), but it's worth every penny to the fans of its home teams, the California Angels and the Los Angeles Rams. Designed for comfort, easy visibility, and smoother traffic flow within the stadium, it seats 70,000 in chair-type seats for baseball and football games. For daily tours call 714/937-7333.

DISNEYLAND

Even the most jaded nose can hardly turn up at Disneyland, 1313 Harbor Blvd. (tel. 714/999-4565), in Anaheim off the Santa Ana Freeway (Hwy. 5). It's that special: a world of charm and magic, an open sesame to one's lost childhood, an extravagant doorway to yesterday and tomorrow. Can you believe that in 1988 Mickey Mouse had his 60th birthday?

Opened in 1955, Disneyland—the creation of Walt Disney—has steadily grown until it ranks today as the single top attraction in all of California. Total attendance has passed 250 million. It sprawls across many acres and is constantly expanding.

It is split into seven themed lands: Main Street, Adventureland, New Orleans Square, Bear Country, Frontierland, Fantasyland, and Tomorrowland. Do-it-yourselfers will find it less confusing to progress clockwise, starting with the point of entry on Main Street. However, some of the attractions, such as the Disneyland trains and the Disneyland Monorail, take guests around the perimeter of the park.

The general admission to Disneyland is $27.50 for adults, $22.50 for those 60 and over daily except Saturday, and $22.50 for children 3 to 11. There is no charge for children under 3. Admission includes unlimited rides and entertainment.

During the fall, winter, and spring seasons (mid-September through May), Disneyland is open Monday through Friday from 10 a.m. to 6 p.m., from 9 a.m. to midnight on weekends. During the Thanksgiving, Christmas, and Easter holidays, and during the summer season, Disneyland is open every day on an extended operating schedule. The parking lot ($4 charge) may be entered from Harbor Boulevard.

Perhaps before you plunge into the Fantasia of Disneyland, you'll board the **Disneyland Railroad** at the Main Street Station. The train chugs into the turn-of-the-century station—evocative of many a western movie—complete with black smokestack and bright-red "cow-ketcher." Circling the "kingdom" for 1½ miles, the train goes by Adventureland, Bear Country, Frontierland, Fantasyland, Tomorrowland, including the Grand Canyon diorama (with a more than 300-foot-long painting of the world-famed canyon), plus the steamy "Primeval World," when dinosaurs walked on the earth.

On **Main Street,** there are a series of old-fashioned vehicles that will take you through the remarkable re-creation of a late 19th-century American town: a horse-drawn carriage, a fire wagon that answers an alarm, a horseless carriage, and a double-decker omnibus.

Many begin their adventure by calling on the corner Market House where Main Street life centers around a potbelly stove (you may want to join in on a checker game while listening to the harmonizing of a barbershop quartet).

After sunset there's a Main Street Electrical Parade spectacular —fabulous whirling lights followed by Fantasy in the Sky fireworks.

Walking down the streets of colorful shops, you'll pass a penny arcade, and can enjoy the "Walt Disney Story featuring great moments with Mr. Lincoln," at the Disneyland Opera House—an "audio-animatronics" figure of the 16th president. Light refreshments and dinner are available at the Carnation Ice Cream Parlor, Plaza Gardens, Plaza Pavilion, the Plaza Inn, and the Town Square Café. You can also stop off at the local cinema to enjoy a silent movie of bygone days.

At **Adventureland** you can—among other thrills—take a river cruise through the jungle, be threatened by wild animals and hostile natives, visit the "enchanted" Tiki Room, or even scale the treehouse of the Swiss Family Robinson.

On the **Jungle Cruise** you'll feel like Katharine Hepburn in *The African Queen* as you glide through tropical vegetation, pass waterfowl, a Cambodian temple in ruins, and a host of other surprises.

The **Enchanted Tiki Room** is a delightful musical fantasy, with "audio-animatronics" personalities in a South Seas world. One of the least-heralded but most skillfully designed attractions of Disneyland is the **Swiss Family Robinson Treehouse,** where you climb to lofty heights around a wide-spreading tree, on whose limbs rest the bedrooms and "parlor" of the legendary family.

For refreshments, there's the **Tiki Juice Bar** (try Tonga punch), and for Polynesian viands, the **Tahitian Terrace.**

The **New Orleans Square** evokes a glamorized Hollywood version of the French Quarter of the Louisiana city, complete with lacy iron balconies, old town house patios, and semitropical plantings behind wrought-iron gates.

One of the most exciting attractions in the park is the **Pirates of the Caribbean.** You can go for a hair-raising sail that recaptures the lore of piracy, including the blood-letting takeover of a Caribbean town and a swampy bayou setting with drooping Spanish moss. One of the best restaurants in Disneyland is the **Blue Bayou** overlooking the Pirates of the Caribbean. At the **French Market** you can feast on an array of tempting Louisiana specialties or try a special Disneyland mint julep.

The **Haunted Mansion** is a tall, gray-and-white mansard-roofed house, where you enter between great fluted columns. For a "spook adventure supreme," you'll find it an imaginative experience. You start by meeting the members of the family, going from room to room. Finally, you're taken on a long graveyard ride in cars

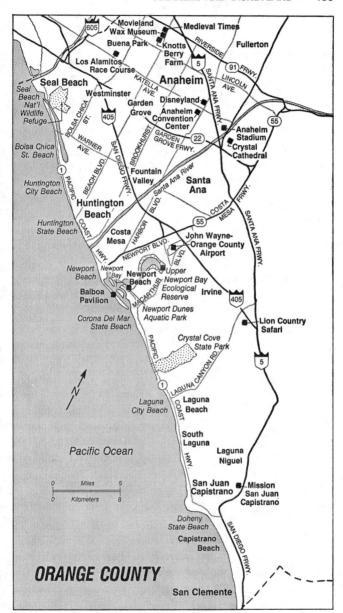

through the spirit world, with ghosts rising, wailing, and calling to you!

Critter Country hosts the **Country Bear Jamboree,** featuring such entertainers as "Liverlips McGrowl." In addition you can paddle yourself along the "Rivers of America" on **Davy Crockett's Explorer Canoes.** Best of all, there is the new **Splash Mountain**—the brand-new flume ride attraction located in Bear Country between the Haunted Mansion and Country Bear Playhouse. It is the largest towering log-flume attraction in the world, the most elaborate and possibly the most thrilling. Each log vehicle sends eight guests speeding through twisting backwoods waterways and scenic chutes. There's a chase through swamps, caves, and beehives of backwoods bayous before rising to a 52-foot plunge into a briar patch pond. The huge terraced hill towers 60 feet above the Rivers of America, crowned with the burned-out tree-stump lair of Brer Fox. Splash Mountain is a fantastic extravaganza combining music, water, sudden falls, snapping alligators, angry bees, and a 10-foot tall Brer Bear.

In **Frontierland** the folklore of America comes alive. A popular attraction is the **Mark Twain Steamboat,** a 108-foot-long sternwheel, triple-decker paddlewheeler, accommodating 350 passengers. You cruise the rivers of America past the shores of Tom Sawyer's Island (complete with a waterfall), woodlands, Indian territory, Fort Wilderness, and a floating barrel bridge.

For an adventure on cave-riddled **Tom Sawyer's Island,** you'll be poled across the river on a raft. Once there, you can explore Fort Wilderness. Or take **Big Thunder Mountain Railroad** on a journey through a deserted turn-of-the-century mine imperiled by clusters of swarming bats, wild animals, a flood, earthquake, and rockslide.

A don't-miss attraction is the **Horseshoe Revue,** an old-time music hall, complete with a stage show—a nostalgic glimpse of what amused the '49er—with can-can girls and a sultry soubrette known as "Slue-Foot Sue." Mae West would be right at home here. Sponsored by the Pepsi-Cola company, the saloon charges no admission, but make your show reservations as soon as you arrive in the park.

Fantasyland evokes some of the great Walt Disney films. Cross the moat of the turreted **Sleeping Beauty Castle** and you're suddenly transported into a world of make-believe. Here the big attraction—certainly terrifying fun—is the **Matterhorn Bobsleds,** a race down and around twisting, ice-coated mountain slopes. Bobsledders experience two meetings with the Abominable Snowman, sudden temperature drops, and drifting banks of fog.

Here you can experience the same adventures as **Alice in Wonderland,** meeting some mad, wonderful characters; board the **Casey Jr. Circus Train,** sail over Fantasyland in a wing-eared **Dumbo Flying Elephant,** take a spin on **King Arthur's Carousel,** "whirl and twirl" at the **Mad Tea Party,** steer a **Motor Boat** across dangerous currents and rapids, take **Mr. Toad's Wild Ride** through the London of another era, fly over the English capital in a **Peter Pan Flight** into a never-never land, or share in **Snow White's Adventure.** You can also take a trip through the world of fairy tales on the **Storybook Land Canal Boats.**

"It's a Small World" takes guests in a slow-moving boat past small groups of miniature "children" from around the globe—all singing the same theme song—climaxing in a united earth of total harmony.

In **Tomorrowland,** the romantic past gives way to the wonders of the future. See the exciting 3-D motion picture *Captain Eo,* a musical space adventure starring Michael Jackson performing his original score, and a cast of merry, mythical space characters. The super-realism of the 3-D makes it seem as if Michael Jackson is dancing right off the screen and into the theater, and as if lasers are firing overhead at hovering spaceships. Add to that the new *Star Tours* — you actually believe you are aboard a StarSpeeder as it takes off for the Moon of Endor, only to encounter a spaceload of misadventures. As you enter the Tomorrowland Spaceport, C3PO and R2-D2 (the endearing and dynamic duo from *Star Wars*) are on hand to greet you. You board your own 40-passenger StarSpeeder, fasten your seat belts and you're off on your intergalactic adventure through the universe, with visual special effects and actual motion combining to create a fantastic thrill—hard to believe until you've tried it. For a preview of the way you'll be traveling in the world of tomorrow, take the **Disneyland Monorail** all around Disneyland for a bird's-eye view of the park. Here most guests want to take the **Submarine Voyage,** a breathtaking adventure through "liquid space" on an underwater cruise to the **North Pole.**

Heralded as Disneyland's most spectacular attraction is **Space Mountain,** which allows you to become an astronaut and explore the cosmos.

You can also book a **Mission to Mars,** which will give you a seat in a tremendous rocket for a visit to Mission Control on this faraway planet. Among the free shows and exhibits, you can visit the United States, through film, in the 360° **America the Beautiful** presentation.

And don't forget to visit the **Wonders of China,** a marvelous morning tour of all the remarkably beautiful and historical wonders of this extraordinary land.

By all means, don't miss Disneyland!

WHERE TO STAY

In Anaheim

Many a family has settled into a nearby Anaheim motel with a swimming pool for their stay in Southern California. They buy big books of tickets, savoring Disneyland in bits and pieces, alternating their adventure there with day trips in other directions. If you'd like to make Anaheim your home base, you'll want to consult the following accommodation recommendations.

Disneyland Hotel, 1150 W. Cerritos Ave., Anaheim, CA 92802 (tel. 714/778-6600). Coming from Disneyland via the Monorail—"the highway in the sky"—you arrive at this complete resort. It's a dazzling array of buildings, containing 1,132 rooms and suites set in 60 acres of gardens. Single rooms cost $130 to $198; doubles, $140 to $219; suites begin at $400.

The real story here is the extent of facilities available. Of course, you'd expect the Olympic-size pool, but there's also a two-level cove beach surrounded by sand and tidal pools evoking the Pacific shoreline. A cluster of 35 shops and boutiques lures visitors to the resort's shopping mall. The Disneyland Hotel also has 10 night-lighted tennis courts. Meals are offered in 16 restaurants and cafés, and you can enjoy entertainment and the view from the Pavilion cocktail lounge. A complimentary water show—"Dancing Waters"—is staged nightly.

A Bit of Olde England

The **Sheraton-Anaheim Hotel,** 1015 W. Ball Rd., Anaheim, CA (tel. 714/778-1700, or toll free 800/325-3535), is a Tudor extravaganza. It's a western version of an English coach inn, right on the freeway. The English inn-castle theme permeates both the interior and the black-and-white timbered exterior.

A somewhat unusual 500-room luxury motel, it incorporates bits and pieces of Olde England. A Midlands castle, Larden Hall, built in 1460, was torn down and shipped to the United States piece by piece to become part of the Sheraton (previously the Royale Coach Motor Hotel). In addition, the motel includes a collection of more than 50 stained-glass windows removed from a boys' school in the environs of London. An architect capped the weirdly shaped and gabled melange with a stone tower lined with battlements. There are reflection pools as well, and a formal English garden.

The designer of the public rooms imported tapestries, fireplaces, old paintings, and antique furniture. The rear of the castle opens onto a courtyard, which has a vast oval-shaped swimming pool.

The cost of accommodations at the inn is $100 to $115 for a single, $105 to $125 for doubles. Children 17 and under can stay free in a room with their parents. More expensive suites are available as well. The rooms—all containing color TV, some with a refrigerator—are widely spread out on three floors, and the individualized furnishings are comfortable.

Opening onto the courtyard is the Falstaff Room for dining and the adjoining Falstaff Tavern for cocktails. There's also a nightclub at the Sheraton called Merlin's Happy Yeoman.

Howard Johnson's Motor Lodge, 1380 S. Harbor Blvd., Anaheim, CA 92802 (tel. 714/776-6120, or toll free 800/654-2000), is one of the most elegant hostelries in Anaheim. In a six-acre parklike setting, its contemporary design was the creation of the award-winning architect W. L. Pereira. It's almost like a resort, and it's just opposite Disneyland. Coved-roofed balconies open onto a central garden with two swimming pools for adults, another for children. Garden paths lead under eucalyptus and olive trees to a splashing circular fountain. During the summer, you can watch the nightly fireworks display at Disneyland from the upper balconies. The 320 rooms are equipped with direct-dial phones and tub/shower baths; a small living area, individually controlled air conditioning, and large-screen color television sets with alarm clock and radio round out the amenities.

There's a Howard Johnson's restaurant on the premises, open around the clock and serving all the famous flavors. A bar/lounge adjoins.

Rates are $85 single, $87 double, and $98 for double-doubles. Children under 18 sharing a room with their parents stay free.

The **Inn at the Park,** 1855 S. Harbor Blvd. (at Katella Avenue), Anaheim, CA 92802 (tel. 714/971-4560, or toll free 800/421-6662, 800/352-6686 in California), is a fine example of resort-style architecture. Across from Disneyland, it rises 14 floors and is endowed with parklike grounds and an immense swimming pool. In addition to 500 rooms, facilities include a western-themed restaurant called the Overland Stage, plus the Sunshine Pantry coffeeshop, a game room, and shops.

Rooms have every modern amenity. Singles are $85 to $114; doubles and twins, $95 to $124; suites, $170 to $400.

Anaheim Aloha TraveLodge, 505 W. Katella Ave., Anaheim, CA 92802 (tel. 714/774-8710, or toll free 800/255-3050). Just one block from Disneyland and half a block from the Convention Center, this branch of the TraveLodge chain provides reliable and reasonably priced accommodations. There are 50 nicely furnished rooms, all of which are equipped with color TV, free cable movies, direct-dial phone, modern bath, and coffee makers. An outdoor heated swimming pool is on the premises, complete with a slide. A complimentary Continental breakfast is included in the rates.

Rates are seasonal. In summer single rooms are $59; doubles and twins (double-doubles), $69. Off-season rates are lower, and children under 17 can stay free in a room with their parents. Call direct to find out the off-season prices. Two-bedroom units that can accommodate up to eight persons are $110 in summer. Pets are welcome.

As you might expect, there's a **Motel 6** close to Disneyland and Knott's Berry Farm. It's located at 921 S. Beach Blvd. (between Ball Road and Hwy. 91), Anaheim, CA 92804 (tel. 714/220-2866). It's easy on the budget, clean, efficient, comfortable, and has a pool. Singles are $30, plus $6 for each additional adult.

In Nearby Fullerton

The ultimate in economy near Disneyland and Knott's Berry Farm is the **Fullerton Hacienda AYH Hostel,** 1700 N. Harbor Blvd., Fullerton, CA 92635 (tel. 714/738-3721), adjoining Anaheim. It's located on the site of an old dairy farm, surrounded by greenery with lemon trees, rabbits, squirrels—lots of friendly country life. As with all the AYH hostels I've been to, accommodations are comfortable, and the manager is congenial and helpful. The hostel provides a complete kitchen and bathroom facilities. It operates under a self-help system. You're expected to clean up after yourself, leave the hostel tidy, and do some chores each morning as requested by the houseparents. The maximum stay is three consecutive days. Rates are $10 for AYH/IYHF members and $13 for non-members. If you travel often and enjoy the very simple life, I suggest that it's worth joining the AYH—just ask for the application information. They welcome members of all ages.

Note: No alcohol, drugs, or weapons are allowed on the premises. Smoking is not allowed in the building.

WHERE TO DINE

If you're in Anaheim to see Disneyland, you'll probably eat there; however, most hotels offer satisfactory dining choices. The Disneyland Hotel, alone, has 16 restaurants and lounges.

One other alternative for lunch or dinner is **Mr. Stox,** 1105 E. Katella Ave., between the Santa Ana Freeway (Hwy. 5) and State College Boulevard (tel. 714/634-2994). It lavishly lays on the charm of early California when missions dominated the culture. At night, there's entertainment while you dine, usually a singer performing with a trio.

At lunch you can order salads like a smoked seafood or Cobb salad for $7 to $13. Hot entrees such as fresh seafood or leg of lamb are $10 to $12.

For an appetizer at dinner I'd suggest freshly made fettuccine with three cheeses. Dinner entrees include a wide range of choices such as veal with wild mushrooms, fresh halibut, or prime rib, at $12 to $19. Desserts are homemade. The Mr. Stox wine list is impressive, including over 550 selections.

Open for lunch weekdays from 11 a.m. to 3 p.m., and for dinner nightly from 6:30 to 10 p.m. Reservations suggested.

2. Buena Park

Three major sights—**Knott's Berry Farm,** the **Movieland Wax Museum,** and the tournament/banquet **Medieval Times**—are clustered in the tiny community of Buena Park, 20 miles southeast of Los Angeles City Hall on the Santa Ana Freeway. In Orange County, the small area in flatlands (once orange groves) is just a few miles south of Santa Fe Springs (the oil town that produced a coterie of millionaires).

Since Anaheim, with its super-colossal attraction, Disneyland, is only five miles beyond Buena Park, many visitors are tempted to combine all the adventures into one day. But unless it's the longest day of the year, and you have unlimited energy, I suggest that you divide the trek into at least two days—a full day at Buena Park, another day at Disneyland—if not more, plus one extra day for each two children.

From the Santa Ana Freeway (Hwy. 5), turn off when you come to Hwy. 39 (Beach Boulevard). The first sight will be the Movieland Wax Museum, on Beach Boulevard. Knott's Berry Farm is between four streets: La Palma Avenue, Knott Avenue, Beach Avenue, and Lincoln Avenue.

To go to Disneyland, in Anaheim, continue on La Palma till you join the Santa Ana Freeway.

To reach Buena Park and Anaheim by bus, take "Freeway Flyer" no. 56 from the downtown Los Angeles terminal at 6th and Los Angeles streets. It's an hour's trip.

WHAT TO SEE AND DO

The Movieland Wax Museum

At 7711 Beach Blvd., which is also called Hwy. 39 (tel. 714/522-1155), you can see previews of past attractions—everything from Bela Lugosi as Dracula to Marilyn Monroe in *Gentlemen Prefer Blondes*.

Self-billed as "the biggest gathering of stars in the world," and in keeping with the Silver Screen it honors, the museum creates the illusion of a big Hollywood première. Over 250 movie and TV stars are depicted.

"America's Sweetheart," Mary Pickford, dedicated the museum on May 4, 1962. It has steadily risen in popularity ever since, with new stars added yearly, taking their place next to the time-tested favorites. The museum was created by a film addict, Allen Parkinson, who saw to it that some of the most memorable scenes in motion pictures were re-created in exacting detail in wax, with such authentic touches as the ripped dress of Sophia Loren in *Two Women*.

As you walk along the Stars' Hall of Fame, you'll encounter Charlie Chaplin in *The Gold Rush*, Harold Lloyd in *Mad Wednesday*, Jean Harlow in *Dinner at Eight*, Charles Laughton in *The Private Life of Henry VIII*, Valentino in *Son of the Sheik*, Shirley Temple in *Bright Eyes*, Edward G. Robinson as *Little Caesar*, Tony Perkins in *Psycho*, Gene Kelly in *Singin' in the Rain*, Tyrone Power in *Blood and Sand*, Elizabeth Taylor in *Cleopatra*, Newman and Redford in *Butch Cassidy and the Sundance Kid*, and Ed Asner as "Lou Grant."

In tableaux are some of the most popular teams: Bogart and Katharine Hepburn in *The African Queen*, Myrna Loy and William Powell in *The Thin Man*, Garbo and Gilbert in *Queen Christina*, Clark Gable and Vivien Leigh in *Gone with the Wind*, not to forget Laurel and Hardy in *The Perfect Day*. Later sets include *Star Trek* and *Superman*.

Other intriguing exhibits are the chariots used in the Charlton Heston version of *Ben Hur* and a tableau depicting the incomparable Gloria Swanson attending the world première of *Sunset Boulevard*. Her wax counterpart is seen getting out of a sedan with her co-stars in the film, William Holden and Erich von Stroheim.

Among the newer exhibits are Bette Davis, Marlon Brando, Jimmy Stewart, and Clint Eastwood.

Final warning: Beware of one of the Keystone Kops. He's for real!

The museum is open every day, rain or shine. Hours are from 9 a.m. to 8 p.m. Once in, you can stay till 9:30 p.m. Admission is $10.95 for adults, $8.95 for seniors, $6.95 for children 4 to 11 years, under 4 it's free. Parking is free. Movieland is located one block north of Knott's Berry Farm in Buena Park, Orange County. Take the Beach Boulevard exit south from the Santa Ana Freeway (Hwy. 5) and the Riverside Freeway (Hwy. 91).

Knott's Berry Farm

Spend a wild day in the West at 8039 Beach Blvd. in Buena Park, just south of the Santa Ana (Hwy. 5) and Riverside/Artesia (Hwy. 91) freeways (tel. 714/220-5200). At Knott's, the rip-roarin' Wild West is brought back to life for the whole family to enjoy. You can pan for gold or take a spine-tingling ride down Timber Mountain. Walk through **Old West Ghost Town.** Suddenly shots ring out! It's a shoot-'em-up showdown between the sheriff and two "gunfighters."

On the street a pretty girl plays a steam calliope. A barker hustles you into the **Birdcage Theater** for an old-time melodrama where you boo the villain and cheer the hero. Clamber aboard the old **Butterfield Stagecoach** for a journey through the Old West, then amble over to **Timber Mountain** for a free-floatin' log ride through sawmills and logging camps that winds up with a wild plunge down a 42-foot chute. For daredevils there's Montezooma's Revenge, a shuttle loop roller coaster that not only turns you completely upside-down, but even goes backward! Thrillseekers will also like the Corkscrew, a coaster with two 360° loops, and the Sky Tower, a parachute jump that drops riders 20 stories at free-fall speeds.

Knott's began in 1920 when Walter and Cordelia Knott and their family arrived in Buena Park in their old Model T. Starting with 10 acres of leased land, the Knotts began to eke out a living by farming and selling berries at a roadside stand.

Fourteen years later, in 1934, Mrs. Knott served her first eight chicken dinners, which marked the beginning of the now world-famous **Chicken Dinner Restaurant.** Today the restaurant serves up to 6,000 dinners in a single day. And Knott's other major restaurant, the **Steak House,** has earned a reputation all its own. In addition to these eating places, Knott's offers the **Garden Terrace Buffet, Cable Car Buffet,** and **Ghost Town Grill** restaurant, among others, plus many fast-food takeout stands.

What began as a small family affair more than half a century ago has become the nation's third-largest family-themed entertainment park. Knott's is still owned by the Knott family.

A major attraction at Knott's Berry Farm is the full-scale brick-by-brick replica of Philadelphia's famed **Independence Hall.** Completed in 1966 as the fulfillment of Walter Knott's life-long dream, Independence Hall is furnished with an authentic reproduction of the Liberty Bell, complete with crack.

A truly high point in the development of Knott's has been the construction of **Knott's Toyota Good Time Theatre,** a 2,100-seat indoor facility opened in 1971. A top show is presented daily in the summer. Entrance is included in Knott's admission price.

Still another attraction is **Knott's Fiesta Village,** a Mexican-themed area in tribute to our south-of-the-border neighbors. A fiesta atmosphere prevails, and rides include the Happy Sombrero, the Tampico Tumbler, the Merry-Go-Round, and the above-mentioned Montezooma's Revenge. And you can catch your breath as you watch the new "Incredible Waterworks Show"—a sound, light, and water spectacular held on the park's Reflection Lake.

The $1 million **Pacific Pavillion,** with 1,200 seats, features *Splashdance,* with Dudley the sea lion and co-starring two dolphins. It's also the home of the 2,100-seat Good Time Theatre and the $7 million Kingdom of the Dinosaurs ride.

There's also the 5½-acre **Roaring '20s Amusement Area,** featuring 16 air-themed rides and attractions. Its highlight is the 20-story Sky Tower. Thrill seekers will want to try the XK-1, the ultimate participatory flight ride (you pilot the aircraft with a control stick), as well as the Whirlpool.

Then there's the new Boomerang, a state-of-the-art coaster that turns riders upside down six times—three forward, three backward, in less than one minute. If that doesn't shake your lunch around, nothing will. After boarding, you're pulled backward to the top of a nearly 11-story tower, then the seven-car train is released to dive down, go through two twists and a vertical loop up to the top of another vertical tower. Then the entire trip is repeated—backward.

For the less adventurous, there's an enclosed Sky Cabin that revolves 360° as it travels up and down the tower.

And don't miss **Wild Water Wilderness,** the theme area opened in May 1988. It's a $10 million, 3½-acre, turn-of-the-century California wilderness park with an exciting white-water rapids ride.

Camp Snoopy is Knott's themed area of the picturesque California High Sierra, a home for Charles Schulz's beloved beagle, Snoopy, and his pals, Charlie Brown and Lucy. With 30 rides, shows, and attractions, it's six rustic acres of fun for the young of all ages.

Admission is $22, $16 for seniors over 60, with unlimited access to all rides, shows, and attractions. Children (ages 3 to 11) pay $17 (those under 3 are admitted free).

Knott's is open year round except December 25. In summer, Sunday through Friday it's open from 10 a.m. to midnight and on Saturdays to 1 a.m.; winter hours are 10 a.m. to 6 p.m. weekdays, to 10 p.m. Saturday, and to 7 p.m. Sunday.

Medieval Times

Great fun at 7662 Beach Blvd. (tel. 714/521-4740, or toll free 800/826-5358, 800/438-9911 in California), right near the Movieland Wax Museum in Buena Park. If you haven't already collapsed from the excitement of the rides, the walking, and the gawking, Medieval Times offers entertainment straight out of the 11th century (or thereabouts) in a castle setting. And here, while you eat (albeit with knives and forks instead of bare hands), you will be entertained with tournaments, sword fighting, jousting, and feats of skill by colorfully costumed knights on horseback.

Shows are Monday through Thursday at 7:30 p.m.; Friday and Saturday at 4, 6:30 and 9:15 p.m.; Sunday at 1, 4:45 and 7:30 p.m. The price for adults is $27 to $32, for children 12 and under, it's $19 to $21. Medieval Times is an extremely popular year-round attraction, so I suggest that if you plan to cheer on your favorite knight, make reservations at least two months in advance. A good time will be had by all.

WHERE TO STAY

Farm de Ville, 7800 and 7878 Crescent Ave. (at Hwy. 39), Buena Park, CA 90260 (tel. 714/527-2201). Conveniently located at the south entrance to Knott's Berry Farm, with buses to Disneyland running right out front, the Farm de Ville is popular with visitors to Buena Park and attracts a considerable number of honeymooners (yes, many people do spend their honeymoon in the Anaheim/Buena Park fantasyland). Its 130 rooms, housed in two separate buildings, are immaculate and attractive—stylishly furnished with print spreads, shag carpeting, and large dressing areas. Every room has a color TV, radio, direct-dial phone, tub/shower bath, and individually controlled air conditioning and heating. Facilities on the premises include two swimming pools with slides and diving boards for the kids, two wading pools for very little tots, two sauna baths, a coin-operated laundry, and a Bakers Square restaurant.

In summer, singles are $42, and doubles run $44 to $52, with each additional person in a room charged $4. Family units that accommodate four to six persons cost $80.

---

3. Irvine

Wild Rivers Waterpark is Orange County's newest family theme park and its only waterpark. Located in Irvine off the San Diego Freeway (Hwy. 405) at 8770 Irvine Center Dr. (tel. 714/768-9453), Wild Rivers is a 20-minute drive from Disneyland.

Wild Rivers has more than 40 exciting rides and attractions in a tropical setting on 20 acres. Wild Rivers Mountain is over five stories high with 19 thrilling rides. You can inner-tube down the side of the mountain, shoot through an underground tunnel, or slide down the length of a football field.

Thunder Cove features the only two side-by-side wave-action pools in the country, allowing for gentle body surfing or powerful body boarding—take your pick.

Explorers' Island is the perfect place for families with small children. You'll find activity pools and scaled-down rides for little people.

Changing facilities and rental lockers are available, and there are fast food concessions throughout the park. A picnic area is located just outside the main entrance for guests who bring their own food.

Admission is $17 for those 10 and older, $13 for those 3 to 9 years, while children under age 3 are free. Seniors (55 and older) are $9, as is a spectator pass (includes only dry activities). Admission after 4 p.m. is $9. Parking is $4 per vehicle. The Waterpark is open weekends mid-May to June from 11 a.m. to 5 p.m., then daily to mid-June, when hours are extended to 10 a.m. to 5 p.m. The longer hours continue through Labor Day, when days open revert to weekends from 11 a.m. to 5 p.m. until closing for the season in early October.

X

ACROSS THE DESERT TO PALM SPRINGS

1. CROSSING THE DESERT
2. PALM SPRINGS

After busy days along the Pacific, you may be ready for the special appeal of the desert. If so, the best resort to wind down in is Palm Springs, a two-hour drive from Los Angeles. However, if you long for more excitement, you can head east to Las Vegas. If that is your plan, consider stopping off at either Apple Valley or Calico Ghost Town, or both, on your trip along Interstate 15.

1. Crossing the Desert

Even if you're not planning to go all the way to Las Vegas, but would like to drive out to the desert, here are two places to head for.

APPLE VALLEY

Doesn't it sound like the happiest place in the world? Rimmed by the snow-capped San Bernardino Mountains, this land is for those who want to bask in the sun and breathe pure desert air. The town rose from the desert right after World War II, and uses its vast underground water supply to create this oasis. Horseback riding over desert trails, an 18-hole championship golf course, a haywagon ride to a western steak fry, songs around the campfire—these are but some of the activities that occupy the vacationer. Apple Valley is some 90 miles from Los Angeles (take Interstate 15, turning onto 18 at Victorville). The drive should take under 2 hours if you don't hit bad traffic.

CALICO GHOST TOWN

One of the most famous ghost towns of the Old West still lives. Halfway between Los Angeles and Las Vegas, ten miles north of

Barstow, and just off Interstate 15 (under 3 hours by car with reasonable traffic), Calico was a boom town from 1881 to 1896, when it was abandoned by the silver miners who had settled it so hastily. In its heyday the town was visited frequently by Wyatt Earp, trailed by a string of admiring children. Grubstaked by the county sheriff, a trio of prospectors discovered a silver lode in 1881 that was to produce $86 million of the precious metal in just 15 years.

Today—thanks to Walter Knott of Knott's Berry Farm fame—as in the 19th century, people walk the streets of Calico, past the general store, the old schoolhouse, Lil's saloon, the pottery works, even Boot Hill. The most popular attraction is the Maggie Mine, where it's possible to explore tunnels dug into the old silver lode. You can also see an oldtime melodrama at the Calikage Playhouse featuring the maiden, the villain, and the hero. There are snackshops and a restaurant, and many of the buildings have now become shops selling interesting merchandise. It's pretty touristy, but it's fun, and kids especially love it. Admission is $5 per car, and there's no additional charge to park. There are campgrounds on the premises. For information call 619/254-2122.

2. Palm Springs

People go to Palm Springs just for fun. One of the world's most renowned resorts, Palm Springs combines sunny deserts with palm-lined canyons. Shaded by rugged Mount San Jacinto and surrounded by a dry, invigorating climate, the resort offers days that are sunny and clear.

Palm Springs is also "the golf capital of the world." More than 100 tournaments are held in the area, including the $100,000 Bob Hope Desert Classic.

Its honorary mayor is Bob Hope. President Eisenhower considered the Eldorado Country Club his favorite vacation retreat, and as many movie stars have homes here as they do in Beverly Hills.

Palm Springs lies 104 miles southeast of Los Angeles, about a 2-hour drive via the San Bernadino Freeway (Interstate 10). You can also go by bus and Amtrak (to Indio, 20 miles south). A multi-million-dollar airport is served by several airlines. The plane trip from Los Angeles takes 36 minutes.

To gain perspective—that is, see for yourself that every sixth family (at least) has a swimming pool—you can glide along the **Palm Springs Aerial Tramway** (tel. 619/325-1391 for a recorded announcement, or 325-1449), a distance of 2½ miles up the slopes of Mount San Jacinto. A cable car will carry you and 79 others to a height of 8,516 feet on the world's largest tramway operating on a single span. You'll leave a world of cactus, Joshua trees, date palms, and grazing bighorn sheep, passing through a climate that its promoters have claimed is like going from Mexico to Alaska. At the end of the line, you emerge into the snow, with a panoramic vista of the Coachella Valley, Nevada, Arizona, even Mexico. The tramway

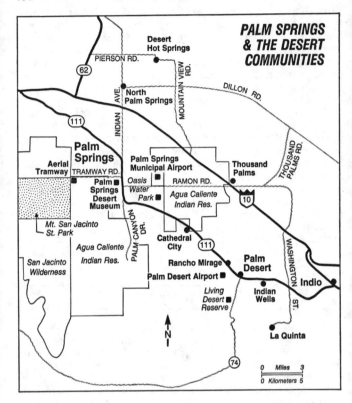

opens weekdays at 10 a.m., weekends at 8 a.m. From May 1 to Labor Day the last tram goes up at 8 p.m., the last one comes down at 9:45 p.m. The rest of the year, the last cars go up and down an hour earlier. The round-trip price is $13.95 for adults, $8.95 for children 3 to 11. To reach it, go to Tramway Drive, at Chino Canyon, off Hwy. 111.

There are two places to eat at: a snackbar at the bottom of the tramway and the Alpine Restaurant at the top. You can purchase a special ride-and-dinner combination ticket after 2:30 p.m., costing $17.95 for adults, $11.50 for children (a great bargain).

For a down-to-earth perspective of Palm Springs, not to mention maps, brochures, and information, stop in at the **Palm Springs Desert Resorts Convention and Visitors Bureau** in Suite 201, 69730 Hwy. 111, Rancho Mirage, CA 92272 (tel. 619/327-8411).

If you don't want to traipse out to Rancho Mirage for information, the people at the **Palm Springs Chamber of Commerce** can be very helpful. The chamber is near the heart of town, 190 W. Amado Rd., at the corner of Belardo (tel. 619/325-1577), and is open Monday through Friday from 8 a.m. to 5 p.m., Saturday and Sunday from 10 a.m. to 2 p.m.

For a fascinating tour of the Palm Springs area, the place to start is **Palm Springs Celebrity Tours,** 333 N. Palm Canyon Dr., Suite 204A (tel. 619/325-2682).

Celebrity Tours have been around since 1963. They take pride in their professional guides, who know all the in's and out's of Palm Springs and who will escort you around in comfort. Groups are small and service is personalized. Their deluxe coaches are air-conditioned and seat up to 14.

The one-hour tour of Palm Springs includes the homes of movie stars and celebrities. The two-hour tour not only has everything you'd see during the one-hour version, but the estates of Frank Sinatra and the very wealthy and well-connected Walter Annenberg, who has his own golf course. You'll also see the Tamarisk, Canyon, and Thunderbird Country Clubs, where the international elite meet to play. Then on to the Eisenhower Medical Center and beautiful date groves, with a brief stop for refreshments.

The one-hour tour meets at the office at the above address. For the two-hour tour, Celebrity Tours will pick you up at any hotel in Palm Springs. Rates for the one-hour tour are $10 for adults, $9 for seniors, $5 for children to 11 years. The two-hour tour is $14 for adults, $12 for seniors, $7 for children to 11 years.

Reservations are required. You must make them at least a day or two ahead for either tour. They fill up especially quickly during the "high season." For daily departure times, check when you make your reservations.

WHERE TO STAY

The **Ingleside Inn,** 200 W. Ramon Rd. (at Belardo Road), Palm Springs, CA 92262 (tel. 619/325-0046), offers the most romantic accommodations in Palm Springs. Once you enter the imposing wrought-iron gates, you're in a gracious world of tranquility and fine service. Each of the 28 rooms (some are villas) is furnished in antiques, many left over from the days when this was the Humphrey Birge estate. Perhaps your room will have a canopied bed or a 15th-century vestment chest. Many have fireplaces, and all have in-room steambaths and refrigerators stocked with complimentary light snacks and beverages, not to mention all the other luxuries you might desire *plus* a complimentary Continental breakfast.

On the premises is one of this town's most acclaimed restaurants, Melvyn's, a celebrity haunt which was chosen by Frank and Barbara Sinatra for their "intimate" after-wedding dinner party (only about 70 close friends were invited). The decor is most attractive, with wicker and tapestry-upholstered furnishings, lace curtains on the windows, lots of plants, and a turn-of-the-century oak-and-mahogany bar with beveled mirrors.

At dinner you might begin with the goose liver pâté (with truffle) or the deep-fried brie with jalapeño jelly, and then a veal chop grilled and accented with Madeira wine, green peppercorns, and a wild French mushroom sauce. Your entree, ranging from $18 to $27, is served with soup or salad. The wine list is distinguished. The dessert selection changes daily, but the chocolate mousse pie, when available, is excellent. If that meal sounds like a bit of a strain on your budget, come at lunch when you can have a French dip sandwich, au jus, with french fries or breast of chicken on sourdough bread and other hot entrees and cold plates for $8 to $15. It's also known for its Saturday and Sunday champagne brunch ($14 to $19), when you can have such entrees as eggs Florentine, or its very popular prime rib hash with poached egg and mushroom sauce. All dishes are served with fresh fruit and unlimited Melvyn's champagne.

Other notable facilities are a swimming pool and Jacuzzi, croquet, and shuffleboard; golf, tennis, and horseback riding can be arranged. Evenings there's entertainment at the piano bar and dancing in the lounge.

Singles and doubles are $85 to $225 in season (October 1 to June 1); mini-suites $195 to $250; suites $295 to $500; summer rates are lower.

The **Spa Hotel & Mineral Springs,** 100 N. Indian Ave. (at Tahquitz McCallum Way), Palm Springs, CA 92262 (tel. 619/325-1461, or toll free 800/854-1279, 800/472-4371 in California), offers among the best contemporary spa facilities in Palm Springs. It's situated on land that was formerly considered a shrine by the Cahuilla Indians because of the magical properties of its spring waters. The spa has two outdoor pools filled with the revitalizing, mineral-filled waters from its underground natural springs, as well as a conventional Olympic-size outdoor swimming pool and a sundeck. In addition, there are 30 indoor sunken Roman swirlpools, also filled from the springs. Rounding out these healthful facilities are a eucalyptus vapor-inhalation room, a rock steamroom (where mineral waters are turned to steam), a completely equipped gymnasium, health club, and daily fitness classes, and a staff to pamper guests with massages, facials, manicures, pedicures, and other beauty treatments for both men and women. There are also three night-lighted tennis courts, and golf is available at a nearby country club. Of course, after you've done all those healthy things, you'll have to be careful not to pile on pounds at the lavish Rennicks' Dining Room.

Rooms at the spa are suitably luxurious and elegantly appointed. All are equipped with refrigerators, direct-dial phones, color TVs, baths with Travertine marble sinks, and turndown service. The views are spectacular. Complimentary ground transportation is provided to the airport.

Rates for all this basking and luxuriating are as follows: $145 to $215 during winter months, $105 to $190 during spring and fall, $55 to $100 during the summer. If you don't choose to stay at the spa, you can use the mineral baths for $25.

The **Villa Royale,** 1620 Indian Trail, Palm Springs, CA 92262 (tel. 619/327-2314), spread across 3½ acres, has an elegant Old-World charm and the atmosphere of a European-style country inn. It is one of those rare facilities where everything gets better with each passing year.

Each of the 31 units reflects the colors, the spirit, and the beauty of a particular country. The owners spent six years buying in Europe and sending their treasures back to Palm Springs—you'll find them in every room—carvings, sculptures, woven hangings, even the custom-designed quilts and ruffled pillows. Several rooms have their own Jacuzzis on private patios. All rooms have color TV and private phones. There are two large swimming pools. Room service is available for all meals.

This extraordinary bed-and-breakfast resort has a series of interior courtyards all framed with statuesque pillars, shade trees, bougainvillea, and pots of flowers. There's even a fountain courtyard where you can quietly listen to classical music. An attractive roofed patio, resembling a living room, has a fireplace and comfortable Italian wicker chairs. There's a water garden and a small waterfall beside it.

As you might expect, dining facilities are attractive. There is a poolside breakfast room as well as a full-service dining room (the Europa room) for serving lunches and dinners. To enhance your dining pleasure, the Villa Royale has amassed a collection of fine California and European wines and champagnes. Imported and domestic beers are also served. You can arrange (in advance) for a romantic candlelight private dinner in your room or in the water garden gazebo. The dining room kitchen can also pack a picnic lunch for you (with knapsack) to take on your excursions. A complimentary Continental breakfast is served daily at the Europa. Luncheon and dinner ranges from $10 to $22. The menu changes daily.

Other pleasant touches—*The Los Angeles Times* is at your door each morning, bicycles are available for your use at no charge, and golf and tennis reservations can be made at nearby courts and courses. If you wish to have outside guests for dinner at the Villa Royale, this can be arranged in advance; however, outside guests cannot use other facilities such as the pool.

Standard guest rooms, single or double occupancy, are $65 to $220, with a Jacuzzi $140 to $200; one-bedroom suites are $145; one-bedroom villas $155 to $200, with Jacuzzi $250; two-bedroom villas (four persons) are $200 to $310. Two large private villas, each with its own pool (one 20 feet and the other 36 feet long), patio, and enclosed yard, are $280 and $380; both offer great privacy. Extra person occupancy is $25 per person.

Casa Cody Hotel, 175 S. Cahuilla Rd., a half-block south of Tahquitz Way, Palm Springs, CA 92262 (tel. 619/320-9346), is an attractive, newly restored inn with some interesting historical touches. The original inn was built by Harriet Cody, a relative of Wild Bill Cody, and was once owned by Polly Bergen.

The restoration took almost a year and created 17 lovely, spacious, relaxed accommodations with such elegant touches as wood-burning fireplaces, private patios, Saltillo tile floors, dhurri rugs, and original art displayed against a background of gentle desert colors. Furnishings are in a comfortable Santa Fe style befitting a handsomely decorated apartment.

Accommodations range from studios to two-bedrooms, two-baths. Each has a fully equipped kitchen (with the exception of the "room" category, which has small refrigerators) plus the expected touches of cable TV and private phones. And there are two swimming pools—one at the center of each of the two segments of the inn—plus a tree-shaded whirlpool spa. There are complimentary poolside breakfasts and Saturday night wine-and-cheese parties.

Casa Cody, nestled in the heart of Palm Springs just at the base of the mountain, is close to the Desert Museum, the new Desert Fashion Plaza, and the Palm Canyon Drive shops, restaurants, and galleries. Arrangements can be made for tennis, golf, and access to a private health spa. Bicycles are available without charge for exploring the surrounding elegant neighborhoods. And for those with an urge to trek up the mountain, the Carl Lyken desert trail begins nearby. Indian canyons have reopened and add to any hiking adventure.

The staff at Casa Cody is a remarkably helpful source of information on where to go, what to do, etc. If you communicate more easily in French or Dutch, both are spoken by staff members.

Season rates range from $60 to $160; rooms begin at $60, studios at $75, one-bedrooms at $105, and two bedrooms for one to four persons begin at $150. Charge for an extra person is $10. Rates are modestly higher during the winter (mid-December through April) and considerably lower from July through September. If you require transportation from the airport, Casa Cody provides pickup.

Le Petit Chateau, 1491 Via Soledad, at Palmera, Palm Springs, CA 92264 (tel. 619/325-2686), is, as far as I know, the only clothes-optional bed-and-breakfast inn in the country, bringing the tradition of the French Mediterranean auberge to sunny Southern California. Le Petit Chateau is located in a very quiet, residential part of Palm Springs, about one mile from the downtown center. It's a charming secluded environment, a "cocoon," as its owners, Don and Mary Robidoux, describe it, surrounded by bougainvillea-covered walls and hedges. Access is only for guests so that privacy and security are assured. The harmonious aura of Le Petit Chateau emerges from the peace and solitude it affords, from the charm of its owners, and from the tasteful French-countryside style of each of its comfortable rooms—most of which offer delightful brick patios. And of course guests especially appreciate the option to enjoy the sun at poolside the way nature intended—"au naturel." (Nude sunbathing is obviously optional and you may bask with clothing if you prefer.) And to enhance your tan, Le Petit Chateau also has a unique Mist Tanning System to keep you cool and your skin moist and soft. Just so you won't dwell on age and shape, guests range in age from early 20s to late 60s. Most are world travelers with a love for an all-over tan.

Mary Robidoux's morning breakfasts are a combination of goodies to suit almost any appetite. She prepares a complete European-style breakfast with eggs, sausages, ham, muffins, sweet rolls, fresh-ground coffee, and fresh fruit. In the late afternoon there's a buffet table with wines and a variety of fruits and cheeses.

There are ten rooms, so don't expect to call at the last minute and find accommodations. It's precisely the inn's petite size that generates such a comfortable and appealing social atmosphere.

Rates are $110 for larger rooms with a kitchen, Friday and Saturday; $92 Sunday through Thursday. For the smaller rooms without a kitchen, it's $103 Friday and Saturday; $85 Sunday through Thursday. All rooms have TVs. There are three phones for common use by guests. Prices are the same year round. All rates include double occupancy, the European breakfast, and afternoon wine and hors d'oeuvres. Prior reservations are necessary. To repeat, you cannot simply drop in: It just doesn't happen that way—besides which, the front gate is locked.

The **Estrella Inn,** 415 S. Belardo, Palm Springs, CA 92262 (tel. 619/320-4117), is a fine small hotel. Though it's only a few minutes from the action on Palm Canyon Drive, its location near the base of the San Jacinto mountains affords peace and quiet. A wide variety of rooms, suites, and deluxe cottages is available, all individually decorated and furnished. Some rooms feature lanai decks, wet bars, kitchens, and fireplaces (which come in handy on cool winter evenings), and all are equipped with air conditioning, cable color TV, and direct-dial phone.

The Estrella Inn has two adult swimming pools, one for children, and two hydrotherapy pools. A lawn- and court-games area is decked out with a flood-lit fountain, and there is a barbecue area.

A complimentary Continental breakfast is served daily in the inn's small lounge. Rooms with two queen-size beds are $125, a one-bedroom cottage is $160, and two-bedroom cottages are $195. Off-season rates (June 1 to October 30) are about 30% lower. Weekly and monthly rates are also available off season, monthly rates in season.

One of the best buys in Palm Springs is **El Rancho Lodge,** 1330 E. Palm Canyon Dr., Palm Springs, CA 92264 (tel. 619/327-1339). Accommodations are pleasant, roomy, and nicely maintained (quite possibly because the manager is also the owner). All are situated around a large heated pool and spa. El Rancho Lodge has only 19 rooms, which may account for the congenial community feeling, plus the fact that most guests seem to be of the relaxed, over-50 generation.

Accommodations termed "hotel rooms" have one king-size or two twin beds. Furnishings are pleasant and comfortable, with the added luxury of a small refrigerator. The color TV has remote control, which is not fastened down to a piece of furniture (bless their hearts). Studios have the same sleeping arrangements as the above hotel room and remote-control color TV, but they also have a full kitchen. Two-room suites have the above sleeping arrangements, or offer two king-size beds. Suites have two full baths, a luxury rarely found even in pricey hotels, and a full kitchen.

A Continental breakfast, served poolside each morning, is included in the rates.

Rates vary seasonally: Winter season is October 1 through May 31, summer season is June 1 through September 30. Summer rates range from $40 for the hotel rooms to $85 for a two-room suite. Winter rates are $56 to $121. Monthly discount rates are available.

Westward Ho Hotel, 701 E. Palm Canyon Dr., Palm Springs, CA 92264 (tel. 619/320-2700 or toll free 800/854-4345, 800/472-4313 in California), is pleasant, comfortable, and moderately priced. The motel (they're all "hotels" in Palm Springs) has 208 rooms with a modified western look. Most have attractive Indian print spreads, hanging cylinder lamps, upholstered chairs with casters, dark wood bedsteads and furnishings, and warm brown carpeting. All of the rooms have both tub and shower, and those with two beds have a separate sink facility set apart from the bathroom. Each room has individually controlled air conditioning, satellite color TV, allowing for extra channels, and direct-dial phones. A heated "therapy" pool for guests is at the center of the complex surrounded by comfortable lounges, and there is a small wading pool for children.

One of the conveniences of the motel is that it adjoins a Denny's Restaurant, open 24 hours. If you've never eaten at Denny's, try it. The food is consistently good and the prices are modest.

Rates at the Westward Ho Hotel are $60 to $75 from October through the third week of December, and $70 to $86 for the balance of the year. During holiday periods and special events there is a two-night minimum and rates are slightly higher than above.

And forever there will be a Motel 6. In Palm Springs, however, it's **Hotel 6,** at 595 E. Palm Canyon Dr., Palm Springs, CA 92262 (tel. 619/325-6129). Advance planning is the key if you hope to stay here during the season—reservations should be made 12 months in advance. Singles are $29, plus $6 for each additional adult. It's clean, efficient, and convenient, and it has a pool. All local calls are free.

In 1989 a new **Hotel 6** opened at 666 S. Palm Canyon Dr. (tel. 619/327-4200). There are 149 units and a pool. As with the other Hotel 6 on East Palm Canyon Drive, all rooms have cable color TV, are comfortably furnished, have individually controlled air conditioning, and are close to downtown Palm Springs as well as the golf courses and resort attractions. Singles are $32, plus $6 for each additional adult; no charge for color TV or local calls. To stay here, plan well in advance.

If Hotel 6 in Palm Springs can't accommodate you, try **Motel 6** at 78100 Varner Rd., Bermuda Dunes, CA 92201 (tel. 619/345-0550)—it's about a 15-minute drive west to Palm Springs, has a smaller pool, but is just as clean and efficient and a bit less per night. Singles are $26, plus $6 for each additional adult.

In Rancho Mirage

Just a short drive south from Palm Springs via Hwy. 111, Rancho Mirage is fast developing into an ultra-chic southward expansion of Palm Springs. Its famous residents include Gerald and Betty Ford, it has a growing "restaurant row," and it contains one of the area's most beautiful and luxurious accommodations, the **Marriott's Rancho Las Palmas Resort.** Opened in 1979, this Marriott showplace at 41000 Bob Hope Dr. (off Hwy. 111), Rancho Mirage, CA 92270 (tel. 619/568-2727, or toll free 800/458-

8786), has 450 spacious rooms housed in two-story terra-cotta–roofed white stucco buildings. The resort itself is set on 26½ verdant garden acres with lush flower beds everywhere. Facilities include two large outdoor swimming pools, two outdoor Jacuzzis, and three restaurants: the Sunrise Terrace for outdoor buffets overlooking the garden; the Old Mexico hacienda-style Fountain Court; the posh Cabrillo Restaurant for dinner; plus Miguel's for cocktails and dancing. A hospitality desk, shops, tour and car-rental desks, free airport pickup and return, and nightly turndown service are further amenities. And that's not to mention the Rancho Las Palmas Country Club down the road, of which guests become automatic members. It has 25 tennis courts (eight lit for night play), including three red clay, a 27-hole championship golf course, pro shops for both, a driving range and putting green, a restaurant and snackbar, and an additional swimming pool. Anything you'd like to do that's not offered at the resort or country club—from horseback riding to ballooning—the folks at Marriott will be happy to arrange.

All the rooms overlook the golf course or one of the pools. All have separate sitting areas with a sofa and easy chair, oversize beds, remote-control color TVs with in-room movies, and all other luxury hotel fixings. They're decorated with desert colors against white stucco walls hung with paintings of desert scenes.

Rates for single or double occupancy are $260 to $280 from January through early May, $195 to $215 from May through early June, $110 to $130 from early June through the beginning of September, and $175 to $190 through late December. Extra adults pay $10 year round; there's no charge for children under 18 occupying the same room as their parents. Be sure to ask about any special packages that might be available.

A more economical choice in Rancho Mirage is the **Allstar Inn,** 69–570 Hwy. 111 (between Date Palm Drive and Frank Sinatra Drive), Rancho Mirage, CA 92270 (tel. 619/324-8475). As with all the Allstar Inns, the guest rooms are nicely furnished and spotlessly clean, and have a full tub and shower and free color TV. At Rancho Mirage there is a small pool and Jacuzzi. Singles are $33, doubles $36; summer rates are $6 lower. Reservations for the winter season (October through May) should be made well in advance.

WHERE TO DINE

As noted, several of the above-mentioned accommodations have fine restaurants. There are many other attractive restaurants in Palm Springs, and more in the offing, but now and then the food doesn't quite measure up to the look. And if you're a lover of fish, you'll find the entree frequently described on the menu as "fresh." Be advised that fresh in most instances refers to fish that is "fresh frozen," which in fact means "frozen" and does not taste like "fresh." Obviously there are occasions where the fish will, indeed, be fresh. My advice is to ask.

If you'd like to enjoy reasonably priced, hearty home-style cooking, and don't mind waiting, go where the locals go: **Billy Reed's,** 1800 N. Palm Canyon Dr., near Vista Chino Drive (tel. 619/325-1946). It has the ambience of a fancy but quaint coffeeshop, with lots of plants flourishing under skylights, shelves of crockery and knickknacks, framed paintings on brick and cedar-paneled walls, and crystal chandeliers. They take no reservations, and even though the place is huge, it's usually mobbed. You can start the day here with ham and eggs with hash browns and toast, a stack of buttermilk pancakes, a three-egg omelet, or perhaps Billy's delicious homemade cornbread for under $7. At lunch a bowl of chili with cubed sirloin and beans, served with garlic toast or cornbread, a roast beef and Swiss cheese sandwich on sourdough with potato salad or coleslaw, a large shrimp Louis salad, a delicious chicken pot pie, or baked noodles with tomato sauce and Cheddar cheese, served with soup or salad and cornbread or garlic toast, make a filling meal for $7 to $14. Dinner entrees cost $12 to $20 and include soup or salad, fresh vegetables, and a baked potato or rice pilaf. Among the options are jumbo prawns, prime rib, top sirloin, and fried chicken. The entire menu is served all day, every day (except major holidays), from 7 a.m. to 11 p.m.

Cedar Creek Inn, 1555 S. Palm Canyon Dr. (tel. 619/325-7300), is one of the most popular dining establishments in Palm Springs and with good reason. The number of local residents who frequent Cedar Creek Inn is appropriate testimony to its fine food, comfortable attractive surroundings, excellent service, and reasonable prices.

Cedar Creek Inn has the tone of casual desert elegance with its high ceilings, slate floors, ficus trees decorated with thousands of tiny lights, potted plants, floral wall patterns, and beamed ceilings. Dining areas are separated with decorative metal railings.

The entry area is a more attractive foyer for greeting guests than one generally expects at a restaurant. Above is an enormous decorative metal chandelier of leaves and flowers, and the reservation desk is graced with a sculpted swan faced in gold. The bar area to the right of the entry has the look of a handsome pub with its unstructured seating arrangement and stone walls, and it features live music Tuesday through Thursday from 7 to 11 p.m., Friday and Saturday from 8 p.m. to midnight.

Each of the dining rooms is decorated in a different spring tone —green with green floral drapes tied back for access to French doors; pink with pink floral drapes tied to enhance the vast expanse of window. Decorative plates and plants add color to each of the rooms; high-backed chairs at the tables point up the remarkable height of the ceiling. Polished wood booths along one wall are semi-enclosed and provide a touch of intimacy.

As for the food, the fish is generally fresh; when fresh frozen, the waiter will advise you so. A special fresh chicken entree is offered each evening; the prime rib is excellent—slowly roasted choice, Eastern-fed, served with horseradish sauce. Or consider the extraordinary Veal Swiss prepared from milk-fed veal seasoned with bread crumbs, sautéed and topped with avocado, tomato, Swiss cheese and béarnaise sauce. Dinner entrees range from $15 for the chicken special to $18 for the New York steak or the delicious scampi sautéed in lemon butter with lots of garlic, capers, bread crumbs, and parmesan. Dinners include a hearty soup or the Cedar Creek's Greek salad, plus vegetables, and homemade batter bread or garlic toast. Then there's a choice of baked potato, creamed corn, or rice pilaf.

Cedar Creek serves sandwiches all day, and what sandwiches they are! Consider the thinly sliced rare roast beef served cold, open-faced on pumpernickel with Brie cheese, butter lettuce, tomato, and Bermuda onion with Dijon horseradish sauce on the side; or a chili patty melt, a large patty covered with chili and beans, grated cheese, and sour cream on batter bread or garlic toast. All sandwiches are served with warm applesauce. If you'd prefer a salad, there's an exceptional Cobb salad, a Greek salad, and best of all, the inn's spicy chicken tostada salad. It's assembled in a large tortilla shell filled with refried beans, shredded chicken, and lettuce, and covered with cheese, tomato, guacamole, sour cream, black olives, and—to warm the blood—sliced jalapeños. Sandwiches cost $5.25 to $8.50, salads $4.50 to $8. And for a happy end to it all (if you still have room), ask to see the dessert list with about a dozen entries made fresh daily on the premises.

The Cedar Creek Inn is open for lunch and dinner daily from 11 a.m. to 9 p.m. Dinner is served from 4:30 p.m.

The **Otani,** 266 Avenida Caballeros, at Tahquitz Way (tel. 619/327-6700), refers to itself as "a garden restaurant" and indeed this is the feeling you have when you enter. The decor is Japanese architecture blended with the best in contemporary design. There is an open, airy atmosphere with bamboo trees that rise to what certainly must be at least a 50-foot ceiling. Rich dark woods, slate floors, marble counters, stylized fish sculptures, and muted grass green carpeting create an aura of comfort visually and spiritually. At the perimeter of the restaurant is a modest garden with a waterfall and brook.

There are four areas of preparation and dining, each with its own chef: *teppan-yaki,* where grilled dishes are served; *tempura,* for the deep-fried, delicately battered seafood and vegetables; *yakitori,* for the grilled meats on skewers; and *sushi/sashimi* for seafood in its various modes. You can dine at a marble bar in any of the four areas and watch the preparation and artful design of food, or take the Occidental approach and be served at a table in the main dining area. I happen to prefer the former. Wherever you choose to sit, Otani offers selections from an à la carte or set menu.

The dinner menu will tell you that sushi dates back to the theaters and "pleasure houses" of the Edo period, tempura was introduced by the Portuguese Monk in the 16th century; and yakitori had its origins with the Dutch, who introduced falconry to the Japanese nobility (the falcon's catch was prepared and quickly grilled over charcoal in the field).

The set menu for tempura may include an assortment of shrimp, white fish, and seasonal vegetables; or you may choose the vegetarian approach with 10 kinds of seasonal vegetables ($12 to $25). The à la carte selections offer delectable choices ranging from tempura garlic (that's what I said, *garlic*) to over 20 other choices, including Japanese eggplant, several varieties of mushrooms, oysters, and lobster tail ($1.50 to $9).

As to the yakitori, here again you can order à la carte or from a set menu. A special 12-skewer course ($23) features 10 different items including a particular favorite of mine, the bacon-wrapped quail egg. This is not to exclude other toothsome items such as the chicken vegetable roll stuffed with minced chicken rather like a dim sum. For those with a lesser-size appetite, consider the eight-skewer assortment, which includes an excellent asparagus beef roll, among others.

If you believe that sushi or sashimi should be the premier dish at a Japanese restaurant, you won't be disappointed at Otani. There are over 25 seafood and vegetable variations on sushi ranging from tuna, sea urchin, to fresh water eel and including a number of rolls. For the diner who thought that sushi is synonymous with raw fish, Otani is the place to review a number of outstanding cooked possibilities. There's a superb Manhattan roll with cooked tuna and daikon sprouts lovingly enclosed in a nori wrapper, or on the dinner à la carte menu, Dynamite, a delicious assortment of seafood and mushrooms assembled in an abalone shell and baked in a heavenly creamy sauce. For the indecisive, Otani offers a sampler menu with a dish from each of the four categories plus dessert ($16 to $25). Service is attentive and helpful.

If you have room for dessert, there's a first-rate cheesecake (as strange as it may seem) with various fruit sauces, an apple sundae, fresh fruit, and ice cream. At the end of my luncheon, I was presented with a work of art in the form of a cone-shaped peeled orange with a strawberry perched on top and a cucumber slice floral leaf.

Otani is open Monday through Friday for lunch from 11 a.m. to 2 p.m.; for dinner Sunday through Thursday from 5 to 10 p.m., Friday and Saturday to 10:30 p.m.

A favorite of Mexican-food lovers, both locals and out-of-towners, is **Las Casuelas Terraza,** 222 S. Palm Canyon Dr. (tel. 619/325-2794). It's redolent with the flavor of Old Mexico, with white stucco walls, flowered archways, hanging plants, papier-mâché birds (as well as live ones—two brightly colored macaws live on the premises), and Mexican art. Waitresses sport south-of-the-border dresses, and a band plays Mexican music in the bar (sometimes there's even a strolling mariachi group). The entire effect is natural and delightful.

There are six separate dining areas at Las Casuelas, including the bar and two patios, one with a softly splashing fountain. *Especiales de la casa* include a *machaca* burrito (a specially seasoned beef burrito served with guacamole and sour cream) and a *tostada suprema* (a tortilla heaped high with chicken or beef, shredded lettuce, cheeses, tomato, and sour cream). There's a wide variety of Mexican appetizers—nachos, guacamole, quesadilla, and Mexican platters with a variety of combinations. More unusual fare includes *camarones diablos* (shrimp marinated in adobo sauce and wrapped in crisp bacon), and steak *picado* (cubes of New York steak cooked with bell peppers, tomatoes, and onions). Entrees cost $13 to $20, with

Mexican dishes at the low end of the scale, and steak and seafood at the top. Lunch is less expensive at $7 to $12. To top off your meal, there's flan, or an *empañada*—a Mexican deep-fried apple pie. Or you can linger over a delicious liqueur-laced coffee topped with whipped cream.

Las Casuelas Terraza is open daily from 11 a.m. to 10 p.m. for dinner (to midnight for drinks on Friday and Saturday). Reservations advised.

There are two other **Las Casuelas** in the Palm Springs area: the original, at 368 N. Palm Canyon Dr. (tel. 619/325-3213), and the more formal **Las Casuelas Nuevas** at 70050 Hwy. 111, in Rancho Mirage (tel. 619/328-8844). The latter is larger than the other locations, with a lovely 200-seat formal Spanish garden.

Sorrentino's, 1032 N. Palm Canyon Dr. (tel. 619/325-2944), is undoubtedly the best seafood restaurant in Palm Springs. The fish is truly fresh. As you may have inferred from its name, its origins are Italian-American—a fact that's amply demonstrated by the restaurant's stylish decor and delightful cuisine. Banquettes are apple green against rust-red walls, some walls are paneled, and there's a multitude of potted plants throughout. Tables have fresh flowers, lavender cloths, and seating is on red vinyl straight-backed chairs. Overhead lighting, including the chandeliers, is enclosed in interestingly shaped wrought-iron designs. All in all, the restaurant has a cozy, familiar feeling that makes dining a very pleasant experience.

Virtually all the fish is fresh, and when it's "fresh frozen" Sorrentino's tells you so. The menu is extensive and varied with some great choices—there's a hearty seafood and chicken gumbo with andouille sausage and steamed rice, sauteed sand dabs (a particular favorite of mine), king crab legs, swordfish steak, shrimp scampi-style, Maine lobster, abalone steak, and of course cioppino. While Sorrentino's is primarily a seafood house, the quality of their meats is excellent. There's a fine selection of veal dishes including veal osso bucco Genovese; there's Steak Sinatra with peppers and mushrooms, filet mignon, and a roast rack of lamb that's tender, moist, and delicious. Sorrentino's also has a children's dinner (under 12) offering a choice from among four varied entrees ($7.50 to $11.50). Entrees and specials for grown-ups range from $11.95 to $26.95. There's the usual choice of desserts, with one notable and pleasantly surprising anomaly—English Trifle (in an Italian seafood restaurant?).

Whether you're a party of one or eight, service is very attentive without being overbearing. The wine list, domestic and imported, is limited but good.

Sorrentino's has a huge bar adjacent to the main dining room, so if you must wait for a few minutes, you will be comfortable. Sorrentino's is open nightly from 5:30 to 10:30 p.m. Reservations are necessary.

You can't and shouldn't miss **Alfredo's,** 292 E. Palm Canyon Dr., at Via Entrada (tel. 619/320-1020)—its exterior is simple, uncluttered, and inviting with the forthright statement,

"Alfredo's," in neon script. The restaurant is just as handsome inside, with a subdued, congenial charm, and a menu that's perfectly suited to almost any taste.

Among the several appetizers, you might begin with Mama's fave beans or a Sicilian style artichoke ($3.50), or opt for the antipasto Alfredo at $7.95. Right in the middle at $5.95 is a favorite of mine—mozzarella marinara—deep-fried cheese cooked with the chef's special marinara sauce. Specialty salads offer an interesting selection ranging from the house's dandelion salad at $3.95 to a cold seafood and linguine combination for $11.50.

There are entrees to satisfy all appetites from veal Marsala or filet mignon "Alfredo style" to pizza. And the Buffalo chicken wings have to be the best this side of Buffalo, N.Y. (Alfredo's home town). They come hot, medium, or mild. I chose "medium" and they were just right—spicy, but not enough to create an unredeemable scorch. The wings are served in true Buffalo style, with celery sticks and blue cheese dip, and they were absolutely delicious ($5 for 10 pieces, $11.95 for 30 pieces, $16.50 for a bucket of 50 wings).

Now you would think that spaghetti and meatballs would hardly be an inspired choice for dinner. What makes this combination unique at Alfredo's is the toothsome flavor and texture of the homemade meatballs. Mother's never quite matched up. Not to be ignored is a magnificent veal "Alfredo"—veal cutlets and eggplant lightly battered, sautéed, separated with prosciutto, topped with mozzarella, baked, and finished with Alfredo's special sauce. Alfredo's prepares veal in a multitude of time-honored Italian forms. For the somewhat conventional chicken lover, the chicken à la Nardizzi is a delectable combination of pieces of chicken breast sautéed with seasonings, mushrooms, and Marsala wine, served with the pasta of the day.

And when was the last time you had steak and dandelions? Try it here for a light dinner. You'll enjoy choice tenderloin broiled to order, smothered in Alfredo's house specialty—sautéed dandelions—and served on a special Italian roll. For the somewhat reluctant dandelion gourmet, go for an appetizer-size order or the fresh dandelion salad. Seafood entrees, including calamari, are served with Alfredo's pasta and artichoke sauce. Pasta specialties come with salad or soup.

Alfredo's has something to intrigue almost any palate. And the delightful surprise is that no matter what you order, you'll find it to be exceptional. Dinner entrees are $14 to $19 and include salad or soup, pasta, chef's vegetable, and fresh Italian bread. All recipes are cooked to order. There's a good selection of wines to accompany your meal.

Alfredo's is open nightly from 5 to 11 p.m. A small parking lot is located right behind the restaurant, off Via Entrada.

Got a big appetite for some really great deli food? Head on over to **Nate's Delicatessen and Restaurant** (also known as Mister Corned Beef of Palm Springs), 100 S. Indian Ave., at the corner of Tahquitz Way (tel. 619/325-3506). Unlike the New York, Los Angeles, or San Francisco delis, Nate's looks more like a restaurant, but with all the great aromas of a super deli. Seating arrangements are very comfortable, and the decor is easy on the eyes. Overhead are ceiling fans and hidden indirect lighting. The dining room is quiet even when crowded. Service is efficient, knowledgeable, and pleasant.

If you like deli food, you'll want to eat your way through the entire menu. For breakfast, there are omelets in every conceivable combination—with salami, pastrami, corned beef, chopped liver, etc.; and then there are eggs with onions, with lox, whitefish, even grilled knockwurst. If you insist, there's always eggs, french toast, or pancakes, served with ham, bacon, or sausage.

And when it comes to lunch, there are sandwiches piled high with meats of your choice and served on Nate's hot rye bread (or whatever bread or roll you prefer) plus a relish tray of kosher pickles and sauerkraut. What kind of sandwiches, you ask? What else but corned beef, pastrami, chopped liver, tongue, salami, pepper beef, and on down the list; single decker; triple decker; a "1½ sandwich" including three "halves" of classic deli meats—one of chopped liver, one of pastrami and one of corned beef; and the Fresser Sandwich—any combination of up to three items on three deckers. You want a salad, they have eight varieties. You have a taste for blintzes, a cold gefilte fish plate, potato pancakes, a knish, Nate's has those, too.

Save room for dinner. Nate's has a nine-course meal for $11, including the aforementioned relish tray and sauerkraut, an appetizer of juice or homemade chopped liver, soup or salad, entrees ranging from baked or fried chicken, corned beef, and brisket, to seafood catch of the day and so on—all served with a vegetable, potato, hot rye bread, dessert and coffee. Or you might simply have a taste for boiled chicken "in the pot" with matzo ball, noodles, rice and carrots accompanied by salad or appetizer and beverage. Nate's also serves a daily dinner special for $7 available from 4 to 8:30 p.m.

Breakfast prices range from $3.50 to $9.50, though some of the delicatessen specialties such as the combination plate of lox *and* whitefish *and* cod *plus* two eggs with bagel and cream cheese will raise the rate to $17.50. Luncheon sandwiches are in the range of $6 to $9, salads about $9. Dinner is a bargain at $7 to $12. Beer and wine are available.

Nate's is open daily from 7:30 a.m. to 8:30 p.m.

The **Hamburger Hamlet Bar-Grille,** 105 N. Palm Canyon Dr. (tel. 619/325-2321), is virtually the only place of its kind at the center of town. There's no question that much of the popularity of Hamburger Hamlet rests on the quality and variety of its food as well as the singularly large portions of its drinks, nonalcoholic and alcoholic. Add to that the look of the interior—it's a bit like a well-groomed pub, comfortable, lots of wood, a working rotisserie in the center of the activity, and all sorts of interesting things to look at apart from its other customers. There are framed playbills dating back to Richard Burton's performances, and a fascinating collection of other reminiscences of the theater. In good weather, you can dine at the tables on the patio out front under attractive yellow and white umbrellas. And finally there is good service—especially attentive to the order of things if you're ordering several small dishes (grazings).

Hamburger Hamlet has excellent choices for brunch, lunch, or dinner. There is a good selection of grazings, their famous lobster bisque soup, salads, spa salads (low-cal), big appetizers great for sharing, about 20 hamburgers including one served in a pita pocket, and of course the hamburger platters. Of all the sandwiches, I particularly enjoy the Stella Special, a perfect combination of a "halfer" sandwich with several options, plus soup (French onion, du jour, or pea) and a green salad.

Excellent chili dishes include a "prison chili" dinner with everything on it: sour cream, shredded lettuce, chopped red onion, and Cheddar cheese served with garlic toast. You can even combine chili with breakfast—scrambled eggs and hot chili served with guacamole, tostaditos, chopped onions on the side, salsa, and hash browns.

And speaking of eggs, there are eggs and omelets galore from huevos rancheros to a "hangover omelet" with diced ham, jalapeño pepper (sure to wake you up), melted cheeses, and hash browns.

Several inspired vegetarian dishes include a favorite of mine, a casserole of double mushrooms with fresh leaf spinach covered with Jack and Muenster cheese, served with a house salad and garlic toast.

The rotisserie provides chicken that's a specialty of the house. The dinner platter serves up a plump half of a chicken with baked potato, or ratatouille, or french fries, plus garlic toast or homemade corn bread, a green salad, and a sherbet compote. Lunch or brunch will cost about $5 to $8. Dinner specialties are $9 to $11.

Last of all (or perhaps first, depending on the time of day), Hamburger Hamlet has a full bar, which serves some exceptional creations such as a frosted margarita with tequila and triple sec, a red-eye special that's part tomato juice and part Michelob beer, and an Amaretto freeze of ice cream with Amaretto. As a matter of observation, all of the establishment's drinks are quite generous in size and attractively presented. Premium varietal wines and champagne can be had by the bottle or the glass. Bass ale or Michelob is on tap and served by the mug or by the schooner (a two-hands container).

Hamburger Hamlet is open daily, Monday through Thursday 11 a.m. to 9 p.m.; Friday to 10 p.m.; Saturday 9 a.m. to 10 p.m., Sunday to 9 p.m.

A fine alternative to the better known Mexican eateries in Palm Springs is **El Mirasol** at 140 E. Palm Canyon Dr. (tel. 619/323-0721). It's decorated simply with dark wood chairs and tables, a beautiful desert mural on one wall, a few small paintings, potted plants, and a Mexican tile design on the floor.

El Mirasol serves classic Mexican combinations of tacos, enchiladas, chile rellenos, tostadas and burritos, and for the benefit of brunchers egg dishes including huevos rancheros or chorizo and eggs. But the excellence of the menu is in the many *especialidades de la casa* whether you choose the pork chile verde cooked with green chiles and tomatillos or the perfectly seasoned shrimp rancheros, a special treat prepared with bell peppers, onions, olives, and tomatoes. Topping the menu is *pollo en mole,* boneless breast of chicken beautifully prepared in an elegant blend of dried mild chiles, almonds, sesame seeds, and other seasonings.

The Mexican combinations ($5.25 to $10.25) are all served with rice and beans. Specialties of the house ($8 to $11) are accompanied by corn chips and salsa, rice, beans, and corn or flour tortillas. Beer and wine are available, as are other beverages.

El Mirasol is open Monday through Saturday for lunch from 11 a.m. to 3 p.m., dinner 5 to 9 p.m.

A fixture in Palm Springs since 1942, **Louise's Pantry,** 124 S. Palm Canyon Dr. (tel. 619/325-5124), is a warm, cheery place that few can resist. It's not hard to spot—just look for the long line out front. The tiny dining area is decorated in cheery yellow with homey print curtains, a row of booths, and an eating counter. Home cooking is the order of the day. Louise's squeezes fresh orange juice daily, grinds their own beef, and bakes the sweet rolls, cornbread, pies, and cakes on the premises.

Louise's serves food that almost everyone likes. There are three to six specials each evening plus choices from a regular list of eight selections—roast beef, grilled pork chops, New York steak, deep-fried jumbo shrimp, grilled halibut, meat loaf, and sautéed baby beef liver with bacon or onions. Specials of the day may include lamb shanks, roast turkey, pork tenderloin, braised short ribs, Swiss steak, sirloin tips with buttered noodles, veal cutlets parmesan, grilled ham steak, roast leg of lamb, and fried chicken. And each of the above is served with a choice of soup or seafood cocktail plus dinner salad, potato, fresh steamed vegetables, dessert, and beverage. Dinner selections cost from $7.75 to $10.50; top of the line is the New York steak.

Daily lunch specials ($6 to $7) include baby beef liver, petrale sole, deep-fried shrimp, roast beef, omelets with ham and cheese or bacon, plus a ½-lb. ground chuck steak. The changing choices may include chicken or beef steak pot pie, stuffed bell peppers, chicken livers, corned beef and cabbage, beef stew, chicken and dumplings, macaroni and cheese, or sirloin tips with buttered noodles. Luncheon specials are served with soup or salad, fresh steamed vegetables, and homemade cornbread.

But the luncheon possibilities don't end there. Hot and cold sandwiches, cold plates, salads, light lunches, all in the range of $4.75 to $7, are available.

Louise's Pantry also serves breakfast with all sorts of accompaniments. If you're so inclined, you can even create your own omelet from a lengthy mix-and-match list of goodies.

And then there are sundaes, shakes, sodas, banana splits, floats, ades, fresh juices, and a Palm Springs Special—a super-nutritious milkshake made with crushed dates.

You can order to take out. If it's a large order, call at least one hour prior to pickup.

In case you're wondering, Louise's Pantry does not serve beer or wine.

Louise is no longer around to oversee the cooking and baking, but the current staff still maintains the same exacting standards and service.

Louise's Pantry is open daily from 7 a.m. to 9:45 p.m.; it's closed every year from about mid-July to mid-August. No reservations, just join the line.

There's another Louise's Pantry (with the same menu) in Palm Desert at 44-491 Town Center Way.

XI

ALONG THE COAST FROM SANTA BARBARA TO SAN DIEGO

1. PACIFIC PALISADES
2. SANTA BARBARA
3. MALIBU
4. SANTA MONICA
5. VENICE
6. MARINA DEL RAY
7. REDONDO BEACH
8. THE WAYFARERS CHAPEL
9. SAN PEDRO
10. LONG BEACH
11. CATALINA ISLAND
12. NEWPORT BEACH
13. LAGUNA BEACH
14. LA JOLLA
15. SAN DIEGO
16. ON TO TIJUANA

The beaches of Greater Los Angeles are as varied as the general topography—ranging from wide, golden sands, with gentle waves, to narrow rocky strips where the surf dashes high toward the sky. Chances are you'll find a beach for any whim, aquatic sport, or pleasure. If you drive out curvy Sunset Boulevard, you'll reach the Coast Highway and the Pacific. While in the area, you can visit the Will Rogers State Park in the **Pacific Palisades.**

Afterward, if you continue north up the coast, you'll reach **Santa Barbara** (a 92-mile drive from L.A.) with its beautiful town, beaches, and mountain backdrop. Heading south again, you come to **Malibu,** a 27-mile "strip" studded with the homes of numerous movie and TV stars and home to the J. Paul Getty Museum. The southern part, **Castle Rock,** was used as the background for many a Mack Sennett comedy and its attendant bathing beauties.

Below Malibu is **Santa Monica** with its municipal pier and excellent public beaches. It is the locale of an occasional star's home (in days of yore, Marion Davies's "colonial palace" and Cary Grant's villa were there). Continuing south, you'll pass through **Venice, Manhattan, Hermosa,** and **Redondo Beaches,** with lifeguards and bathing facilities.

Beginning at Palos Verdes Estates, you can head southwest toward the Pacific along **Palos Verdes Drive,** a curving coastline road that evokes the Riviera. At the end of the drive, you'll pass through **San Pedro,** the port of Los Angeles (visit the Ports O'Call and the Whaler's Wharf) and then reach **Long Beach.**

Farther south, **Huntington Beach,** another popular stopover, is the scene of the world surfing championships in September (sleeping bags line the beach during the "grunion hunts"—I can personally attest to the existence of grunion). **San Pedro, Long Beach, Newport Beach,** and **Balboa** are jumping-off points for the offshore **Santa Catalina Island.** The public beach at **Corona del Mar** is relatively uncrowded, the area a haven for yachtsmen. The coves near the art colony of **Laguna Beach** provide top-notch swimming and sunbathing.

This coastal tour won't really end at **La Jolla** and **San Diego,** but will continue across the border for bullfights at **Tijuana.**

Note: There are privately operated bathhouses at most of the public beaches, where you can rent a locker, shower, and towel. State beaches provide lifeguards, and I'd strongly advise staying within the areas supervised by them. The surf in many rocky places is only for the very experienced, if at all. Swimming in much of Southern California is quite possible all year round if you're accustomed to very cold water. This is not Florida. Many swimmers wear wet suits on winter days.

1. Pacific Palisades

After leaving Beverly Hills on Sunset Boulevard, you will soon pass sprawling **U.C.L.A.** on your left—one of the campuses of the University of California, the largest in the United States. Before you reach the coast you can stop off for three widely varied, but fascinating, visits at the following attractions.

WILL ROGERS STATE HISTORIC PARK

At 14253 Sunset Blvd. (tel. 213/454-8212), Will Rogers State Historic Park perpetuates the memory of the "cracker-barrel philosopher." Will Rogers, of course, became a legend to a whole generation of Americans, going from trick rider to rope-trick artist, eventually becoming a philosopher of sorts, with such down-on-the-farm observations as "Americans are getting too much like Model 'A' Fords. They all have the same upholstery—and they all make the same noise."

He began in show business as a trick roper in traveling rodeos, an act he later brought to the Ziegfeld Follies in New York. Eventually he settled in Hollywood, buying his own ranch and making films, which led one cinema critic to write: "Will Rogers upheld the homely virtues against the tide of sophistication and sex." He was killed in an air crash with his friend, Wiley Post, in Alaska in mid-August 1935.

Mrs. Rogers lived at the 31-room ranch until her death in 1944, at which time the home and grounds of the "Cherokee Kid" were willed to the state, and they are now supervised as a historic site by the Department of Parks and Recreation. Visitors may explore the grounds, seeing the former Rogers stables, even watching polo games, usually on Saturday afternoon and Sunday mornings, weather permitting. The house is filled with the original comfortable furnishings, including a porch swing in the living room and many Indian rugs and baskets.

The park is open from 8 a.m. to 7 p.m. during the summer, till 6 p.m. the rest of the year. The house is open from 10 a.m. to 5 p.m. daily, except on Christmas, Thanksgiving, and New Year's Day. There is a $4-per-vehicle fee for entry, including all passengers. The fee includes a guided tour of the Will Rogers home, an audio tour, and a film on Will Rogers shown in the Visitor Center. There are picnic tables, although no food is sold, and a small gift shop in the Center. Incidentally, Charles Lindbergh and his wife hid out here in the '30s during part of the kidnap craze that surrounded the murder of their first son.

2. Santa Barbara

Already blessed with the Santa Ynez Mountains as a magnificent backdrop, and a mostly gorgeous coastline, Santa Barbara has, with careful planning, become one of California's most beautiful cities. It is also (at least part time) the residence of some notable personages—one former president, and a bevy of show business personalities (Jane Russell, Karl Malden, Steve Martin, Robert Mitchum, Jonathan Winters), and one remarkable chef, Julia Child.

The beauty of the Santa Barbara beach area cannot be disguised, even on an overcast day: Then the ocean and mountains to either side have the same blue haze often seen in Japanese paintings. The only blight on the scene are the oil rigs out on the ocean—difficult to ignore whether the sun is shining or not.

As you drive along State Street (a plaza boulevard, and the town's main drag) from U.S. 101, you'll first pass through the old section of town, which is in a continual state of redevelopment. But once you get into the heart of the city, life changes. The sidewalks are wide and landscaped, enhanced by flowering trees and planting beds, store signs are limited in size, mailboxes and newsstands are built into stucco walls, and at every pedestrian crossing is a living Christmas tree that serves as just a regular tree the rest of the year. Even billboards have been banned in this delightful city.

Just 92 miles north of Los Angeles and 332 south of San Francisco, Santa Barbara is reached by car via Calif. 1 or U.S. 101. Several airlines link both major cities with Santa Barbara, as do Greyhound buses and Amtrak. (See Chapter II, Section 1.)

There's so much to do and see in this lovely beach resort city that I advise you to take a moment to visit the **Santa Barbara Visitor Information Center,** 1 Santa Barbara St., Santa Barbara, CA 93101 (tel. 805/965-3021), for maps, literature, and a calendar of the many and varied events taking place at all times. Among other things, they've planned out a scenic drive that takes in 15 major points of interest, and a suggested walking tour of Santa Barbara's historical landmarks. Don't forget to stop at Mission Santa Barbara (described in Chapter VI, Section 12). One of the most recent additions to Santa Barbara's calendar of annual events occurs early in October—the **International Jazz Festival.** Don't miss it if you're around in the fall. The Information Center is open daily, Monday through Saturday from 9 a.m. to 5 p.m., Sunday from 10 a.m.; however, it's wise to call before you stop by.

Be forewarned: On-street parking in the downtown area can be a real hassle. You can drive around forever (well almost), day or evening, looking for a spot. So the city has provided municipal parking lots conveniently located with pedestrian walkways to State Street and the surrounding areas. Parking facilities are open 24 hours a day. Rates are computed beginning at 8 a.m., Monday through Saturday. In most lots, parking is free for the first 90 minutes (courtesy of the downtown businesses), 50¢ for the next hour, $1 for each additional hour with a maximum of $8.50. *Note:* In certain lots if you park before 9 a.m. the rates can be steep. The first 90 minutes are still free, but thereafter it's $5 for each additional hour, or part thereof, with a maximum of $25! This is to deter local employees from filling the lots. The Visitor Information Center has a guide to downtown public parking, but be sure to ask which lots charge a premium before 9 a.m.

WHERE TO STAY

Upper Bracket Accommodations

If you fall in love with the special Spanish charm that hangs over Santa Barbara, you might want to splurge and spend the night, checking in at **Four Seasons Biltmore,** 1260 Channel Dr., Montecito, CA 93108 (tel. 805/969-2261, or toll free 800/332-3442), one of America's most outstanding hotels. It's a garden paradise, between the Pacific and Santa Ynez mountains on 21 acres of lawns and floral gardens. During 1988 the hotel underwent a $16 million face-lift that would satisfy even the most discriminating client.

Each guest room or suite offers a view of the Pacific, the Santa

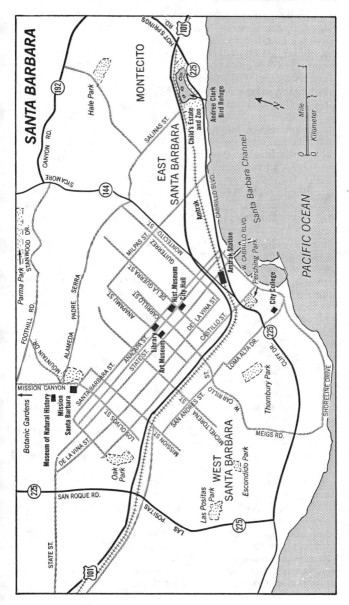

Ynez mountains, a garden, or the Olympic-size pool. All accommodations are deluxe, with every convenience plus mostly marble bathrooms. Rooms are appointed with plush furnishings in Iberian style, and they have remote-control color TV, ceiling fans, and individual climate controls. Elegant touches include terry robes, hair dryers, a mini-bar, twice-daily maid service, overnight shoe shine, 24-hour room service, and full concierge service. Many of the guest rooms have romantic Spanish balconies and/or fireplaces; some have private patios. And then there are cottages for those who desire the ultimate in luxurious privacy. There is, of course, a women's and men's beauty salon, as well as a gift shop and boutique.

Daily resort activities include tennis clinics conducted by a tennis pro, toning exercises, arts and crafts, and special events for the children. There are three lighted tennis courts, two swimming pools including a 50-meter Olympic pool at the hotel's Coral Casino Club, a putting green, and shuffleboard and croquet courts. The Coral Casino Club has beachfront cabanas and a sundeck.

The La Marina restaurant offers elegant evening dining. California-inspired specialties range from smoked rack of veal with a red pepper flan served with batter-fried golden beets, to seared sea scallops with wild rice and roasted peppers. Less formal but casually elegant is The Patio, a glass-enclosed atrium, rather like an indoor garden with palms and flowers and a roof that rolls back for year-round dining. The Patio serves breakfast, lunch, dinner, and Sunday brunch. The La Sala lounge serves an afternoon high tea daily with pastries made on the premises, as well as cocktails. La Sala also has live entertainment during the cocktail hour, and nightly except Sunday. The La Perla Dining Room affords poolside dining at the Coral Casino Beach and Cabana Club, or you might have a casual snack at The Raft. For all this elegance, beauty, and comfort, singles or doubles and twins are $290 to $375 depending on the view; cottages cost $325, cottage suites are $695 to $850.

A second luxurious getaway sits nestled in the hills above the town and it's definitely not easy to find—ask directions. So lush is **El Encanto Hotel and Garden Villas,** 1900 Lasuen Rd., Santa Barbara, CA 93103 (tel. 805/687-5000), that it provided the Caribbean setting for the filming of *A Caribbean Mystery,* a made-for-TV Agatha Christie movie that starred Helen Hayes. The hotel's 100 cottages and villas occupy numerous small terra-cotta–roofed buildings scattered throughout 10 acres of gardens. The decor varies from room to room, but all are charming and cozy, and many have fireplaces to cuddle by. You'll find all the amenities too—color TVs, direct-dial phone, modern bathroom with special soaps and other luxuries, room service, and turndown service.

There's an outdoor heated pool secluded by fencing and trees, a tennis court, and nearby golf. Behind the lobby lounge, a veranda overlooks Santa Barbara and the Pacific beyond; the Channel Islands, often shrouded in clouds, hover in the distance like fairy castles. Sunset out here is a special time, and in the morning you can tarry over breakfast.

The El Encanto dining room is a gourmet's delight. It's decorated like a French country inn and specializes in California cuisine with a French flair.

Accommodations are priced from $120 to $155 for the "small and cozy"; $180 to $235, "spacious and special"; and $235 to

$375, "magnifique." El Encanto lives up to its name—"The Enchantment."

Moderately Price Accommodations

The **Franciscan Inn,** 109 Bath St. (at the corner of Mason), Santa Barbara, CA 93101 (tel. 805/963-8845), has to be one of the best buys for a stay in Santa Barbara. It's hard to beat the convenient location, reasonable price, attractive accommodations and very pleasant personnel.

The inn is situated just off Cabrillo Boulevard, one short block to the marina and beach. You can get there from Hwy. 101 by exiting at the Castillo Exit (going south) or the Cabrillo Boulevard Exit (if going north).

There are 53 rooms at the Franciscan Inn and no two are alike. Each is decorated in delicate pastels, sand colors, and white. All are airy, comfortable, and spacious, and most have ceiling fans. You'll have a phone with no charge for local telephone calls, color TV plus free HBO, a complimentary copy of *The Los Angeles Times,* and a complimentary Continental breakfast served in the lobby.

The heated pool has an adjacent snack bar. If luxurious soaking suits you more than swimming, there's a hot whirlpool (otherwise known as a spa). And last, but certainly not least for those on the go, is a coin-operated guest laundry on the premises.

Among other amenities is an attractive, comfortable lobby with a settee, wing chairs, and palms. A friendly desk person dispenses advice on where to eat (there are several excellent restaurants within walking distance), sights to see, things to do, and who can arrange for transportation to the airport.

Singles and suites range from $65 for one person (during the week and depending on the season) to $155 for a bi-level suite with a living room, a separate kitchen, and sleeping quarters for four. Several rooms have fully equipped kitchenettes. The Honeymoon Suite has the added charm of a fireplace. I suggest reservations well in advance if you plan to travel from May through September.

For those who enjoy the beauty of historic inns, there is the **Bath Street Inn,** 1720 Bath St. (between Valerio and Mission), Santa Barbara, CA 93101 (tel. 805/682-9680), a handsome Queen Anne Victorian built over 100 years ago. This historic residence has such unusual architectural features as a semicircular "eyelid" balcony and a hipped roof, unique even for Santa Barbara. And the century-old trees, flower-filled patio with white wicker furniture, and brick courtyard add to the inn's charm, as does the graciousness of the innkeepers.

Great care was taken in expanding and renovating the inn to incorporate modern safety features while preserving the atmosphere of the original home. The living room is comfortable and inviting. The fireplace, Chinese rug, period prints, sideboard with attractively displayed crystal, ivory-and-white wallpaper, and fresh flowers create a pleasant warmth. The dining area has a traditional blue-and-white floral-print paper that complements the finely crafted woodwork and furnishings.

There are seven guest rooms in the Bath Street Inn, all with private baths. Each room has its own character: one with a king-size canopied bed, another under the eaves with a superb sunset view from a historic balcony, others with a mountain view or a window seat with a glimpse of the ocean.

Room rates, single or double, are $80 to $125 and include breakfast, evening refreshments, and the use of the inn's bicycles. Pets are not accepted.

Budget Accommodations

Budget travelers to Santa Barbara can seek refuge at **Motel 6**—two in Santa Barbara proper, and one in nearby Carpinteria about 10 minutes away by car.

The **Motel 6** at 443 Corona del Mar, Santa Barbara, CA 93103 (tel. 805/564-1392), is located right near the beach. It offers basic, clean accommodations; rates are $36 for a single, $6 extra for each additional adult. There is a small pool. No charge for local calls or for TV. Be sure to reserve far in advance, as this motel gets booked up quickly.

A second **Motel 6** is at 3505 State St., between Las Positas and Hitchcock Way, Santa Barbara, CA 93105 (tel. 805/687-5400). Prices are the same, there is also a large pool, and no charge for local calls or TV. There are free cable movies.

The **Motel 6** in Carpinteria is, as I mentioned, about a 10-minute drive from Santa Barbara, at 4200 Via Real, Carpinteria, CA 93103 (tel. 805/684-6921). Prices here are $27 for a single, plus $6 for each additional adult. Carpinteria also has a pool, and no charge for local calls or TV.

Another budget blessing, also in Carpinteria, is the **Allstar Inn,** at 5550 Carpinteria Ave., Carpinteria, CA 93103 (tel. 805/684-8602). It's spotlessly clean and nicely furnished, and has full tub/shower baths, free color TVs, and a pool. Singles are $27; doubles, $31.

WHERE TO DINE

There are many excellent places to eat at in Santa Barbara—elegant places, traditional places, some dripping with decor—but there is one place where the food is head and shoulders above anything of its kind between California and New York—**La Super-Rica Taqueria,** 622 N. Milpas St., between Cota and Orgega (tel. 805/963-4940). What makes it so? The incredible soft tacos and the cooking of the Gonzales family. If you ever thought that a tortilla is a tortilla is a soft taco you were wrong, oh were you wrong. La Super-Rica's soft tacos are as soft as crepes, about twice as thick, and so delectable you could make a meal of these alone with the fresh salsa.

There's nothing grand about La Super-Rica except the delicious quality of whatever you order. As you enter, eyes right, you face the menu and kitchen. The daily specials on the chalkboard are great reading and it usually takes a while to pore over the list of unusually toothsome dishes. While you're at it, you can watch chicken, pork, and beef being grilled over an open flame. If you need help in the decision-making process, the folks behind the counter are very obliging as are other customers.

As to the decor, forget about it if you require white tablecloths, flowers, cutlery, and glasses. The neighborhood once was a barrio before being gentrified, and the restaurant remains unadorned, though the clientele is now a mix of the very affluent and the somewhat less so. (It has been reported that even Julia Child comes for the frijoles—a joyous mix of pintos, sausage, chilis, bacon, and herbs.) The floors are simple wooden planking. Past the kitchen out back is a canvas-topped patio, wooden tables with glass tops, comfortable white plastic chairs, and a bit of greenery. Plates are paper, cups are styrofoam, and forks are plastic. But the soft corn tacos are homemade, just thick enough to be leak-proof, and perfect for holding the delicious contents.

Now, about the basics. I had the Taco de Rajas—sautéed strips of chili pasilla with onions, melted cheese and herbs on two soft tacos. Had I the appetite for two, I would also have ordered the Alambre de Pechuga—grilled chicken breast with bell pepper, onions and mushrooms served on three corn tortillas. If you're inclined to simpler fare, there's the Taco de Costilla—tender strips of charbroiled top round served on two fresh homemade tortillas. On the other hand, if you want to go for it all, order the Super-Rica Especial of roasted chili pasilla stuffed with cheese and combined with charbroiled marinated pork served with three soft tacos. For the vegetarian, the Cordita de Frijol has the handmade thick corn tortillas filled with spicy ground beans. Prices for the above range from $2 to $4.50.

And to accompany the food, the assortment of Mexican beers is first-rate. (If you enjoy Mexican beer, be sure to try the Chihuahua.)

La Super-Rica Taqueria is open Friday through Wednesday from 11 a.m. to 8:30 p.m. If you plan to come late, call first.

All right, so you want something a bit tonier with respect to decor and you're looking for delicious New Mexican food—head straight for **The Zia Café**, 421 N. Milpas St., at Reddick (tel. 805/ 962-5391), the culinary child of Douglas and Jane Scott of Santa Fe.

Zia's has the colors of an outdoor cafe—sand-washed pink walls, light wood chairs, green leather seats, rust-colored floor tile, and bunches of chilis drying in the windows. Handsome desert-colored poster prints, New Mexican in tone, decorate the walls; there are mirrors with brass Mexican frames and overhead star glow lighting. It's all very inviting, comfortable, and relaxed. The counter seats face an open kitchen where you can see the food preparations, and you can even sample their New Mexican chili.

Zia's offers a wide variety of enchiladas, burritos, and tamales served with red or green chili. But there is nothing commonplace about any of the house specialties. The chilis rellenos are prepared from two green chili peppers stuffed with cheese and piñon nuts, dipped in batter, deep-fried and served with red or green chili. And the green chili chicken enchilada is worth a mention in a letter home —layered chicken and sour cream served flat with blue corn tortillas, topped with more sour cream and guacamole. What's more, when you order a Zia specialty with chicken, you get a large portion of hot breast meat, enough to satisfy the appetite of most any diner.

If you long for a breakfast burrito, Zia's serves a flour tortilla with three scrambled eggs covered with red or green chili; or you may choose huevos rancheros with blue corn tortillas topped with two fried eggs and your choice of red or green chili. Personally, I opt for the green chili, the best of which is found along the Southern Rio Grande and served at the Zia Café. The New Mexican favorites range from $5.25 to $9, combination plates are $9 to $10.50. Beer and wine are available by the glass, the pitcher (beer), or the liter.

The service is as warm, friendly, and helpful as you would expect in a Santa Fe restaurant. The Zia Café is open daily from 7:30 a.m. to 2:30 p.m. and 5 to 10 p.m.

You couldn't possibly treat yourself to a more pleasant spot to have breakfast, lunch, or an early dinner and watch the passing parade than at **Andersen's Danish Bakery and Restaurant,** 1106 State St., near Figueroa (tel. 805/962-5085). You'll spot it by the red-and-white Amstel umbrellas protecting the outside diners seated at the white tables on spanking clean wrought-iron garden chairs. Even mid-November can be warm enough to eat out at 9 a.m.

The food is delicious, the portions are substantial, the coffee is outstanding, and the service is prompt and thoughtful. Andersen's "Goodmorning Breakfast" ($3.95) includes bacon, eggs, cheese, fruit, jam (homemade), and bread. Andersen's bakes delicious Danish, strudel, pastries, rich croissants, cinnamon rolls, and bread, to name just a few of the daily choices. If you'd simply like fresh fruit for breakfast, there's that too. Fresh strawberries with cream (when available) or a compote is $2.95. The fresh fruit plate ($8.95) is enormous—enough for two—and generally includes bananas, cheese, grapes, slices of orange and kiwis, bread, and a bit of ice cream.

There's always a soup and sandwich of the day, Andersen's quiche, liver pâté. For vegetarians there are omelets with Danish Havarti cheese and a vegetable sandwich, a warm vegetable platter with a salad, or a cheese plate with fruit. For those interested in seafood, there's a catch of the day, which may be halibut, cod, trout, or you may prefer the daily offering of Scottish smoked salmon with dill sauce ($8.95). A selection of European dishes changes daily and may include Hungarian goulash, *frikadeller* (Danish meatballs), schnitzel, duckling, chicken with caper sauce, Danish meat loaf, and roast turkey with caramel sautéed potatoes. But if you yearn for smörgåsbord, Andersen's is a first-rate choice. The mini-smörgåsbord for two ($14) includes pickled herring, shrimp, smoked salmon, homemade liver pâté, cold cuts, and several warm surprises.

Luncheon and dinner choices range from $3.95 to $8.95. Any order can be prepared to go. Wine is available by the bottle or glass, beer is also served.

Andersen's is open daily, Monday through Saturday from 8 a.m. to 6 p.m., Sunday from 9 a.m.

You'll have to search up and down the coast to beat the first-class food served at **Brophy Bros. Clam Bar & Restaurant** (purveyors of fresh seafood) in Santa Barbara, which may have something to do with its Boston origins. Brophy Bros. is situated at the yacht basin and marina behind the breakwater off Harbor Way (tel. 805/966-4418). Directions to get there may sound a bit complicated, but bear with me. Heading west on Cabrillo Boulevard, you'll pass Castillo Street (there's a traffic light), then make a left at the next light, which is Harbor Way. Parking next to the marina and yacht basin is limited, but there's ample space in a lot on your left, which you'll spot as soon as you turn onto Harbor Way. It's a short walk right along the yacht basin to Brophy Bros., on the second floor of the small light-gray building ahead on your right.

Depending on which entrance you pick, you'll see the open kitchen to one side, a multitude of photos of fishing vessels, fish, and unidentified fishermen, and a bar that runs the length of the small restaurant. The windows behind the bar swing open in good weather. If you're dining al fresco on the balcony overlooking the yacht basin, overhead heaters keep you comfortable. There's nothing grand about the restaurant, but it is nicely done in light grays, beamed ceiling, and happy diners.

Brophy Bros. serves fresh seafood (and I mean fresh) plus two good meat selections, a Brophy Burger and a choice top sirloin. The seafood includes oysters and clams on the half shell, peel-and-eat shrimp, oyster shooters, steamed clams and mussels, oysters Rockefeller, to name just a few, or combination platters of cold or hot appetizers. Individual appetizers, or clam bar selections, range from $5.50 to $9.50, with the exception of the oyster shooter at $1.30. As you might expect, there's also New England clam chowder or cioppino (fish stew). An assortment of seafood salads and sandwiches includes such goodies as a crab melt of snowcrab meat salad with Jack cheese, a deep-fried West Coast snapper sandwich, and even a simple fried clam sandwich.

For dinner, you might prefer half of a fresh local lobster, stuffed and baked, then topped with hollandaise. Scampi is one of the consistent favorites, sautéed with garlic, lemon, Chablis, and a bit of tomato. The selection of the day's fresh catch may include albacore, sea scallops, white sea bass, swordfish, or thresher shark. The swordfish is the best I have eaten in any restaurant in California. It was moist, beautifully seasoned, and delectably tender, having been marinated with olive oil, basil, oregano, and lemon, then broiled and topped with garlic butter. Entrees cost $12 to $16 and are served with tossed green salad, cole slaw, and rice pilaf or fried potatoes. A good assortment of beers and wines is available.

Brophy Bros. is a fun, friendly, noisy, convivial scene of locals and tourists on almost any night. A romantic, quiet dinner for two is not to be had here, but with all the commotion and general milling about, the service is excellent and remarkably attentive in light of the crowd. And apart from the beauty of the food, it's hard to beat the view of the fishing boats, sailboats, power launches—enough to turn any confirmed landlubber into a sea lover. If you want to avoid the rush, plan on eating early, at about 4 p.m., or after 9 p.m. especially on weekends, when you're competing with the locals for a table. On the other hand, you can eat at the bar, a good alternative during those hours when tables are at a premium. Brophy Bros. is one of the select California establishments I never miss when I'm in town. And in case you should wonder, dress is about as casual as you can get.

Brophy Bros. is open from 11 a.m. to 10 p.m. Sunday through Thursday, to 11 p.m. Friday and Saturday. They don't take reservations, so expect at least a one-hour wait during the usual dinner hours. I promise, it's worth it.

The **Palace Café,** 8 E. Cota, between State and Anacapa (tel. 805/966-3133), is a fine Cajun-Creole-Caribbean restaurant, busy, relaxed, and fun. The café opened in 1985 and has been doing a booming business ever since. Dress is casual whatever the hour. Background music is jazz. The scene is busy, fun, noisy, and great for people watching.

The café is divided into two rooms: hot pink on the left and cool cream on the right with a carpeted platformed area. As to the decor, the high ceilings, overhead fans, wood tables, bentwood chairs, posters, paintings, murals, sustain the Cajun "N'Awlins" look with a French touch of wine racks and street lamps. There's a superb Frank Ashley painting that reflects the jazz glories of the horn with the New Orleans touch. On each table, the Palace Café features a huge bottle of McIlhenny Co. Tabasco, the ultimate symbol of Cajun cuisine. Service, like the clientele, is young.

Before your first course or entree arrives, an assortment of delicious, hot, freshly baked muffins appears including molasses, jalapeño, among other varieties.

On to the menu. In addition to the standard items, selections change as fresh products are flown in daily. The choice is always difficult because everything is so good, but I have two favorite starters, the Cajun popcorn (Louisiana crawfish tails dipped in cornmeal buttermilk batter and flash fried) served with creamy sherry-wine sauce, and the Bahamian conch chowder served with a pony of sherry. As to the main courses, emphasis is on seafood, but if you must have meat the café affords several good choices. There's a blackened filet mignon served with a side of browned garlic butter; panéed veal Acadiana (now and then it's rabbit), a pair of tender scallopines lightly floured, then flambéed with sherry and finished with the Palace's oyster-sherry cream sauce; or the chicken Tchoupitoulas, a breast sautéed with garlic and white wine and topped with a Creole tarragon sauce. The Palace usually also lists a pasta main course daily. As to the seafood specialties of the house, oysters Palace baked in the half-shell with a mixture of crawfish tails, mushrooms, green onions, and topped with a jalapeño beurre blanc sauce are unlike any I've ever had and are absolutely delicious. On the other hand, if "hot" is what you seek, the Louisiana barbecued shrimp are sautéed with the café's three-pepper butter sauce and served with white rice. For the more delicate palate, a real treat is the stone crab claws (when available), which are hard to find beyond the Caribbean. These are served chilled with a traditional mustard sauce and drawn butter. If there's a vegetarian in your party, the chef will prepare a vegetable platter to satisfy even the choosiest.

Should you still have space for dessert, the tart, tasty Key Lime pie is a good finish with coffee. If it happens to be on the night's menu, consider the Louisiana bread pudding soufflé with whiskey sauce, which must be ordered at the beginning of dinner. It's a magnificent creation.

Starters cost $3.50 to $8.50, main courses $12 to $22, desserts $2.50 to $10. If you have a special place in mind for noshing or dinner like the beach or your boat, just telephone the Palace Café and they'll have your favorite dish ready in 15 minutes.

The café has a good selection of California wines and several imports, beer is also available.

The restaurant is open Sunday through Thursday from 5:30 to 10 p.m. for dinner, to 11 p.m. for dessert and coffee; Friday and Saturday for dinner to 11 p.m., dessert and coffee to midnight. I suggest you make reservations, but if you don't, the restaurant will do its best to accommodate you.

Mousse Odile is just a bit east of State Street at 18 E. Cota St. (tel. 805/962-5393). The plants in the storefront window perched on red carpeting provide an attractive touch at the entry. Breakfast and lunch are served on the brasserie side of the restaurant, nicely done with oak flooring, red-and-blue checked tablecloths, fresh flowers, pink walls bearing an assortment of prints, an overhead fan, and more plants scattered here and there. The brasserie is not fancy, but has a pleasant, simple, French provincial air. Should you want wine or other drinks with your lunch, there's a bar along one wall and a refrigerated case and counter to the rear.

Mousse Odile serves breakfast, lunch, and dinner. Among other gifts, the French make some of the most delicious coffee I've ever had and that served at Mousse Odile is no exception. To add to your gustatory pleasure the food is presented beautifully, for which I am always grateful, especially at breakfast. As with all of the *specialités de la maison,* my single egg arrived with slices of banana, orange, and strawberries. Croissants can be ordered separately and are characteristically domestic—about three times the size of the Gallic variety. Mousse Odile offers some exceptional choices including a quiche du jour, waffles with crème anglaise (a delicious light custard sauce), and a variety of 2- or 3-egg omelets served with French bread, applesauce, and potatoes au gratin. One of my favorites is the *bucheron* omelet with ham, cheese, and mushrooms.

Luncheon choices are delicious and distinctive. Cold plates include a marvelous pasta salad with smoked salmon and peas, and the "Celeri Victor" with fresh cooked celery, egg slices, anchovy, capers, olives, and tomatoes. And there is always the duck pâté accompanied by green salad. All cold plates are served with French bread and butter, and cost $5.75 to $6.75. Mousse Odile also offers "Les Ficelles" (12-inch-long Parisian sandwiches), a great choice for picnicking with a bottle of wine or for munching at the restaurant. Ficelles can be prepared with cold roast lamb, cold roast chicken or turkey, barbecued ham and Swiss, or egg salad with celery and cucumbers. Each of the foregoing ($4.25 to $6.25) is finished with lettuce, tomato, pickles, and a Dijon sauce. If you are in the mood for a hot lunch, there's a delicious *boudin blanc,* white sausage made with pork and veal. Or you might choose the boneless breast of chicken with basil butter or a petit filet mignon with vegetables, each of which comes with a green salad. Prices are $7 to $9.75. Several kinds of quiche are also available at lunch, as are eggplant parmesan and a number of croissant combinations.

The main dining room for dinner adjoins the brasserie. It, too, is very simple but a bit more formal in its decor. White cloths over checked ones cover the tables. Walls are a delicate pink, complementing the mostly French poster prints. Art deco lamps furnish soft lighting. Green plants against the walls and fresh flowers and candles on each table provide the finishing touches. Waiters with red bistro aprons over black trousers and white shirts attentively bustle about at a somewhat livelier pace than the background music of Paris beginning with Edith Piaf and "La Vie en Rose."

As with lunch, there is nothing commonplace about the dinner menu. Mousse Odile offers such excellent choices as leg of lamb roasted with garlic and herbs (*gigot Provençale*); several varieties of mushrooms served on a pastry shell (*crouté aux champignons*); and some truly exceptional specials, for example, Norwegian salmon poached in champagne and port wine; veal en crouté with oyster mushrooms, shallots and Madeira wine; and a personal favorite, sweetbreads with mushrooms, shallots, and Madeira wine sauce. If you must have steak, there is filet mignon with pepper sauce and cognac. Entrees range from $13.25 to $17. Appetizers from julienned celery root in mustard sauce to marinated mussels or warm smoked salmon with pasta, caviar, and chives will add another $4 to $6.25. A good selection of wines is available.

Mousse Odile is open Monday through Saturday for breakfast from 8 to 11:30 a.m., lunch from 11:30 a.m. to 2:30 p.m., dinner from 5:30 to 9 p.m.

Another spot you don't want to miss, especially if you yearn for barbecue, is **Woody's,** 229 W. Montecito St., on the beach side of Hwy. 101 (tel. 805/963-9326). Woody's is woody all right, sort of "early cowpoke" with wood paneling, post-and-beam construction, wood booths, and wood plank floors. Lighting is by overhead industrial lamps. It is the ultimate in friendly, casual style—red-checked vinyl tablecloths, captain's chairs, sawdust on the floor, and beer posters covering the walls. Jukeboxes over 25 years old play oldie classics such as *Stardust* with Artie Shaw's orchestra (you have to be over 55 to remember that one), or *Chattanooga Choo Choo* with Glenn Miller. All in all, Woody's is a fun, casual, unassuming place, and portions are big, so come in hungry.

What's to eat? First of all, it's pretty much do-it-yourself service. There's a counter with all the menu items listed. Put in your order, take a number, and have a seat while you wait. There are barbecued ribs (giant beef, meaty pork, or lean St. Louis–style), baby back ribs, chicken, shrimp, ham, beef, turkey, duckling, a variety of burgers, and all sorts of combinations thereof; plus draft beer by the glass, jug, bucket, or by the bottle. There's also chili by the bowl plus fries, with or without a trip to a huge salad bar. If you're on a diet, but the rest of the family isn't, the lunch salad bar offers all you can eat for $3.75; at dinner it's $4.50.

For most patrons, lunch or dinner can cost anywhere from $3.50 for a Woody Burger to $7.25 for shrimp kebob, or a half slab of ribs, or one-half of a smoked duckling. For those who can down a full slab of ribs, or who may want to share, the tab is $12.50. A glass of draft beer ($1.50 for 16 oz.) comes in a Mason jar, the ½-gallon frothy size shows up in a huge Kern jar ($4), and the bucket (over a gallon) is $8.50.

Woody's has a children's menu for those under 12 including a kidburger (a mite smaller than the usual), or a quarter-chicken, both served with beans or fries and a kid-size soft drink; the cost for either is $2.50.

I can attest to the delicious smoked chicken, which is almost addicting, but if you enjoy shrimp go for the shrimp ke-bob, skewered, smoked, and grilled. The ribs, chicken, duckling, shrimp, and the combinations of ribs and chicken come with coleslaw or bar-becue beans, fries, and bread. If you still have room for dessert, both the pecan pie and carrot cake are excellent choices for $1.75. Woody's will pack orders to go for a charge of 50¢ per order.

Woody's is open Monday through Saturday from 11 a.m. to 11 p.m., on Sundays to 10 p.m. There's another Woody's at 5112 Hollister Ave., near Patterson Avenue (tel. 805/967-3775). Both locations will deliver to Santa Barbara or Goleta; $10 minimum plus $1 delivery charge.

Your Place, 22-A N. Milpas, near Mason (tel. 805/966-5151), has the look of a restaurant designed for the tourist, too much decoration, albeit authentic, for too little space, with a menu that belies its appearance.

Traditional Thai dishes with distinctively fresh ingredients, at-tractively presented, are the specialty of the house. The menu is considerable and includes appetizers, soups, salads, curries, meat sautéed with vegetables, a variety of seafood entrees including a siz-zling seafood platter, noodle dishes, rice prepared with beef, pork, chicken, or shrimp, and an exotic dish prepared with fruit scooped from a pineapple, fried with shrimp, chicken, cashew nuts, and rice, and returned to the pineapple shell before serving. You may find the scope of the menu somewhat overwhelming (there are over 100 dishes). If so, review the specialties of the house listed in the various categories.

You might begin with Golden Wing—a small chicken stuffed with ground chicken and bean thread, deep-fried, and served with sweet plum sauce; or the Regal B.B.Q. spareribs marinated in a deli-cious "royal" sauce. Of the soup choices, I thoroughly enjoyed the Tom Kah Kai—hot and sour chicken soup with coconut milk and mushrooms. Here you can order soup by the bowl or by the hot pot, which is more than enough for two; however, because the variety is so interesting, I'd order by the bowl, assuming you're dining with friends, and do some sampling. Among the meat and poultry dishes, the Siamese duckling is difficult to resist—prepared with vegetables, mushrooms, and a ginger sauce. However, above all, the seafood specialties are a great treat. The seafood hot platter is excellent and arrives served on a hot stove. Other favorites are the yellow curry crab claws or the sweet and sour fish—deep-fried and served with a sweet and sour topping with onion, bell pepper, pineapple, and tomatoes. Several of the dishes on the menu are spicy and may be ordered mild, medium, hot, or very hot.

Prices are moderate and entrees range from $5 to $12. The restaurant serves wine, sake, beer (including Thai beer and ale), plus the usual beverages—hot ginger tea among them. The restaurant is open Tuesday through Thursday and Sunday from 11 a.m. to 10 p.m., Friday and Saturday to 11 p.m.

Piatti's Ristorante is an elegant country beauty at 516 San Ysidro Rd., at East Valley Road (tel. 805/969-7520) in Montecito, about a 10-minute drive from Santa Barbara. It's located at the east end of a small smart collection of fashionable shops situated at the northeast corner of the intersecting roads. The trip is definitely worth the time.

As you walk up to the restaurant, there's an inviting patio neatly appointed with white chairs, faux marble-topped tables, and handsome cream-colored umbrellas displaying the restaurant's name. All of which conveys the impression that dining will be a pleasant treat, and indeed it is.

The spacious interior of Piatti's is polished country. It's airy, comfortable, warm, relaxed. Everything from the small bar on the left as you enter to the exhibition kitchen will attract your eye. Chairs are rough-cut with a natural finish and cushioned with light multicolor covers. Mini-murals in pastels depict things that make the restaurant and the region special—vegetables, sausages, pasta, beach scenes. Floors are of terra-cotta tiles and to one side a fireplace and pine sideboards add to the attractive country look. One patio decorates the entry, while at the rear of the restaurant is another lovely patio and garden with overhead heating for outdoor dining.

Beginning from the top of the menu, appetizers are exceptional whether you prefer the eggplant rolled with goat cheese, arugula, and sun-dried tomatoes, the fresh sweetbreads with assorted mushrooms, or the homemade ravioli filled with white truffles and eggplant. For lunch you might consider one of the antipasti accompanied by a salad or the pizza of the day. But then consider the entrees, as attractive and as inviting as the setting. There's a marvelous *le orecchiette Piatti,* pasta dumplings with cabbage, pancetta, fontina cheese, garlic, and butter. Or a pasta that caught my eye and appetite—the lasagne al pesto with layers of fresh tomato pasta, pesto, grilled zucchini, sun-dried tomatoes, pine nuts, and cheeses —very rich, but very delicious. A specialty of the house is *la zuppa di pesce,* seasonal fresh fish and shellfish cooked in a light tomato broth and served with grilled polenta. If pasta or fish is not to your taste, a tenderly grilled porterhouse steak served with Tuscan white beans may be suitable, or the boneless breast of chicken prepared with fresh herbs.

Whether or not you have room for dessert (sharing is always possible), you should at least consider Il Tiramisu, ladyfingers with mascarpone cheese, rum, and chocolate. For those counting every calorie, there is fresh seasonal fruit with or without gelato.

Entrees range from $8 to $18, but the average is about $12. Antipasti will add about $6 to the check, dessert about $4.

The restaurant has an excellent selection of wines, primarily California, a few Italian, and a full bar. The majority of still wines are in the range of $18 to $32 per bottle. Select wines are available by the glass.

Piatti's is open Monday through Friday from 11:30 a.m. to 2:30 p.m. for lunch and 5 to 10 p.m. for dinner; Saturday and Sunday hours are from noon to 11 p.m. Reservations are advised.

---

3. Malibu

During the "Panic of 1857," a shrewd Irishman purchased Malibu—then a sprawling rancho—for 10¢ an acre. Today its streets and coastline are covered with platinum. A canny Yankee from Massachusetts, Frederick Hastings Rindge, first saw (in 1891) the possibility of an "American Riviera" developing at Malibu. But a step in that direction didn't occur until his widow (who fought a long, bitter legal battle with California to prevent a coastal road from going through her spread) leased property to actress Anna Q. Nilsson in 1927. In time, a host of other stars, including John Gilbert and Clara Bow, built homes on the Malibu strip, and parties here intrigued tabloid readers during the Roaring '20s.

The movie colony, though not as celebrated as it once was, is still ensconced at Malibu, as are many TV stars. The area stretches along the West Pacific Coast Highway from the Los Angeles city line to the extreme frontier of Ventura County. Flanking the coastal road are a string of motels and restaurants, which are especially crowded in summer. Malibu lies about 25 miles from the Los Angeles Civic Center.

At its greatest point, the strip is only three miles wide; at its narrowest, just one mile. Malibu's wide, sandy beaches delight thousands of yearly visitors, who engage in every activity from nude sunbathing to grunion hunting.

WHAT TO SEE

J. Paul Getty Museum

It's been waggishly dubbed "Pompeii-by-the-Pacific," but the spectacular reconstruction of a Roman villa hidden in the hills above the Pacific is a serious—and successful—attempt to create an ideal setting for the magnificent J. Paul Getty collection. The museum is just 20 miles from downtown Los Angeles, at 17985 Pacific Coast Hwy. (a mile north of Sunset Boulevard), Malibu, CA 90265 (tel. 213/458-2003). Opened in January 1974, the museum re-cre-

3(0

ates the splendor of the Villa dei Papiri, a Roman villa which was buried in volcanic mud when Mount Vesuvius erupted in A.D. 79, destroying Pompeii and Herculaneum.

Completed in 1974, the present museum—the world's wealthiest—replaced a ranch house that Getty had opened to the public as a showplace for his collection. The museum is heralded by a colonnaded peristyle garden with a graceful reflecting pool and replicas of bronze statues unearthed at the site of the original villa. Reproductions of ancient frescoes adorn the garden walls, and over 40 different types of marble were used in the halls and colonnades. The museum's gardens include trees, flowers, shrubs, and herbs typical of those that might have been found at the villa.

Set on 10 acres, the museum houses the magnificent J. Paul Getty collection, which fittingly is strong on Greek and Roman antiquities. Notable works include a 4th-century B.C. Greek sculpture, *The Victorious Athlete* (known as the Getty Bronze), possibly done by Lysippus, court sculptor to Alexander the Great; and a rare Greek statue dating from the 5th century B.C., thought to be of the goddess Aphrodite.

In addition to the Greco-Roman pieces, the collection is also rich in Renaissance and baroque paintings from Europe and decorative arts from France. Recently acquired collections include medieval and Renaissance illuminated manuscripts, sculpture, and drawings (15th century to the end of the 19th), and 19th- and 20th-century European and American photographs. The Getty now buys paintings up to 1900, leaving later art to the Museum of Contemporary Art and the Los Angeles County Museum of Art (see Chapter VI).

Antiquities are on the first floor; decorative arts, paintings, a heralded collection of Old Master drawings, and manuscripts are on the second. A recent addition to the manuscript collection is the *Prayer Book of Charles the Bold,* by Lievin van Lathem (1469). The museum's decorative arts collection features 18th-century French furniture and tapestries. The painting galleries contain an extensive Italian Renaissance and Flemish baroque collection as well as several important French paintings by such artists as Georges de la Tour, Nicolas Poussin, Jacques-Louis David, Jean-François Millet, and François Boucher. The museum has the only documented painting in the country by Italian Renaissance master Masaccio.

In March 1990, the museum announced that it had acquired *Irises,* painted in 1889 by Vincent van Gogh. It is the Getty's greatest 19th-century painting and is regarded as one of the most important works of art in the western United States. The *Irises* can be seen in the museum's second-floor galleries together with a growing collection of important 19th-century paintings including Pierre-Auguste Renoir's *La Promenade,* Edouard Manet's *Rue Mosnier with Flags,* Edvard Munch's *Starry Night,* and James Ensor's *Christ's Entry into Brussels in 1889.* Among other recent acquisitions is a watercolor by Honoré Daumier, *A Criminal Case (Une Cause Criminelle),* illustrating one aspect of Daumier's fascination with the French judicial system. The museum also has major examples of styles of French silver, which was fashionable in the late 17th and 18th centuries.

The museum's interactive video technology allows the user to pursue his or her own interests. With this tool you can, for example, have the otherwise forbidden luxury of leafing through the rich world of medieval and illuminated Renaissance manuscripts. Videodiscs feature much of the Getty's collection spanning the 5th to the 16th century. It also includes demonstrations of techniques used in making manuscripts, and discusses the subjects and types of books represented. Five of the museum's greatest manuscripts are presented in detail. I found this new approach to learning fascinating in studying the Getty's extensive Greek vase collection.

For a light lunch or snack, there's the Garden Tea Room in a lovely terraced setting of gardens, fountain, and sunshine (usually). Prices are moderate ($4 to $8) for sandwiches, salads, and snacks served cafeteria style. Wine and beer are available. Seating is inside or al fresco. Luncheon is served from 11 a.m. to 2:30 p.m., light refreshments from 9:30 a.m. to 4:30 p.m. Picnics are not permitted.

Plans for a new home for the J. Paul Getty Center are under way. The site is on top of a cliff overlooking Brentwood and Bel-Air. On completion of the project, the current museum will be devoted exclusively to ancient Greek and Roman art.

The Getty Museum is open Tuesday through Sunday from 10 a.m. to 5 p.m. (the gate closes at 4:30 p.m.), and there is no admission or parking charge. Docent orientation lectures are given at the ocean end of the main peristyle garden every 15 minutes between 9:30 a.m. and 3:15 p.m.

Note: Because there are limited parking facilities, if you plan to come by car and park, *without exception* you must make a parking reservation seven to ten days in advance (by mail or by telephone). Visitors who do not have a car or who are unable to make parking reservations may enter the museum grounds by bicycle (racks are available), motorcycle, taxi, RTD bus #434 (please request a museum pass from the driver), or by being dropped at the gatehouse by car. No walk-in traffic is permitted with the exception of bona fide RTD bus passengers.

WHERE TO STAY

What once was the Tonga Lei Motel and Don the Beachcomber, has been replaced by the new **Malibu Beach Inn,** at 22878 Pacific Coast Hwy., Malibu CA 90265 (tel. 213/456-6444). The inn is on the beach next to Malibu Pier. Malibu's first all-new beachfront motel in some 37 years has oceanfront rooms with private balconies. Amenities include color TV, VCR, and phone. Continental breakfast is included in the rates, which are $135 to $175 for singles and doubles. Suites are available.

Casa Malibu, 22752 Pacific Coast Hwy., Malibu, CA 90265 (tel. 213/456-2219), is like staying at your own beach club. Right on the highway, it's built hacienda-style, with bedrooms and terraces leading down to the surf and sand. There's a restful inner courtyard, with palm trees and cuppa d'oro vines growing up to the balcony. A sundeck adjoins. The 21 units are simple but cheerfully furnished, and many have peaked, beamed ceilings. All have double or king-size beds, shower baths, phones, and color TVs.

Singles or doubles cost $120 to $130 overlooking the water, $85 to $95 if fronting the patio or coastal highway. Rooms with kitchens (minimum three-day stay) are $12 a day extra. An extra person adds on $12.

WHERE TO DINE

Carlos and Pepe's, 22706 Pacific Coast Hwy. (tel. 213/456-3105), is a delightful weathered-wood seacoast structure. Inside you'll find a few touches from south of the border, including papier-mâché banana trees at the bar, complete with tropical birds. The interior is designed so that each table has an ocean view. An immense aquarium filled with tropical fish separates the bar and dining areas. Best place to sit is on the plant-filled, glass-enclosed deck directly overlooking the ocean.

The menu features a wide variety of Mexican dishes, including enchiladas, chimichangas (a burrito fried crisp, just like a fried taco) and "Carlos' Wild Tostada." But the most popular dish here is fajitas, prepared (from bottom up) with flour tortillas, guacamole, salsa cruda, lettuce, beans, and served in a hot skillet containing peppers, onions, tomatoes, and either steak or chicken or both. And for those who are not happy with the previous selection, there are "Gringo Specials"—hamburgers, omelets, and steaks—for $5 to $15. Lunch will cost $7 to $9; dinner $10 to $15. For dessert, there's a delicious mud pie (chocolate), or deep-fried ice cream, plus a selection of great ice cream flavors. A wide selection of wines and imported beers is available, and there's a well-stocked liquor bar. But above all, Carlos and Pepe's is famous for their delicious 16-ounce margaritas—made with fresh-squeezed juices.

Open daily from 11:30 a.m. to 2 a.m., they serve appetizers until 1:30 a.m. Meals are served till 11 p.m. Sunday to Thursday, till midnight on Friday and Saturday. No reservations.

Alice's is still where it has always been for 18 years, at 23000 Pacific Coast Hwy. (tel. 213/456-6646), and is still one of the liveliest restaurants in the area. Facing the Malibu Pier, the dining area is glassed in on three sides, and rear tables are on a raised platform so that everyone can view the ocean, an intoxicating sight at twilight. It's light and airy, but most important the menu is still mostly seafood—as always, beautifully fresh.

There's nothing commonplace on the luncheon or dinner menus. Among the tempting luncheon entrees are yellowtail with spinach, lemon, and tarragon butter, and the grilled chicken breast marinated in garlic, soy, and spices and served with a tomato/cilantro relish. But don't overlook the pasta choices, especially the spaghetti with hot Creole sausage and zucchini with sweet red-pepper sauce. Alice's also has a good selection of salads, warm and cold. There's a warm duck salad, which combines a perfectly grilled duck breast with sautéed mushrooms, mixed greens, cucumbers, and ginger/shallot dressing. Eggs and sandwiches include eggs

Benedict or an exceptional hamburger, but consider the Malibu sausage burger with sautéed onions and peppers, and mustard dressing.

As to dinner, you might begin with smoked Norwegian salmon served with caviar cream, onion, capers, and toast points. Among the salads my choice is the hot roasted goat cheese salad with mixed greens, fresh herbs, walnuts, touched with a sherry vinaigrette. Some of the great entrees are Alice's grilled swordfish with herb butter, a dish I find difficult to resist, and the stir-fried scallops with black bean sauce and sweet peppers over pan-fried angel hair pasta. But Alice's doesn't forget the meat lovers. Take your choice of a grilled New York strip steak served with soy-glazed red onions, or the grilled veal rack chop with shiitake mushrooms, roasted shallots, and Cabernet sauce.

Luncheon salads, eggs, and sandwiches are $5.50 to $7.50, pastas $7.50 to $9. Dinner entrees are $13.50 to $19, pastas $8 to $11.50. Appetizers range from $3.50 to $9.50. The list of delicious homemade desserts and pastries changes daily, so be sure to ask.

Alice's is open weekdays from 11:30 a.m. to 10 p.m., Saturday from 11 a.m., and Sunday 10:30 a.m. to 10 p.m. Reservations are advised.

Inn of the Seventh Ray, 128 Old Topanga Canyon Rd. (tel. 213/455-1311), four miles from the Coast Highway, offers the "best of freshly energized food . . . to raise your body's vibration." The "seventh ray," in case you're wondering, is the energy that will bring the golden age into being. If you'd like further elucidation, the back of the menu explains it all, as well as the quality of the food and drink and its preparation. Suffice it to say that you're getting more than just an ordinary meal here.

The vibes are certainly peaceful and the creekside setting beautiful. Inside it looks like a country church with a peaked ceiling, stained-glass windows, candles flickering on every table, and a fireplace blazing (in season). Carefully selected music—classical or Asian—is played in the background. If you dine outdoors, which most people do, the music is piped through a speaker. The tables overlook the creek and lots of untamed foliage. Trees overhead provide shade, and there are fresh flowers on every table.

As for the food, it is lovingly prepared, using only the finest and purest ingredients, and it's absolutely delicious. All the bread is homemade with freshly ground organic grains. Preservatives, sugar, food coloring, or bleached flours are verboten, and desserts are made with honey and maple syrup. A number of the fruit wines are unpasteurized. I suggest ordering a glass as an apéritif. There are 10 dinner entrees, all served with soup or salad, hors d'oeuvres, lightly steamed vegetables, baked potato or herbed brown rice, and homemade stone-ground bread. They're listed in order of their vibrational value, the lightest and least dense (those are better for you) first. The number one, or purest, item is "Five Secret Rays," lightly steamed vegetables served with lemon-tahini and caraway cheese sauces. Skipping along a vibration or two you'll come to number four, Omritas, described as coming "direct from the violet planet, a space ship of nature's perfect vessel." It turns out to be half an eggplant filled with olives, nuts, mushrooms, shallots, and feta cheese, topped with ruby ray tomato sauce. Numbers five and six are pasta and seafood entrees, seven is coquille St-Germain (fresh scallops, in season, in a cheese sauce with mushrooms and cognac), eight is chicken rosemary, ninth is rack of lamb, and the tenth (market permitting) and densest item is a 10-ounce New York steak, cut from beef fed on natural grasses only, charbroiled, and served with two steak sauces. These vibrational delights range from $12 to $22.

Most luncheon entrees are under $9; they include a variety of salads, open-faced sandwiches served with steamed vegetables, and entrees like cheese fondue with steamed vegetables for dipping. For Sunday brunch, you can partake of a variety of omelets (like spinach, feta cheese, and mushroom; crab and tomato; or cream cheese, olive, and tomato); or quiche, waffles, or cereal, for $5 to $9.

Whether you believe in vibes or not, all the food is excellent, and you're sure to enjoy the tranquil canyon views. The inn is open for lunch weekdays from 11:30 a.m. to 3 p.m., Saturday from 10:30 a.m., Sunday from 9:30 a.m., and for dinner nightly from 6 to 10. Reservations are essential for dinner.

La Scala Malibu, 3874 Cross Creek Rd., off Pacific Coast Hwy. (tel. 213/456-1979), is the venture of Jean Leon, whose ultra-chic Beverly Hills restaurants (see Chapter V) are hangouts for Jacqueline Bisset, Robert Wagner, and Suzanne Pleshette, among others. It's different from its Beverly Hills counterparts. The entry is Italian marble. There are pastel bargello-patterned banquettes, terra-cotta tile floors, and etched-glass area dividers. There's an impressive wood-paneled 1,800 bottle wine room and an exhibition kitchen. Solarium windows overlook the wilds of Malibu Creek with a view of the Pacific. It's a relaxed atmosphere for friendly, leisurely dining.

Lunch at La Scala might begin with gazpacho followed by fresh turkey salad with sliced tomato and hard-boiled egg, a cold plate of broiled chicken, smoked salmon with onions and capers, or a hot entree such as veal and peppers, swordfish, or the daily fresh pasta, for $12 to $15. For dessert, try the homemade ice cream with fresh raspberries. Dinner begins with antipasti such as mozzarella marinara, seafood salad, carpaccio, or a Caesar salad and continues with entrees such as baked sea bass, veal with pepperoni, or the nightly fresh pasta. Entrees cost $17 to $28.

La Scala Malibu is open for lunch weekdays 11:30 a.m. to 2:30 p.m.; for dinner Monday through Thursday from 5:30 to 10:30 p.m., on Friday and Saturday to 11 p.m., Sunday 5:30 to 10 p.m.

For leisurely breakfasts or lunches I'm partial to the **Sand Castle,** just off the pier at 28128 W. Pacific Coast Hwy. (tel. 213/457-2503). Housed in a gray shingled building, complete with weather vane and widow's walk, it's right on the beach and has a wall of windows overlooking the ocean. The interior is rustic with many nautical touches (ship-light chandeliers, rigging, etc.), and a big fireplace (ablaze at night) connects the restaurant and lounge. (The latter sees a lot of action on weekend nights.)

Breakfast can be a big order of steak and eggs with hash browns or home-fries and hot buttered toast; an avocado, bacon, and jack cheese omelet; or buttermilk pancakes with bacon—for $6 to $10.

Champagne brunch ($10), served from 9 a.m. to 4 p.m. daily (till 2:30 p.m. on Sunday), comes with a refillable glass of champagne and a choice of entrees—perhaps a seafood crêpe in mornay sauce served with a fresh fruit cup, or the steak and teriyaki chicken. Lunch fare runs the gamut from a Monte Cristo sandwich to scallops sautéed in white wine for $8 to $18. An excellent buy are the sunset dinners, served from 5 to 7 p.m. (4 to 7 p.m. on Sunday). For about $8 these include soup or salad and a choice of entrees—London broil au jus with whipped potatoes, grilled mahi-mahi with rice pilaf, pasta primavera, etc.

The Sand Castle is open daily for breakfast from 6 to noon, for lunch from 11 a.m. to 4 p.m., and for dinner from 5 to 10 p.m. (till 11 p.m. on Friday and Saturday). Reservations advised at dinner.

4. Santa Monica

In the northwestern corner of Los Angeles, Santa Monica draws both visitors and permanent residents who romp on its three miles of good sandy beaches, basking in an ideal year-round climate.

At the municipally owned **Santa Monica Pier,** fun-seekers go fishing, boating, and swimming.

Santa Monica's history as a resort goes back to the 1870s. Today it's a popular residential and convention city, activities centering around a $3 million **Civic Auditorium,** previously the setting for the Academy Award presentations.

Many hotels and apartment houses, with such Southern California overstatement names as Shangri-La, line the coast. Four major boulevards from Los Angeles (Wilshire, Santa Monica, Olympic, and Pico) lead to the oceanfront and the 14-block-long **Palisades Park.**

Also, right on the beach is a string of palatial homes, many built by movie stars in the '30s. On the north, Santa Monica is bounded by San Vicente Boulevard, on the south by Venice, and it extends 33 blocks inland toward Los Angeles.

WHERE TO STAY

First-Class Accommodations

Located at the foot of Wilshire Boulevard, across the street (and up a cliff) from one of the best beaches in Southern California, the **Miramar-Sheraton Hotel,** 101 Wilshire Blvd. (at 2nd Street), Santa Monica, CA 90401 (tel. 213/394-3731, or toll free 800/325-3535), offers quality service and tasteful surroundings. Part of the Sheraton chain since 1978, the hotel actually dates from 1921, and the charm and leisure of that era are still apparent.

The hotel's main courtyard centers around a beautiful, century-old fig tree. Located as it is in Santa Monica, it's convenient to the airport, Westwood, Beverly Hills, and in fact much of the city. And it's smack in the center of one of the most tranquil and scenic parts of Greater Los Angeles.

The Miramar has 305 guest rooms, including 61 suites. All are spacious and well appointed, with a king-size or two double beds and pastel decor. Little touches are in evidence—special soaps, oversize towels, two direct-dial phones (one in the bathroom), and color TV. All rooms have honor bars and in-room safes as well.

The hotel offers several dining and entertainment choices. The International Room is an intimate dining room offering classic Continental cuisines and traditional American favorites. A limited gourmet menu features veal, fowl, seafood, and steaks, for $16 to $25. The Garden Room, open for lunch only, affords a commanding view of the pool terrace and surrounding gardens. Adjoining is the Stateroom Lounge, complete with piano bar, where you can listen to music and dance the night away Tuesday to Saturday. And there's a coffeeshop, open daily from 6:30 a.m. to midnight, where breakfast, sandwiches, salads, and omelets are available, along with a selection of hot entrees.

Rates at the Miramar-Sheraton are $125 to $200 single, $145 to $220 double. Suites cost $250 to $600. Airport bus service is available.

Medium-Priced Accommodations

The **Pacific Shore Hotel,** 1819 Ocean Ave. (at Pico Boulevard), Santa Monica, CA 90401 (tel. 213/451-8711, or toll free 800/241-3848), is a modern 168-room, eight-story hotel half a block from the beach. All rooms have ocean or pool view visible through an entire wall of tinted glass; you can see out but nobody can see in. They're attractively decorated in cheerful colors. Each has individually controlled heating and air conditioning, a small dressing area, rattan and walnut furnishing, color TV, direct-dial phone, tub/shower bath, and AM/FM radio. On-premises facilities include ice and soft-drink machines on every floor, shops, car-rental and tour desks, a guest laundry, a nice-size outdoor heated swimming pool and whirlpool, a Jacuzzi, saunas for men and women, and a cocktail lounge offering nightly entertainment.

Singles cost $90 to $117; doubles run $94 to $127; and suites are $225 to $375. Rates change with the seasons. Parking is free.

The **Radisson-Huntley Hotel,** 1111 2nd St. (at Wilshire Boulevard), Santa Monica, CA 90403 (tel. 213/394-5454, or toll free 800/556-4011, 800/556-4012 in California), offers 213 rooms and suites right near the beach. You can walk from the Huntley to the Santa Monica Pier, where you'll find over 300 shops, boutiques, and restaurants. There's no swimming pool on the premises, but the ocean is a stone's throw away. The rooms are large and attractive (all have ocean or mountain views), and are equipped with color TV, AM/FM radio, direct-dial phone, and other modern amenities. Running up the front of the hotel is a glass elevator; the view on the way up (or down) is spectacular.

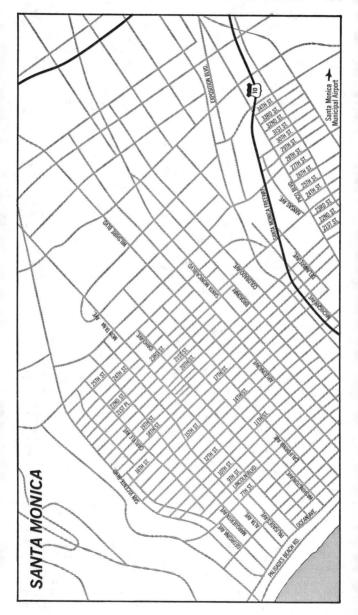

Atop the hotel is a rooftop restaurant called Toppers, with magnificent views—be sure to see the sunset from here. Mexican cuisine is offered at lunch and dinner, but if you choose there's also pasta, seafood, chicken, steak, and hamburgers. Toppers serves a Sunday champagne brunch from 11 a.m. to 3 p.m., and has entertainment nightly from 8:30 p.m. to 1:30 a.m. In addition there's a classy coffeeshop called the Garden Café on the premises.

Single rooms cost $115 to $125, and doubles are $125 to $135; suites rent for $155 to $260. Parking is free.

There are two Holiday Inns (tel. toll free 800/465-4329) in Santa Monica. The **Holiday Inn Bay View Plaza,** 530 Pico Blvd. (at 6th Street, west of Lincoln), Santa Monica, CA 90405 (tel. 213/399-9344), has over 300 guest rooms, with color TVs, direct-dial phones, mini-bars, air conditioning, and private tub/shower bathrooms, plus nice views of the ocean or city. The Bay View Café serves three meals a day; there's a pool and garage parking for guests, and free airport service.

Rates are $80 to $115 single, $85 to $130 double, $225 and up for suites.

A few blocks away is the **Holiday Inn at the Pier,** 120 Colorado Ave. (at Ocean and 2nd streets), Santa Monica, CA 90401 (tel. 213/451-0676). It's the older of the two; rooms and facilities are similar, if less fancy. Its location is convenient, across from the beach and pier and adjacent to the Santa Monica Freeway. Rooms here start at $98 single and $114 double. Parking is free. A restaurant on the premises serves breakfast, lunch, and dinner.

Budget Accommodations

By the time you read this the new **Santa Monica International AYH-Hostel** will have opened at 1436 Second St., P.O. Box 575, Santa Monica, CA 90406 (tel. 213/393-9913). Calls are answered by a clerk between 7 and 11 a.m. and 4 p.m. to midnight; otherwise it's recorded information. An alternative source for information is tel. 213/831-8846 from noon to 5 p.m.

If you don't already know it, be advised that Santa Monica is one of Los Angeles' most popular beach communities. The Santa Monica hostel is one of the largest in this country and accommodates up to 200 guests including groups and families on a space-available basis. Private family rooms have four beds. As with all hostels, showers and bathrooms are dormitory-style. The hostel has guest kitchen facilities, a travel library, and a travel center.

The Santa Monica hostel is just two blocks from the beach and Santa Monica Pier, about one mile to Venice Beach. It's within walking distance of shops and restaurants and about two blocks from regional bus lines including a direct bus to Los Angeles International Airport (about 7 miles). Buses to Los Angeles and its tourist attractions run regularly from stops near the hotel.

Accommodations are $12 per night per person for members, $15 for non-members. Individual membership in the American Youth Hostel organization is $20 per year, which entitles you to stay at the local rate in any of the AYH hostels. If you are not a member, you can join at the hostel. Guests are limited to three-day stays; however, this can be extended to five nights with the approval of the manager.

Reservations are accepted by mail only and are advised for visits during the summer months. Send the first night's fee as a deposit.

WHERE TO DINE

There is a great choice of restaurants in Santa Monica, but don't forget one of the most prestigious is **Michael's,** which I've mentioned in Chapter V.

Zucky's, 431 Wilshire Blvd., at 5th Street (tel. 213/393-0551), is the place to go if you've got a yen for the likes of kreplach or kugel. It's one of L.A.'s top delicatessens, and I particularly like the fact that it's kosher style, not strictly kosher. Which means that you can order dairy items—like cheese blintzes—as well as meat dishes. You can even get a seafood omelet of crab, bay shrimp, and whitefish for lunch. If you're from Manhattan, you'll feel at home here. It's always busy.

The menu offers something for everyone. Zucky's makes a pretty good pastrami sandwich on rye. Other favorites are Hungarian-style stuffed cabbage, potato pancakes with sour cream and apple sauce, and cream cheese and lox on a bagel (what else?). This lighter fare costs $5 to $7. You can also order full meals with soup, salad, entree, potato, vegetable, and bread, for $7 to $10. Or à la carte there are some delicious bargains, like chicken in the pot, with noodles, matzoh balls, vegetables, and kreplach, at $9.50 for two. For dessert there are over 20 choices, including New York–style cheesecake and a chocolate eclair. Drinks range from a traditional Dr. Brown's cream soda or chocolate egg cream to beer and wine.

The decor is typically modernistic Jewish deli in earth tones with leatherette booths, Formica tables, and glass cases filled with salamis, smoked fish, bottles of borscht, halvah, and other Jewish delicacies. The ambience is one of lively hubbub. Zucky's is open 24 hours Friday and Saturday to satisfy your deli cravings. You can also have breakfast around the clock here with freshly squeezed orange juice. Sunday through Thursday hours are from 6 a.m. to 2 a.m. Free validated parking.

Fuji Gardens, 424 Wilshire Blvd., between 4th and 5th streets (tel. 213/393-2118), is a favorite of mine for many of the reasons that one returns time and again to any restaurant—it's pleasant; lunches and dinners are reasonably priced; the food is excellent; and the service couldn't be better. Fuji Gardens is a pretty little place with comfortable booths, bamboo-pattern wallpaper, and the blue flags hanging from a rooflike structure that seem to be a part of many Japanese restaurants.

Combination dinners here are a good value. One such combination is beef teriyaki and lobster tail, which comes with salad, chilled noodles, sashimi or tempura, an appetizer, soup, rice, and green tea. And most of these dinners are in the $10 to $15 range; you can also order à la carte items like salmon teriyaki with vegetable salad and noodles.

Lunches are also a great buy. A Makunochi lunchbox with entree, soup, rice, and tea costs $9 to $12; pork cutlet with tonkatsu sauce comes with the same accompaniments. For dessert with either meal, try the green-tea or ginger ice cream.

Fuji Gardens is open for lunch weekdays from 11:30 a.m. to 10:30 p.m.; Saturday and Sunday from 3 to 11 p.m.

A Santa Monica landmark for over 50 years, the **Belle-Vue French Restaurant,** 101 Santa Monica Blvd., at Ocean Avenue (tel. 213/393-2843), features a quaint French provincial motif with café-curtained, multipaned windows, floral-design carpeting, lots of plants, and shelves of decorative plates and books. The birch-paneled walls are hung with photos of old Santa Monica.

Simple French home cooking is featured. Best buys are the full lunches and dinners. Lunch, priced at $7 to $13, including soup or salad, vegetable, and potatoes, might feature an entree of palace court (artichoke stuffed with crab), French pot roast, or lamb kidneys sautéed with wine. The marine salad is first-rate. Dinners, at $16 to $22, include soup and salad, vegetable, and potato du jour, plus an appetizer—perhaps a seafood cocktail or pâté. Among the entrees are baked oysters, coq au vin, duckling à l'orange, tournedos, and those French delicacies, brains and sweetbreads. On Friday there's a special bouillabaisse, chock full of shrimp, clams, whitefish, and lobster, cooked with a white wine sauce and served in a tureen. French pastries for dessert are served at either meal, and, of course, wines and other drinks are available. There's also a lengthy à la carte listing. On Sunday a brunch is served from 12:30 to 3 p.m. For about $14 you get champagne, melon, pâté, or salad, and a choice of several entrees. A very pleasant cocktail area adjoins the restaurant.

The Belle-Vue is open Monday to Thursday from 11:30 a.m. to 3 p.m. for lunch, dinner 4:30 to 9:30 p.m., on Friday and Saturday till 10 p.m., and on Sunday from 12:30 to 9:30 p.m.

One of the most "in" spots in Santa Monica is **Chinois on Main,** 2709 Main St. (tel. 213/392-9025), a high-fashion restaurant owned and operated by Wolfgang Puck and Barbara Lazaroff of Spago. It's a stunning extravaganza, decorated in green and pink with black touches. There are special details too—a pair of large cloisonné cranes, a Buddha over the bar, a large window full of blossoms, and exotic flowers all around. The superb food is a combination of Asian, California, and French nouvelle cuisines. The à la carte menu is changed seasonally to take advantage of the freshest foods available. You might begin your meal with stir-fried garlic chicken with marinated spinach on radicchio leaves, or sautéed goose liver with warm ginger vinaigrette. First "flavors" (courses) range from $6 to $13. Entrees might include a whole sizzling catfish stuffed with ginger, phoenix, and dragon (pigeon and lobster sliced on watercress with mushrooms and whole shallots roasted in cabernet sauce), or charcoal-grilled Szechuan beef, thinly sliced with hot chili oil and cilantro sauce. Entrees cost $15 to $28. And for dessert, you can partake of a rice tart flavored with lichee wine or assorted sherbets and fresh fruits, among other choices.

Chinois is open seven nights a week for dinner from 6 to 10:30

p.m., and Wednesday to Friday for lunch from 11:30 a.m. to 2 p.m. As at Spago, reservations are essential and should be made as far in advance as possible.

Note: The party atmosphere and acoustical design of the restaurant cause quite a din, so if you're planning on quiet conversation, Chinois may not be your dish. On the other hand, if you can't resist (you really shouldn't) and time is short, the only option is to dine early.

---

5. Venice

Venice is an oceanside community south of Santa Monica, bordered by Marina del Rey. The character of Venice has undergone a remarkable change since the turn of the century, when it was founded with the intention of resembling its namesake in Italy. It was graced with canals, quaint one-lane bridges, and authentic imported gondolas piloted by gondoliers. An Italian-style rococo hotel, the St. Mark's, attracted the celebrated people of its day. Self-enchanted silent-screen star Mae Murray (*The Merry Widow*) became one of the first to build a Venetian-style palazzo there in pistachio colors.

Suddenly oil was discovered, and block after block of residences gave way to derricks. As a beach resort (not to mention a harbinger of Disneyland) Venice died a miserable death. Its canals became slimy and filled with refuse. In the '50s, Venice attracted the beatniks and in the '60s the hippies.

In the last few years Venice has experienced a spotty renaissance, and it has become a chic area in which to live, a trend reflected in soaring real estate prices and the appearance of scores of new restaurants and boutiques. But don't expect to see a Malibu or even a Santa Monica; parts of it are still a bit sleazy. Its boardwalk is more like a mingling of muscle, Coney Island, and a circus with skateboarders, middle-aged skaters, and cyclists of all ages and shapes.

WHERE TO DINE

Nowhere in Venice can you get a better view of the local action than at the **Sidewalk Café,** 8 Horizon Ave., at Oceanfront (tel. 213/399-5547). It's housed in one of the few remaining buildings of the original town of the early 20th century. Along the front is the open-air café, crammed with tables, all with a perfect view of the skaters, bikers, joggers, skateboarders, breakdancers, and sidewalk performers who provide an ever-changing diversion. In the back there's a small bar.

Gracious dining it isn't, but for an interesting insight into Venice, this is it. You can dally here over a drink—a glass of white wine or a fresh strawberry daiquiri, for example—or you can have a bite to eat from the extensive menu. There are lots of omelets, salads, burgers, and sandwiches for $5 to $10.

The Sidewalk Café is open from 8 a.m. to midnight (from 9 a.m. weekdays in winter) daily. Don't miss this Venice institution.

A smashing addition to the Venice restaurant scene is the **West Beach Café**, 60 N. Venice Blvd., one block from the beach (tel. 213/399-9246). It's a trendy eatery that specializes in California nouvelle cuisine. The decor is cool, modern, and minimalist, with white cinder-block walls, track lighting, and simple black chairs and white-clothed tables. The walls of the café serve as a gallery for an ever-changing variety of works of local artists.

Featured at lunch are hamburgers, Caesar salad, pasta, seafood, warm salad, and chicken, as well as many specials, which change weekly. Prices at midday average $9 to $18. Dinner entrees are more elaborate. Among the favorites are grilled Spanish red shrimp in achiote oil with garlic, and ancho chili with steamed potatoes tossed with cilantro and a side plate of steamed spinach. The menu changes weekly. Dinner prices range from $18 to $32. A special brunch is served on weekends, and includes eggs Benedict, Belgian waffles, huevos rancheros, and do-it-yourself tacos (you pick the ingredients), for $10 to $20. There's a fine wine list with selections to complement any meal.

The West Beach Café is open for breakfast (about $6 to $10) weekdays from 8 to 11:30 a.m., weekends from 10 a.m., lunch from 11:30 a.m. to 2:30 p.m., for dinner from 6 to 10:30 p.m., and for late-night pizzas (made with whatever's in the kitchen) after 11:30 p.m. till 1:30 a.m. ($13 to $17).

6. Marina Del Rey

Almost like a community created overnight has Marina del Rey burst onto the scene. Not only are there 6,000 boats (though it seems more like 60,000) in the world's largest small-craft harbor, but a Restaurant Row has sprung up that offers a great assortment of food styles and a waterside view as a bonus. And it's a high-powered, beautifully-tuned-blonde singles bar scene, some of which is at the Warehouse, and the Cheesecake Factory.

The recreation and convention center lies right on the coastal stretch between Santa Monica and Los Angeles International Airport, easily accessible via the San Diego Freeway.

Marina del Rey also has a unique shopping and recreation development known as **Fisherman's Village** at 13763 Fiji Way (tel. 213/823-5411), containing over 30 specialty shops built in the style of an Old English whaling village. Imports from around the world are sold here. These shops line cobblestoned walks along the waterfront and are interspersed with waterside restaurants and picnic tables. In the center is an authentic 60-foot lighthouse.

As mentioned, the village is right on the waterfront, with a magnificent view of the marina and main channel. Visitors can take a **water sightseeing trip** around the marina, aboard the *Marina Belle* excursion boat (tel. 213/822-1151), leaving every hour on the hour from 11 a.m. to 4 p.m. seven days a week. It's a great 40-minute narrated tour. Adults pay $6; seniors, $4; children 6 to 12, $5; under 6, $4.

It's also possible to go out on **fishing trips** (call the *Betty O;* tel. 213/822-3625). Boats going out for the three-quarter-day (6-hour) trips ($24) leave at 7 a.m. and 8 a.m. Half-day (4½-hour) trips ($19) leave at 7:30 a.m. and 12:30 p.m. If you need tackle, it can be rented on the boat for $6.

Rent-A-Sail at 13560 Mindanao Way, one block from Fisherman's Village (tel. 213/822-1868), has sailboat and power boat rentals for both harbor and ocean, including 90 rental sloops, catamarans, and runabouts from 14 feet to 25 feet. Rental rates range from $12 to $34 per hour. Rent-A-Sail is open daily, year round, from 9 a.m. till dark. Rent-A-Sail also has a sailing school at the same facility. Sailing instruction ranges from lessons for the beginner to guidance for the more advanced sailor. Instruction is $28 to $30 per hour, including both the boat and instructor. All instruction is individual and is conducted completely on the water. Reservations are suggested.

WHERE TO STAY

Upper-Bracket Accommodations
The **Marina Del Rey Marriott**, 13480 Maxella Blvd., Marina del Rey, CA 90292 (tel. 213/822-8555, or toll free 800/228-9290), is an excellent choice. It has 283 luxurious air-conditioned rooms, all fitted out with first-run movies on the color TV, tub/shower bath, direct-dial phone, and AM/FM clock radio. The decor is resortlike. Housed in the Villa Marina Center, the hotel offers access to about 30 interesting shops, and it's also convenient to the airport. A beautifully landscaped courtyard is the setting for a swimming pool, hydrotherapy whirlpool, and pool bar, not to mention a pond, a bridged stream, and a rock waterfall.

A notable attraction is Maxfield's Restaurant and Lounge, offering fine American/Continental cuisine and featuring aged, prime beef. There's a fine wine list to complement your meal. Abundant colorful flowers and stained-glass windows further enhance the cheerful ambience.

Rates for singles at the Marriott are $134 to $144; doubles and twins cost $144 to $164; suites $235 to $335.

First-Class Hotels
This emerging resort represents a new way to live in Greater Los Angeles. Those who want a relaxing resort atmosphere will anchor here minutes away from California's famed beaches. The Los Angeles International Airport is only 10 miles away, and you're two

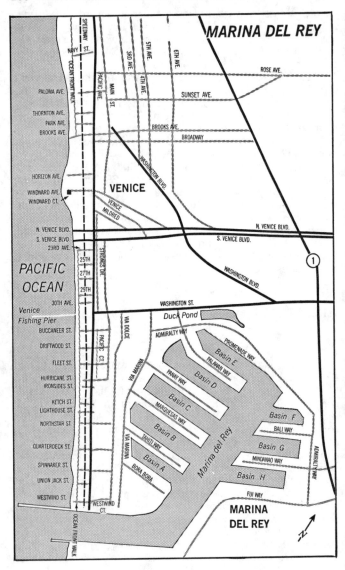

minutes from the freeway system, which will take you to most of the attractions of Southern California.

Marina International Hotel, 4200 Admiralty Way (at Palawan Way), Marina del Rey, CA 90292 (tel. 213/301-2000, or toll free 800/882-4000, 800/862-7462 in California).

There are 127 rooms and suites in this attractive hotel, done in bright, light colors for a look of contemporary elegance. Each room is fitted out with color TV and bedside controls, direct-dial phone, tub and/or shower bath. All junior suites have a phone in the bathroom. The lobby bar and courtyard recently have been refinished in pastel tones similar to those in the rooms with soft lighting, lots of lush plants, and simple, comfortable contemporary furnishings.

The 25 bungalows (originally called villas) were refurbished in 1988. These spacious, luxuriously appointed accommodations are warm and cozy. Their decor is contemporary California casual, with soft pastels of teal, rose, peach, and lavender, and comfortable textured fabrics. Each has a sitting area, bedroom, bathroom, and lots of privacy. All the bungalows are located off a private courtyard.

The hotel's Crystal Fountain offers Continental cuisine in an indoor/outdoor garden setting. The restaurant is open for breakfast, lunch, dinner, and Sunday brunch. A unique service of the Crystal Fountain features selected appetizers, entrees, and desserts prepared tableside. Twenty-four hour room service is available.

Facilities include a heated swimming pool and whirlpool (the beach is right across the street); golf and tennis can be arranged nearby. Free covered parking is available for guests.

A bonus is free shuttle bus service to and from the airport. Rates vary according to room location. Singles are $97 to $109; doubles and twins run $127 to $147. Suites and bungalows are $157 to $177 single; $195 to $285 double.

Marina Del Rey Hotel, 13534 Bali Way (at Admiralty Way), Marina del Rey, CA 90292 (tel. 213/301-1000, or toll free 800/882-4000, 800/862-7462 in California), is under the same ownership as the International. The hotel is on the marina's main channel and is surrounded by water. Rooms have color TV, oversize beds, direct-dial phone, AM/FM clock radio, and harbor-view windows. Many have private balconies and patios, so you can breakfast in the sun, inspecting the yachts moored nearby. Singles cost $125 to $170; doubles, $145 to $190; suites, $375 to $450. There's free limousine service to the airport 24 hours a day. Those who don't want to go to the beach can enjoy a large, landscaped pool on the waterfront.

On the premises is the Dockside Café, a coffeeshop overlooking the harbor open daily for breakfast and lunch. Another choice for dining is the Crystal Seahorse, open daily from 6 to 11 p.m. Its panoramic marina views are reflected in mirrored walls, tables, and ceilings. It has two patios for al fresco dining and drinking, and the Seahorse Lounge.

WHERE TO DINE

The ambience and views at most Marina del Rey harborside restaurants are generally better than the food. Nonetheless, everyone occasionally likes to go there to eat.

The Warehouse, 4499 Admiralty Way, near Lincoln and Bali Way (tel. 213/823-5451), is the creation of photographer Burt Hixson, who traveled 23,000 miles, ostensibly in a quest to find the perfect decor for his dream restaurant. Remembering the exotic wharves he had seen, he erected a two-level dockside structure, where one now dines on casks and barrels, or inside wooded packing crates. Burlap coffee bags line the walls; netting, rope, and peacock chairs further enhance the setting. The place is entered via a tropical walkway of bamboo and palm that extends over a large fish pond. Hixson's photos line the walls in this unusual restaurant, which is not only colorful but surprisingly unfunky and elegant. Most of the tables have a view of the marina, and many are outside right on the water.

Lunches range from $8 to $13. Dinner is $14 to $29, with entrees from the world over: Poulet Dijon, Malaysian shrimp, steak teriyaki. Included are soup or salad, potato or rice, and vegetables. Drink it down with beer from whatever nation you wish, or with an exotic rum concoction. Throughout the afternoon and evening there's the oyster bar for snacks like garlic bread, nachos, or quesadillas, and lots of seafood selections (shrimp, oysters, clams, chowder). Is the Warehouse touristy? Certainly, but with good food and all that atmosphere, who cares?

Open for lunch Monday to Friday from 11:30 a.m. to 2:30 p.m., for brunch Saturday from 11 a.m. to 2:30 p.m. and Sunday from 10 a.m. to 3 p.m. Dinner is served daily, Sunday through Thursday from 5 to 10 p.m., Friday and Saturday to 11 p.m. No reservations except for groups of 10 or more.

There's fancy seaside dining galore, and then there's the great and simple food at **Aunt Kizzy's Back Porch**, 4325 Glencoe Ave., in the Villa Marina Shopping Center (tel. 213/578-1005), which lends credence to "all-American food is in." It's Southern home-cooked food prepared from time-honored recipes (collected from relatives and friends) that will keep your soul, body, and pocketbook intact. The chef is from Cleveland, Mississippi, and she has prepared regional Southern food for 36 years or more.

Nothing is easy to find in the shopping center. You'll find Aunt Kizzy's Back Porch easily if you face Vons (distinctive as you pull into the shopping center parking lot of Glencoe), walk to the right, cross the small driveway, and walk straight on toward a discreet red neon sign with the name of the restaurant.

Though Aunt Kizzy's has moved to larger quarters, they're still close to their original home and within the same shopping center. Fear not, Aunt Kizzy's has the same great food, now served in somewhat snazzier surroundings. Walls are wood paneled (board and batten), there is parquet flooring, a display of antique cooking utensils on a curio shelf, red-and-white checked tablecloths, lace café curtains, and simple wood chairs and tables. The walls are still covered with pictures of entertainers, and as you enter there's a composite scene of several great black performers (you can't miss Whoopi Goldberg). As always, the restaurant is busy.

And what food! For lunch any day of the week, you can have fried chicken, two vegetables, rice and gravy or cornbread dressing and gravy, plus cornbread muffins—all for $5.95. Depending on the day, that same $5.95 buys a choice of smothered steak, chicken and dumplings, some of the best smothered pork chops you've ever tasted, fried chicken, turkey wings and drumsticks with dressing, chicken pot pie, meat loaf, smothered liver and onions, or the fish of the day (Friday only). (There are lots of "smothereds" in Southern home-cooking.)

Specialties of the house (served Sunday only) are baked chicken with cornbread dressing or pungent barbecued beef ribs. As with most dishes on the dinner menu, these are $9.95. The dinner menu includes most of the lunch entrees plus (are you ready?) chicken Creole; chicken and sausage jambalaya; catfish with heavenly hush puppies (fried to order); Uncle Wade's baked beef short ribs—truly lean, meaty, and falling off the bone; red beans and rice and hot links; and for the noncarnivores—an all-vegetable plate. Take your pick—each is $9.95, except the catfish (it's delicious) at $10.95; the Rich Folk's meat loaf is $8.95; the red beans and rice and hot links, $6.95; and the vegetable plate, $5.95. Entrees include two vegetables (fresh steamed), rice or cornbread dressing, gravy and cornbread muffins. Old-Time Country Desserts are extra, but $2 will buy a soul-satisfying portion of Grandmother Zady's peach cobbler, Miss Flossie's floating sweet potato pie, or "Sock-it-to-me cake" filled with walnuts and cinnamon, and served warm.

There's a Sunday down-home brunch for $10.95, served buffet-style, that defies the capacity of most humans. How about some scrambled eggs with cheese or an omelet and a choice of bacon, sausage, grits, or grilled potatoes; possibly followed by smothered pork chops, barbecued beef ribs, or fried chicken (to name just three choices), plus a choice of five vegetables, topped off by peach cobbler or the "Sock-it-to-me cake." All this comes with fruit juice, tea, coffee, or milk. *Note:* No toting privileges.

And Showtime at Aunt Kizzy's is the late-night supper on Friday and Saturday. The Uptown Menu ranges from a short-rib sandwich to a salmon and spinach roulade, which is lightly grilled salmon on a bed of seasoned spinach that is rolled, then topped with a poached egg and a basil hollandaise sauce. There's also a superb hamburger with yam french fries, and some of the fluffiest blackberry pancakes you've ever had. Uptown Menu prices are $3.95 to $8.95. The Downtown Menu Late-Night Supper (otherwise known as a Southern-Style Breakfast) would take Aunt Kizzy's grandparents from the school bus to lunch or through a whole morning of farm chores. There's a fried catfish filet, smothered steak or pork chops, or fried chicken with beef sausage, pork sausage or bacon. All this comes with two eggs any style and biscuits, or toast, grits, or home fries. The single Downtown Menu price is $7.95.

Aunt Kizzy's doesn't serve beer or wine, but their ice-cold lemonade served in a Mason jar is just about the best possible complement for the down-home cooking. Aunt Kizzy's is open for lunch 11 a.m. to 4 p.m. Monday through Saturday, to 3 p.m. Sunday; dinner 4 to 10 p.m. Sunday through Thursday, to 11 p.m. Friday and Saturday.

At the above prices, you can understand that Aunt Kizzy's does not accept credit cards.

There's a superb dessert/food emporium I wouldn't want you to miss—**The Cheesecake Factory,** at 4142 Via Marina Way (tel.

213/306-3344). I've discussed the establishment in detail in Chapter V under "Beverly Hills," which just happens to come before "Marina del Rey." Forget the calories, just go there.

7. Redondo Beach

This oceanside resort is south of Santa Monica, Marina del Rey, and the Los Angeles International Airport. It was established by Henry E. Huntington, the railway tycoon. After a big land boom, the town settled into life as a modest beach resort with King Harbor, which now houses about 2,000 boats. It has always attracted fishermen, and more recently it has become industrial.

The Fisherman's Wharf pier is a maze of architecturally attractive restaurants, shops, and a concert auditorium. For a description of "concerts by the sea" presented here, refer to the nightlife details (Chapter VIII). The restaurants there feature not only seafood but an international cuisine including Polynesian, Mexican, and Japanese.

WHERE TO STAY

Portofino Inn, 260 Portofino Way, Redondo Beach, CA 90277 (tel. 213/379-8481, or toll free 800/338-2993, 800/468-4292 in California), is beautifully situated at the middle of King Harbor so that each of the 169 rooms and the two suites has a balcony overlooking either the yacht harbor or the ocean.

The hotel completed an extensive renovation in 1989, and all of the new accommodations are attractively decorated with furnishings of bleached woods complemented by muted tones of pink, rose, and gray. Each room has a color TV, radio, an honor mini-bar stocked with snacks and beverages, two-line direct-dial phone, and tub/shower bath. The inn provides a useful array of custom bath accessories (shampoo, soaps, hand and body lotions) and a plush bathrobe. Special touches include the complimentary morning newspaper and nightly turndown service.

The hotel also has 20 furnished apartments, each with a living room, one or two bedrooms, a complete kitchen including stove, range, microwave oven, full-size refrigerator, and convenient maid service. The apartments are available by the week or month.

Dining and drinking facilities include the Marina Café (obviously with a marvelous view of the marina), the Marina Grill, and the Marina Lounge. The café serves breakfast and lunch ($4 to $8.50) from 7 a.m. to 3 p.m. The grill serves dinner from 5 p.m. to 1 a.m.; specialties of the house are seafood, pasta, and ribs ($12 to $30). The lounge serves cocktails and hors d'oeuvres and has live entertainment and dancing Wednesday through Sunday from 9 p.m. to 2 a.m.

Portofino Inn has a heated outdoor pool that overlooks the ocean, plus a Jacuzzi. For somewhat more vigorous exercise, the inn has bicycles for the use of its guests. Complimentary health club facilities are just a block away. The inn is within walking distance of some famous beaches, the historic Redondo Pier, several fine restaurants, shops, even sportfishing, and it is only six miles from Los Angeles International Airport (LAX).

Rooms with a marina view are $115 to $135, single or double; with an ocean view $135 to $165; suites are $220. Apartment rates (on request) vary depending on the length of your stay; one week is the minimum.

WHERE TO DINE

The Red Onion, 655 N. Harbor Dr. (tel. 213/376-8813), is zany in concept: It's billed as a "Mexican Restaurant and Social Club." The decor is elaborate in the extreme, with slowly rotating fans suspended from bamboo ceilings; stucco walls hung with hundreds of photos of Mexico; an eclectic selection of chairs, many of them rattan and bamboo; an open brick-and-tile fireplace; Persian carpets; and lots and lots of plants. Though a bit overdone, it works well, and enhancing the ambience even more is the harbor view afforded from many tables.

The fare, in case you haven't guessed from the above description, is Mexican, and it's both tasty and plentiful. An amazing bargain here is the Happy Hour buffet served weekdays between 4 and 8 p.m. For the price of a drink you can eat all you want from a bountiful buffet of salads, rice, beans, enchiladas, tacos, chips, etc.

If you come at other times, or wish to have a regular sitdown meal while the buffet is going, there's an extensive menu. Best to order a margarita right away, and peruse at leisure. You might begin with an appetizer of guacamole. Then go on to one of the combination plates priced between $9 and $13, the latter for a deluxe order that includes a taco, enchilada verde, Spanish rice, and beans.

Another option is a hot entree for $10 to $15, like sea bass sautéed in lemon butter with shallots simmered in julienne tomato sauce, or arroz con pollo—a chicken-and-rice casserole. Both are served with soup or salad.

Open daily from 11 a.m. to 2 a.m. Food is served until 10 p.m.

8. The Wayfarers Chapel

Built on a cliff with a broad, steep face, the **Wayfarers Chapel,** 5755 Palos Verdes Dr. South (tel. 213/377-1650), in Rancho Palos Verdes, is a special oasis. In a spot above the lashing waves of the Pacific, Lloyd Wright, son of a more celebrated father (Frank Lloyd Wright), erected a chapel, leaning heavily on glass, redwood, and native stone, surrounded by lush gardens, to create a stunning effect.

The chapel is a memorial to Emanuel Swedenborg, the Stockholm-born 18th-century philosopher and theologian who claimed to have conversed with spirits and heavenly hosts in his visions.

Surrounding the building, and planted on the hillside, are rare plants, some of which are native to the Holy Land.

The "glass church" is open seven days a week from 9 a.m. to 5 p.m., charging no admission. Escorted tours can be arranged by calling the above number.

9. San Pedro

Farther down the beach is San Pedro, the port of Los Angeles. The partial setting for Richard Henry Dana's *Two Years Before the Mast,* it is nowadays a port handling an estimated two million tons of cargo every month.

PORTS O'CALL AND THE WHALER'S WHARF

In this port city the Ports O'Call and the Whaler's Wharf were created, the latter resembling 19th-century New Bedford, Massachusetts. The wharf has elm-shaded streets, simulating America's past. The shops are skillfully designed, recapturing brilliantly the atmosphere of a New England seacoast village. The 80 stores are shingled, colonial, with lantern lights, tavern signs, and small-paned windows. (For information about shopping here, see Chapter VII, Section 4.)

In a part of the village the promoters attempted to evoke Early California and seaports along the Mediterranean. The latter effect is achieved by bougainvillea and banana plants, bazaar stalls, abundant flowers, and luscious semitropical fruits.

Part of the fun is watching the steady stream of international shipping pass in and out of the port, along with yachts, tuna clippers, and fishing boats.

To reach the Ports O'Call, take the Harbor Freeway (Hwy. 11) to the Harbor Boulevard off-ramp and turn right. The village is at Berth 77 (tel. 213/831-0287). The admission-free village and wharf are open from 11 a.m. to 9 p.m. daily.

There are harbor cruises with **Mardi Gras Cruises** (tel. 213/548-1085 for information).

From January to March **L.A. Harbor Sportfishing,** 1150 Nagoya Way, Berth 79, San Pedro, CA 90731 (tel. 213/547-9916), offers whale-watching cruises. Throughout the year they have half-day, three-quarter-day, and all-day sportfishing charters. If you'd like to know the kind and number of fish they caught the previous day, call 213/547-1318. In addition, there are helicopter rides (Saturday and Sunday only) departing every few minutes from Whaler's Wharf. For information, call 213/831-1073.

For meals, you can stop off at the **Ports O'Call Restaurant,** at Berth 76 (tel. 213/833-3553). Lunch offerings at $9 to $14 include a steak sandwich, Hawaiian glazed ribs, and sautéed filet of snapper, all served with chowder or salad. At dinner you can order such dishes as a Java seafood curry with scallops, shrimps, crabmeat, lobster, and condiments for $14 to $22. Another good dish is baby ribs of pork glazed with a South Pacific sauce. A fine dessert is the chocolate mousse. In addition to wines, exotic rum drinks with names like Tonga Cooler and Bird of Paradise are available. A red Chinese junk is moored in a charming pond near the footbridge to the entrance. Lunch (brunch on Sunday) and dinner are served daily. The restaurant is open daily. Lunch, Monday through Saturday, is from 11 a.m. to 3 p.m.; dinner, Monday through Thursday, from 4 to 11 p.m., Friday and Saturday to midnight; Sunday brunch is from 10 to 2:30 p.m., dinner from 4 to 10 p.m.

An alternative suggestion is **Whiskey Joe's,** Berth 75 (tel. 213/831-0181), a re-creation of a 19th-century waterside pub, situated at the extreme end of the village. Set apart as it is by a little bridge, it misses much of the usual tourist jam. The façade is weathered clapboard and shingle—a northeastern look.

There are five places at which to dine and drink, plus a deck bar with open fireplaces, and a brick terrace on the waterside. Lunch (and brunch on Sunday) and dinner are served seven days a week. Dinner offerings ($14 to $25) include steak, shrimp, mussels, clams, which are accompanied by red-skin potatoes and corn on the cob, plus burgers, chops and chili.

Whiskey Joe's is open weekdays from 10 a.m. to 10 p.m., weekends to 11 p.m.

10. Long Beach

Combining beach resort attractions with oil derricks, Long Beach (20 miles south of Los Angeles on San Pedro Bay), is the home of the **Queen Mary** (tel. 213/435-3511), at the terminus of Pier J in Long Beach Harbor at the end of the Long Beach freeway (Hwy. 710). She completed her final voyage on December 9, 1967, after a 14,500-mile journey that took her around South America via Cape Horn.

The City of Long Beach purchased the vessel at a cost of $3.5 million and has since been billing her as "81,000 tons of fun." The three-hour guided tour takes visitors to an engine room complete with 40,000-horsepower turbines, pipes, pumps, and paraphernalia; the aft steering station; the "viewing room" built around the 18-foot, 35-ton propellor; a restored crew bunkroom as well as officers' quarters; the first-class swimming pool; gold bullion room; the brig; the three-deck-high Queen's Salon; re-creations of the three classes of shipboard accommodations and the contrasting GI quarters used when 800,000 troops were transported by the *Queen Mary* in World War II; and much more.

Next to the *Queen Mary,* under an aluminum dome, is Howard Hughes's fabulous flop, the all-wood 200-ton **Spruce Goose.** It's the largest plane ever built; it was intended to be a troop carrier during World War II—but it barely got off the ground. It has a 320-foot wingspan—that's longer than a football field! In fact there's room for a DC-10 under each wing.

The *Spruce Goose* is now retired and serving as a tourist attraction. Visitors can look into the cockpit and the hold, which was designed to hold 750. There's also a film of the *Goose's* first flight. A special platform built adjacent to the *Goose* allows visitors to see the cockpit, cargo area, and flight deck up close. Surrounding the mammoth plane is a variety of unique displays and audio-visual presentations on the plane's construction, its one-and-only flight, and Howard Hughes's aviation career.

Tickets to these attractions—the *Queen Mary* and the *Spruce Goose*—are $18 for adults, $10 for children 5 to 11 years, under 5 it's free. The sights are open from 10 a.m. to 6 p.m. (the ticket booth closes at 5:30 p.m.). Parking is $4.

Special exhibits include the ship's sound and light show in the Engine Room, re-enacting a near-collision at sea. There's also an extensive World War II display depicting the *Queen's* active role as a troop ship. And if you're at all interested in model-ship building, you'll find a fine exhibit in the Hall of Maritime Heritage.

You can also dine aboard the *Queen Mary* in one of three restaurants (tel. 213/435-3511). The **Chelsea** specializes in fish and seafood. Fare in the **Promenade Café** runs to a variety of entrees. Breakfast, lunch, and dinner are served. The **Sir Winston** serves dinner only; it's basically a steak and seafood house that also features flambé desserts (jackets and ties required for men).

There are many shops aboard ship, and **Londontowne Shopping Village** (designed to look like an English village), with about 25 shops, adjoins. And should you wish to stay overnight, there's even a 365-room hotel on board, the **Hotel Queen Mary** (tel. 213/435-3511, or toll free 800/421-3732). The rooms are actually the original first-class cabins, with many of the luxurious old furnishings plus all modern amenities—phone, air conditioning, color TV, etc. Singles or doubles are $100 to $145; suites, $190 to $650. Parking is $4.

And while you're visiting the *Queen*, head ashore for the **Brighton Carnival.** It's an old-fashioned English fair with all kinds of fun, from rides on a ferris wheel and double-tiered carousel to performances by jugglers, a one-man musical band, death-defying high divers, live musical revues, and a 1939 auto show.

11. Catalina Island

Cove-fringed Catalina lies about 26 miles off the California shoreline. On a clear day you can see it from Long Beach. Noted for its flying fish and porpoises, as well as its undersea gardens, its rise as a resort began when it was purchased in 1919 by William Wrigley, of chewing gum fame. So different is Catalina from the rest of Los Angeles, or, for that matter, from the rest of California, that it almost seems like a foreign country. Because of its geographic separation from the mainland, it actually has evolved indigenous plant life. Part of its uniqueness is due to a determination on the part of residents to keep their lazy island retreat from becoming touristy.

Ownership of 86% of the island by the Santa Catalina Island Conservancy has helped to preserve the island's natural resources. Many people from nearby L.A. have never even visited the place. Nevertheless, its hotels are always filled with in-the-know visitors, so if you plan to stay, reserve early. If you can't stay for a restful week or two, at least plan to spend a day; it will be a memorable part of your Los Angeles vacation.

Catalina offers many resort attractions: miles of hiking and biking trails; camping (by permit only), golf, tennis, and horseback-riding facilities; boating, superb fishing, swimming, scuba-diving, and snorkeling; the above-mentioned undersea gardens; and the picturesque town of Avalon, the island's only city.

GETTING THERE

The **Catalina Express** (tel. 213/519-1212, or toll free 800/257-2227 in California) operates daily year round to Catalina from San Pedro, Long Beach, and in season (about mid-June to Labor Day) from Redondo Beach. They make 19 daily departures; the boat trip takes about an hour. Fares from San Pedro are $14 one way, $13 for seniors, $11 for children 2 to 11, 75¢ for infants. Long Beach/Redondo fares are about $2 higher for all except infants, which stays at 75¢. All round trips are double these fares. The Catalina Express departs from the Sea/Air Terminal at Berth 95, Port of L.A. in San Pedro; in Long Beach from the Catalina Express Port at the *Queen Mary;* and in Redondo from the Catalina Express Port at 161 N. Harbor Dr. Reservations can be made by calling either of the above numbers.

Note: On the Catalina Express, there are very specific baggage limitations. Luggage is limited to 50 pounds per person. If you plan to camp, a camping permit can be obtained from L.A. County (tel. 213/510-0688) or Catalina Cover & Camp (tel. 213/510-0303). Reservations are necessary for bicycles, surfboards, dive tanks, etc. The U.S. Coast Guard prohibits carrying certain commodities on passenger vessels; if you have any questions about what you can take, ask before you arrive for the trip. There are also specific restrictions in transporting domestic pets, so, again, ask.

Service to Catalina is also offered by **Catalina Cruises** from Long Beach and Berth 95 in San Pedro (tel. 213/775-6111), the **Catalina Flyer Catamaran** at the Balboa Pavilion in Newport Beach (tel. 714/673-5245), **California Cruisin'** from San Diego (tel. 619/235-8600), and the **Helitrans Helicopter Service** at Berth 95 in San Pedro (tel. 213/548-1314).

INFORMATION AND TOURS

When you arrive in Avalon, head for the **Catalina Island Chamber of Commerce** on the Green Pleasure Pier (tel. 213/510-1520). They have maps, brochures, and complete information on all of the island's attractions and activities. You can also call them for information and direct phone lines to hotels, boat transportation, sightseeing companies, or to find out about any aspect of the island's offerings. For an extremely useful free 48-page brochure, including a calendar of events, write to the Catalina Island Chamber of Commerce, P.O. Box 217, Avalon, CA 90704.

The **Visitor's Information Center**, just a minute away on Metropole Street, across from the Green Pleasure Pier (tel. 213/510-2000, or toll free 800/428-2566 in California), handles sightseeing tours. These include the one-hour **Skyline Drive** ($10.50 for adults, $9.50 for seniors, $7 for children 5 to 11) and the 50-minute **Scenic Terrace Drive** ($5 for adults, $4.50 for seniors, $3.50 for children). On the 3¾-hour **Inland Motor Tour** ($19.50 for adults, $18 for seniors, $12.50 for children) you'll see pure-bred Arabian horses and possibly buffalo, deer, goats, and boars. The 40-minute **Casino Tour** ($6 for adults, $5 for seniors, $4 for children) explores Catalina's most famous landmark. Not to be missed is the 40-minute **Glass-Bottom Boat Trip** to view Catalina's exquisite undersea gardens and colorful fish. By day the trip is $5.25 for adults, $4.50 for seniors, and $3.50 for children; at night it's $6.25 for adults, $5.50 for seniors, and $4 for children. For the combination package of the Skyline Drive and Glass-Bottom Boat trip, the prices are $14 for adults, $12.75 for seniors and $9.50 for children. Then there's the 55-minute **Coastal Cruise** to Seal Rocks, where you'll see sea lions at play in their natural habitat ($5 for adults, $4.50 for seniors, $3.50 for children); and the one-hour **Flying Fish Boat Trip** ($6.25 for adults, $5.50 for seniors, $4 for children), during which an occasional flying fish lands right on the boat!

There also are three lovely dining cruises. The **Sunset Buffet Cruise** (May through September) takes you aboard a historic paddle-wheeler along Catalina's coastline. Cocktails are served plus a scrumptious buffet and you'll dance to the music of the '50s and '60s. The **Twilight Dining at Two Harbors Cruise** (June through September) packages some of the nicest things about Catalina into one evening. The cruise makes its way along Catalina's coastline to dinner at Doug's Harbor Reef Restaurant, with complimentary wine or beer, music, and a flying fish trip on the way home. The Sunset Buffet Cruise is on Wednesday, Friday, and Saturday; the Twilight Dining at Two Harbors Cruise is on Tuesday and Thursday. Both cruises are $35 for adults, $32.50 for seniors, and $20 for children.

And finally, to get about town on your own, you can rent a U-Drive (a cross between a Jeep and a golf cart) or bicycle (the former for licensed drivers only, the latter for those with good leg muscles) at rental agencies on the Crescent and throughout Avalon. You cannot, however, drive into the island's interior with either of these vehicles.

Consider this about Catalina: The island's residents have a 10-year wait to get a permit to own a car, one interesting solution to the air pollution problem on the mainland.

Since you aren't permitted to drive into the island, the tours are a must if you really wish to explore.

WHERE TO STAY

There are about 30 hotels on the island, none of them in any way modern or luxurious. They are simple, untouristy affairs—not even quaint or charming especially—the kind of places you might expect to find in an unsophisticated English seaside village. Nevertheless, in summer they often achieve 100% occupancy, so reserve in advance.

Most famous is the **Zane Grey Pueblo Hotel,** located off Chimes Tower Road, P.O. Box 216, Avalon, CA 90704 (tel. 213/510-0966), former home of the novelist, who spent his last 20 years in Avalon. Nestled high in the mountains, and offering dramatic ocean views, it is probably the most beautifully situated hotel you'll ever see. Most of the rooms have large windows to let you take in the spectacular scenery, which is just as well because the interiors are nothing to rave about. Vaguely American Indian in theme, they all have private baths (mostly showers), but no phones or TVs. There's a swimming pool and sundeck with "the view," ditto the patio out back.

Summer rates, including Continental breakfast, are $95 to $115 for one or two people, lower amounts the rest of the year.

Innkeepers Martin and Bernadine Curtin have considerably upped the standards of Catalina hotel aesthetics at their **Island Inn,** 125 Metropole St. (just a half block from Crescent), P.O. Box 467, Avalon, CA 90704 (tel. 213/510-1623). Their 36 rooms are tastefully painted in pale blue-gray, a quiet background for the blue carpeting and floral-design blue-and-peach bedspreads. Stained-glass lighting fixtures and shuttered windows add further charm. Even the hallways are cheerful and pretty. All of the rooms have private baths (some with tubs, all with showers), and color TV; most have AM/FM radio. There are no phones, but the desk will take messages. Some have king-size beds, sliding glass doors, and balconies with ocean views. The Curtins provide transportation from the boat (though it isn't very far) and complimentary coffee, juice, and specialty bread in the lobby. There are ice and soda machines in the hall.

May to September, rates for one or two people are $80 to $160, the latter for rooms with ocean views. A room with two queen-size beds that can accommodate up to four people is $145; a balconied mini-suite, also accommodating up to four, $185. October to May, rooms are $30 less, excluding holidays and weekends.

The **Catalina Canyon Hotel,** 888 Country Club Dr., Avalon, CA 90704 (tel. 213/510-0325, toll free 800/253-9361 from Los Angeles only), is set on beautifully landscaped grounds in the foothills of Avalon. There are 80 guest rooms, tastefully decorated and comfortably furnished. All include a tub/shower bath, color TV, AM/FM radio, phone, and a balcony overlooking the outdoor pool and Jacuzzi. The Canyon Restaurant is on the premises for breakfast and lunch, and offers a Continental dinner menu. Room service is available. Cocktails may be enjoyed in the lounge or on the outdoor terrace overlooking the pool. The hotel is adjacent to a golf course and tennis courts, and the courtesy van meets guests at the air and sea terminals.

Rooms are $135 to $165, single or double, based on location and season; $10 for each additional person.

The little **Hotel MacRae,** 409 Crescent, P.O. Box 1517, Avalon, CA 90704 (tel. 213/510-0246), is a pleasant second-floor hostelry right across the street from the beach. It's decorated in brilliant colors—parrot green, orange, yellow, red, and white. There are 23 rooms here, with a wide range of accommodations. Each room has a private bath, color TV, and heater for chilly nights.

A complimentary Continental breakfast is offered every morning, and wine, cheese, and crackers are served in the evening. In the center of the hotel is a large open-air courtyard, perfect for lounging or sunning.

Rates are $65 to $100 for a standard single or double room, $100 to $200 for suites. Kitchen units are available.

WHERE TO DINE

Restaurants, like hotels in Catalina, tend toward an almost affected unpretentiousness. There are several places to eat in and around the Crescent.

The **Busy Bee,** 306 Crescent, at the end of Metropole (tel. 213/510-1983), has been an Avalon institution since 1923. In all those years it's undergone numerous changes. The photos of its incarnations and reincarnations are on the wall of one dining area. Currently the Busy Bee sits on the beach directly over the water. You can eat outside on a great wrap-around patio (perfect for summer lunches), or choose the indoor room furnished with ceiling fans, plants, and tables. Even from here you have a terrific view of the bay through picture windows.

The fare is light deli-style. Breakfast, lunch, and dinner are served all day. The day starts with omelets, five variations on eggs Benedict, and other breakfast dishes for $5 to $10. Throughout the day there are over 80 items to choose from, including sandwiches, salads, Mexican specialties, and pasta. Some of the more popular items are the Chinese chicken salad, Buffalo burger, and a mammoth one-pound hamburger. The Busy Bee grinds its own beef daily and cuts its own potatoes for french fries; salad dressings are also made on the premises. The tab for these tasty dishes ranges from $7 to $17. All this with a harbor view.

The Busy Bee is open daily from 8 a.m. to 10 p.m. in summer, to 11 p.m. on weekends; winter hours are 8 a.m. to 8 p.m. daily.

El Galleon, 411 Crescent (tel. 213/510-1188), is a large, warm, woody nautical affair, with portholes, rigging, anchors, wrought-iron chandeliers, tufted-leather booths, and tables with captain's chairs. There's additional balcony seating and outdoor café tables overlooking the ocean harbor. In summer, the luncheon menu offers fresh seafood, burgers, steak, stews, salads, and sandwiches at $6 to $12. The dinner menu features a goodly assortment of seafood items, like cioppino, fresh swordfish steak, and broiled Catalina lobster tails with drawn butter. There are also a number of nonseafood entrees, ranging from country fried chicken and beef Stroganoff to broiled rack of lamb. Dinner prices range from $10 to $25.

El Galleon is open for lunch from 11:30 a.m. to 2:30 p.m. and for dinner from 5 to 10 p.m. The bar is open from 10 a.m. to 1:30 a.m.

The **Sand Trap,** on Avalon Canyon Rd., just past La Casitas on the way to Memorial Gardens (tel. 213/510-1349), is a local favorite and offers an escape from the Front Street crowds. They serve breakfast, lunch, and snacks that can be enjoyed while looking out over the golf course. The specialties of the house are delectable omelets served till noon and soft tacos served all day. The omelets ($4.95 to $5.50) come with a variety of ingredients like homemade chorizo, or the hearty machaca omelet with spicy shredded beef, Cheddar, sour cream and salsa. The soft tacos ($4.50 to $5.75) offer a choice of fillings, any one of which may make life more enjoyable or at least carry you to dinner with a smile. All in all, the fare can satisfy almost any appetite from burgers to sandwiches, salads, chili ($2.50 to $6.25). Beverages include orange-spiced iced tea, beer, wine, and wine coolers. The Sand Trap is open daily from 7:30 a.m. to 3 p.m.

The **Cafe Prego,** 603 Crescent (tel. 213/510-1218), serves excellent Italian dinners nightly in a rather charming setting of latticework and plants. You can eat well for $11 and up, including soup, salad, pasta, and entree.

The **Dock Café** (tel. 213/510-2755) is directly across from the Casino right at the dock. During the summer it's open daily from 8 a.m. to 7 p.m., weekends the rest of the year. You can sit on the deck, have breakfast, a snack, or a drink, and view the bay and boats that come up to the fuel dock.

The Dock Café serves a breakfast burrito for which there's a lengthy list of tasty accompaniments. If you've never had a burrito for breakfast, you've missed one of life's great start-the-day enjoyments. If you prefer, stick with basic scrambled eggs served with corn tortillas and potatoes or refried beans, granola with yogurt and sliced bananas. Lunch is served all day. There are salads and such sandwiches as a roasted chicken breast on grilled sourdough bread and the one I always have trouble resisting, hot pastrami on a french roll.

Specialties of the house include chicken guacamole tacos, fish tacos, and a crispy tostada with chicken. The Dock Café also has snack ribs, messy and great. Whether you're reviewing the breakfast, lunch, or snack menu, most dishes will cost between $3 and $6. Top price on the menu goes to the tacos ($5.75 to $6.25). As to beverages you will find the usual plus such interesting combinations as cocoa/coffee, and "the blend," a mix of lemonade and iced tea. There's also beer, wine, coolers, as well as the Dock's own sangria.

---

12. Newport Beach

About 35 miles south of Los Angeles, this beautiful resort and yacht harbor (embracing **Balboa** as well) nests on a sandy beach strip opening onto the Pacific. Sheltered in the bay between the sand bar and the mainland are Balboa Island and Lido Isle.

A major point in your exploration should be the **Balboa Pavilion,** at 400 Main St., with its much-photographed landmark cupola.

Established in 1905, it was once a fashionable spot for Mack Sennet-type bathing-beauty contests. Redecorated in 1969, it is the setting for the yearly "Flight of the Snowbirds," and attracts fishermen, sightseers, and hungry diners.

From the Pavilion you can take a ferry to **Balboa Island,** the ride costing 75¢ for cars, 30¢ for adult passengers.

The best way to see the bay is to buy a ticket for a narrated harbor cruise. In summer, there are several trips daily leaving from the **Fun Zone Boat Co.** (tel. 714/673-0240) near the ferry landing. Some of the waterfront homes you pass are owned by motion-picture and TV stars. A 45-minute cruise costs $6 for adults, $5 for seniors, and $1.50 for children 5 to 12 (under 5, free); and a special 90-minute cruise costs $8 for adults, $7 for seniors, and $2 for children.

For information on all Newport Beach activities, stop in at the **Newport Beach Chamber of Commerce,** 1470 Jamboree Rd., at Santa Barbara Drive (tel. 714/644-8211). They're very helpful and some of the nicest people around.

WHERE TO STAY

A major luxury resort is the 400-room **Newport Beach Marriott Hotel & Tennis Club,** 900 Newport Center Dr., Newport Beach, CA 92660 (tel. 714/640-4000, or toll free 800/228-9290). It features the latest mode in hotel architecture—rooms centered around a nine-story atrium and interior balconies hung with ivy and bougainvillea vines. The focal point of the courtyard is a 19th-century Italian Renaissance–style fountain.

All rooms contain oversize beds, color TV, AM/FM radio (both with bedside remote control), direct-dial phone, and tub/shower bath; irons and ironing boards are available upon request. Room decor is striking.

Facilities include two swimming pools and hydrotherapy pools on a palm-lined sundeck, and eight tennis courts (all of them lit for night play), a health club, with adjoining locker room, pro shop, and snack bar. Behind the hotel is the Newport Beach Country Club with an 18-hole golf course, which guests can use. Fashion Island, with four movie theaters, a playground, about 75 shops, and 15 restaurants, is just across the street.

And speaking of restaurants, there are two fine eateries right on the premises. Nicole's Grill, serving the freshest and best in beef and fish, is open for lunch and dinner, as is J. W.'s Sea Grill, serving fresh seafood and American favorites.

Rates at the Marriott are $159 to $179 single, $175 to $195 double.

The **Sheraton Newport,** 4545 MacArthur Blvd. (at Birch Street just ½ mile south of the John Wayne/Orange County Airport.), Newport Beach, CA 92660 (tel. 714/833-0570), or toll free 800/325-3535), has its rooms centered around a courtyard lobby, with ivy-draped balconies reaching seven stories upward to a skylight roof. There are 342 rooms in all, and five beautifully appointed suites, decorated with flair in three colors—mauve, teal, and lavender. Furnishings are oak, with two leather armchairs in each room, and amenities range from color TV to modern bath.

Facilities include two night-lighted tennis courts which guests can use at no charge, a heated swimming pool, whirlpool, use of an 18-hole golf course just five minutes from the hotel, and three restaurants. These are the Palm Garden, offering a steak and seafood menu at lunch and dinner, the Boardwalk Café, a garden-ambience eatery with a skylight roof serving breakfast, lunch and dinner; and the Palm Court for lunch only. There's also the Reefwalker, featuring live music for dancing Monday to Saturday nights.

The Sheraton charges $110 to $145 single, $120 to $155 double, including full buffet breakfast daily, and an evening cocktail party. There are inexpensive weekend packages, including all hotel amenities, for a two-night stay (Friday and Saturday or Saturday and Sunday) at various times throughout the year. Be sure to ask.

Before these two luxury chains planted hotels here, the premier choice was **The Hyatt Newporter,** 1107 Jamboree Rd. (near Backbay Road), Newport Beach, CA 92660 (tel. 714/729-1234, or toll free 800/223-1234). A resortlike complex par excellence, it's still a hub of activity in Newport Beach, and has been renovated to the tune of over $30 million. Facilities include three swimming pools, a children's pool, three whirlpools, a nine-hole golf course, shops, and concierge. The John Wayne Tennis Club on the grounds offers 16 night-lighted championship courts, spa equipment, steam, sauna, and clubhouse. In addition, several 18-hole championship golf courses are located nearby.

The Jamboree Café serves breakfast, lunch, and dinner daily. Classical French cuisine is the highlight of The Wine Cellar as featured in six prix fixe menus, rotated weekly; each five-course menu offers a choice of three entrees. The Wine Cellar is open for dinner Tuesday through Saturday from 6 to 10 p.m. The restaurant has limited seating and reservations are suggested. Dinner is also served at the intimate new Ristorante Cantori.

As for the 410 rooms at the Hyatt Newporter, all are decorated in pastel tones with contemporary furnishings. All have balconies or terraces, and direct-dial phones, color TVs with remote control, in-room movies, oversize beds, radios, and tub/shower baths. Singles are $150 to $170; doubles $170 to $190; suites, $325 to $475. The most luxurious accommodations here are one- to three-bedroom villas complete with wood-burning fireplaces and private swimming pools ($575 to $1,000 a night).

For less expensive accommodations, you might consider staying in the quaint town of Laguna Beach (see below). But whether you stay in Laguna or Newport, be sure to book your room far in advance for the summer, when both towns are packed.

WHERE TO DINE

The Cannery, 3010 Lafayette Ave., at Lido Park Drive (tel. 714/675-5777), is housed in a remodeled 1934 fish cannery that used to turn out 5,000 cases of swordfish and mackerel a day. Now a historical landmark, the two-story restaurant is a favorite spot for locals and tourists alike—for good food, a colorful atmosphere, and friendly service. In the upper lounge tables surround a corner platform where there's live entertainment Wednesday to Saturday from 8:30 p.m.

Fresh fish and local abalone are specialties here. At dinner there's always a super-fresh chef's special catch of the day. Other good choices are eastern beef, chicken champignon, and shrimp scampi. Dinner entrees cost $16 to $22. At lunch you might ask for the house special of the day, shrimp and fries, or sandwiches and salads for $5 to $10. Sunday champagne brunch is popular at $12 to $15, depending on the entree you select. The restaurant also serves a champagne buffet brunch while you cruise Newport Harbor aboard the Cannery's *Isla Mujeres*. The cost is $30. There is a Friday and Sunday champagne dinner cruise for $59.50.

The Cannery is open Monday to Saturday for lunch from 11:30 a.m. to 3 p.m., on Sunday for brunch from 10 a.m. to 2:30 p.m., and for dinner nightly from 5 to 10 p.m. The seafood bar offers a limited menu until midnight. Reservations are advised.

Chanteclair, 18912 MacArthur Blvd., opposite the Airport Terminal between Campus Drive and Douglas (tel. 714/752-8001), is designed like a provincial French inn. A rambling stucco structure with a mansard roof, built around a central garden court, it houses several dining and drinking areas: a grand and petit salon, a boudoir, a *bibliothèque,* a garden area with a skylight room, and a hunting-lodge-like lounge. Furnished in antiques, it has five fireplaces.

The cuisine is Continental. At lunch you might order double-ribbed lamb chops, creamed chicken in pastry, or steak tartare for $12 to $20.

Dinner is an experience in fine dining—a worthwhile splurge, with entrees costing $19 to $30. You might begin with the game bird and pistachio pâté, or perhaps an order of beluga caviar with blinis and garniture (if you have to ask, you can't afford it). I'm also partial to the salads—a spinach salad flambé or hearts of palm. For an entree I recommend the rack of lamb served with a bouquetière of fresh vegetables and potatoes Dauphine. There's a considerable listing of domestic and imported wines to complement your meal; if you don't know what to select, the captain will be happy to help you choose. A soufflé Grand-Marnier is the perfect dessert, which should be ordered ahead.

Chanteclair is open for lunch weekdays and Sunday from 11:30 a.m. to 2:30 p.m., for dinner nightly from 6 to 10 p.m. Reservations are essential.

Marrakesh, 1100 W. Pacific Coast Hwy., near Dover Drive (tel. 714/645-8384), is a variation on the theme of Dar Maghreb, a Moroccan restaurant previously described in Chapter V. The decor is exotic, with dining areas divided into intimate tents furnished with Persian carpets and authentic Moroccan pieces. Moroccan music enhances the exotic ambience. Seating is on low cushioned sofas, and the entire meal is eaten without silverware—you use your hands! It's something of a ritual feast, which begins, appropriately enough, when a server comes around to wash your hands. Everyone in your party shares the same meal—an eight- or nine-course feast priced at $18 to $26 per person. It consists of Moroccan soup, a tangy salad that is scooped up with hunks of fresh bread, b'stila (a chicken-filled pastry topped with cinnamon), or kotban (a lamb shish kebab marinated in olive oil, coriander, cumin and garlic), a choice of four entrees (baked squab with rice and almonds, baked chicken with lemon and olives, baked fish in a piquant sauce, or rabbit in garlic sauce), lamb and vegetables with couscous, fresh fruits, tea, and Moroccan pastries.

Open for dinner daily from 5 to 11 p.m. Reservations suggested.

Reuben E. Lee, 151 E. Pacific Coast Hwy., near Bayside Drive (tel. 714/675-5790), is a free-floating replica of the famous Mississippi riverboat *Robert E. Lee.*

Blue-and-white awnings shelter the gangplanks outside, and the promenade decks have turn-of-the-century ornate cut-out wood trim.

The restaurant specializes in fresh fish, shellfish, steaks, and prime rib, all of which are prepared to perfection. A featured entree is the New Orleans bouillabaisse, a tasty concoction made with whole shrimp, lobsters, scallops, clams, fresh fish filet, and crab legs, all skillfully blended with tomato sauce and laced with wine. Steaks and prime rib come in all sizes and for all tastes. Dinner entrees cost $14 to $28. At lunch sandwiches, salads, and hot entrees are in the $9 to $14 range.

On Sunday the champagne brunch is not to be believed. There is a spectacular buffet: Whatever you enjoy or have ever wanted for brunch is probably there, plus all the champagne you'd like, and a glass of schnapps to boot. The spread is $17.95 for adults, $9.95 for children—and worth every penny. The Sea Food Deck is open Monday through Sunday for lunch from 11:30 a.m. to 3 p.m. and for dinner from 4:30 to 10 p.m. for dinner. Sunday brunch is from 10 a.m. to 3 p.m.

---

13. Laguna Beach

Laguna (about six miles from Newport Beach via Pacific Coast Highway) has long been the gathering point for painters, potters, sculptors, and other artists who have created a colorful colony where the leisure life reigns supreme. Its boutiques, galleries, little theaters, and coffeehouses date from about the same time that Greenwich Village began attracting attention as a haven for New York's artists. Tall eucalyptus trees, palms, and bougainvillea grow abundantly.

For a rundown on the town's many attractions and frequent festivals, stop in at the **Laguna Beach Chamber of Commerce,** 357 Glenneyre St., at Laguna Avenue (tel. 714/494-1018). The staff here can answer all your questions, and you can also pick up maps and a helpful publication called *This Week in Laguna*. There's much to do in Laguna; don't miss it. In summer, be sure to reserve hotel rooms far in advance.

WHERE TO STAY

Capri Laguna, 1441 S. Coast Hwy. (between Mountain Road and Calliope Street), Laguna Beach, CA 92651 (tel. 714/494-6533, or toll free 800/225-4551), is a five-story, 42-room hostelry facing a sandy beach. Almost all rooms open onto balconies or patios, some private. Many units have complete kitchens, dining areas, and ocean views, and all are equipped with direct-dial phones, color TVs, and tub/shower baths. They're pleasantly furnished. There is no elevator, so if you must have a room on a lower floor, be sure to make your need known. Also, there is no air conditioning. The courtyard contains a small outdoor swimming pool and sauna. In 1989 new beachfront sundecks were added. And across the highway is a shopping complex of boutiques, art galleries, and studios.

Rates, which include a complimentary Continental breakfast, vary widely. In high season (mid-June to mid-September) one or two people pay $75 to $250 for a room, depending on location (some with kitchenette). For a studio with kitchenette and double or queen-size bed plus hide-a-bed couch (the studio sleeps up to four), you pay $120 to $180. The balance of the year (low season), rates drop to $60 to $150. Additional persons in a room pay $10.

The **Inn at Laguna Beach,** 211 N. Coast Hwy. (near Cliff Drive), Laguna Beach, CA 92651 (tel. 714/497-9722, or toll free 800/544-4479), is right on the beach, and about two-thirds of its 37 rooms offer ocean views. They're standard modern accommodations, well equipped and comfortable with paintings or prints adorning the white walls. All have color TV, direct-dial phone, and tub/shower bath, and some have a complete kitchen. Upper-floor rooms face out on a large sundeck with umbrella tables and chaises longues. There's a pool with a sundeck overlooking the ocean.

Rates for one or two people in high season (mid-May to mid-September) are $139 to $249 depending on the view. The rates drop to $99 to $199 off-season.

Laguna Beach Motor Inn, 985 N. Coast Hwy. (at the corner of Fairview Avenue), Laguna Beach, CA 92651 (tel. 714/494-5294), is right on the coast road, with oceanside terraces, plus a 20-by 40-foot outdoor swimming pool and a secluded beach cove. It's a quiet retreat with a patio garden ideal for sunny breakfasts. The 22 rooms have color cable TVs and shower baths, but no phones; eight units have kitchens. In summer they cost $85, single or double; $5 for an extra person. The rest of the year rooms are $58 to $65.

One of the most luxurious digs in town, replete with casual elegance, is the **Surf and Sand Hotel,** 1555 S. Coast Hwy. (a mile south of Laguna Canyon Road), Laguna Beach, CA 92651 (tel. 714/497-4477, or toll free 800/524-8621), with 160 units situated in four buildings. The remodeled guest rooms are attractively done in restful sand tones with raw silk fabrics, and beautifully finished with plantation shutters. A few of the very nice touches are the marbled entries and baths, and stocked honor bars. Each room receives a lovely basket of niceties for the bath and there is turndown service each evening. Most rooms have a private balcony overlooking the ocean. There is a Concierge Desk and the Surf & Sand Shopping Village is on the premises. In addition to being right on the beach, the hotel has a heated swimming pool and sundeck.

Two handsome restaurants are on the premises. The elegant Towers Restaurant, as the name implies, offers a spectacular panoramic view of the pounding surf from both below and above—in the mirrored ceiling. The decor is gorgeous too—a cool green-and-brown art deco—and there's an adjoining piano lounge for pre- or post-dining pleasantries. Breakfast, lunch, and dinner are served daily in the Towers Restaurant, which specializes in contemporary French cuisine with a fresh California touch. A new beachfront restaurant, scheduled to open in mid-1991, will allow guests to enjoy casual dining in the oyster bar or the California-style dining room.

In high season (May 1 to Labor Day) rates for one or two people range from $170 to $225, $150 to $210 the rest of the year. Penthouses and suites are also available. High season rates are $390 to $500, otherwise $300 to $440.

WHERE TO DINE

The Cottage, 308 N. Pacific Coast Hwy., at Aster Street (tel. 714/494-3023), is a landmark—a time-worn Early California frame building with an Oriental roof. A tall star pine tree shades the patio garden. The interior is pretty and quaint, furnished with lovely antiques. For example, the table lamps were originally made for the Del Coronado Hotel in San Diego at the turn of the century. The theater seats served for 40 years in the Laguna Playhouse. Be sure to see the photographic collection in the waiting room. Other walls are decorated with original oils by local artists.

Open from 7 a.m. to 3 p.m. and 5 to 10 p.m. daily, the Cottage serves very good food. There's a wide choice of breakfast fare, running the gamut from an omelet filled with cheddar cheese, fresh mushrooms, and avocado, served with cottage fries, toast, and jam, to three slices of extra-thick french toast with bacon or sausages. Lunch and dinner choices include sandwiches, burgers, and salads. A full dinner of spinach lasagne or roast duck glazed in orange sauce comes with soup or salad, potatoes or brown rice, vegetables, and a dinner roll, for $9 to $15. For dessert there's pecan pie à la mode. Beer is available, as well as a nice selection of California varietal wines. Reservations are essential, even at breakfast, during summer and on holidays.

14. La Jolla

"La Hoya" (that's how it's pronounced) is an oceanside residential portion of the coast, at the northern edge of San Diego. It successfully retains its "old-money" image, although adventurous young people are moving in on the coterie of millionaires, Navy families, and retired citizens. For half a century the wealthy have been building beautiful retirement estates here, having selected the site for its lushness and rugged coastline, its beaches and cultural facilities. Along Prospect Avenue, running parallel to the coast, are about five blocks of boutiques, shops, restaurants, cafés, and art galleries. A tasteful, restful, interesting place to visit.

The **Scripps Aquarium Museum,** 8602 La Jolla Shores Dr. (tel. 619/534-6933 for a recorded message with general information, or 534-3474), at the Scripps Institution of Oceanography, is world renowned for the research it does in the oceans. It invites visitors to view its aquarium of marine life and outdoor tidepool exhibit, many of whose specimens were captured on scientific expeditions. The aquarium bookshop (tel. 619/534-4085) specializes in ocean-related books for students and scholars of all ages—preschool to postgraduate to "just interested." The aquarium is open daily from 9 a.m. to 5 p.m., with admission by donation. Nearby are excellent beach and picnic areas.

WHERE TO STAY

La Valencia, 1132 Prospect St. (at Herschel Avenue), La Jolla, CA 92037 (tel. 619/454-0771, or toll free 800/451-0772), is a minor miracle. Too often great old hotels are allowed to deteriorate until they are torn down. La Valencia has been beautifully kept up, its rooms (for the most part with ocean views) refurnished in European antique reproductions and fitted out with every modern amenity to enhance the hotel's quiet elegance. In truth, La Valencia is the "jewel of La Jolla."

The hotel's entrance is in the center of the village, though its rear faces the ocean. You enter via a tiled loggia with a vine-covered trellis. On your left is a dining patio in a small garden with a fountain and flowering subtropical shrubbery. It's old Spain revisited. Old-World charm, outstanding personal service, and an impressive scenic location have made the hotel a frequent haven for celebrities and entertainers.

At the back of the hotel, garden terraces open toward the ocean. Here, a free-form, heated swimming pool is edged with lawn, flowering trees, shrubs, and a flagstone sunning deck. Other facilities include sauna, whirlpool, shuffleboard, and a mini-health club.

La Valencia has 100 guest accommodations including 10 suites. Guest rooms are decorated in subdued tones with a distinctive European flavor. Amenities include terry-cloth robes, oversize towels, bathroom telephones (bless them), Lancôme toiletries, nightly turndown service, and a daily complimentary newspaper. Select accommodations also have mini-bars, bathroom TVs, make-up mirrors and safes.

There are four delightful spots for dining. The elegant rooftop Sky Room serves lunch including soup du jour or salad, and a superb prix fixe dinner. The light French cuisine is enhanced by the spectacular beauty of the California coastline and the La Jolla Cove. The Mediterranean Room, with its adjoining patio for al fresco dining, offers excellent variety with a number of delicious choices at both lunch and dinner. For lunch there's an exceptionally large selection of salads, some fine sandwich plates including chicken or crab quesadilla with green chile pesto, seafood, pasta, and several house specialties such as paella Valencia. Dinner offerings include seafood, spring lamb and poultry, eastern beef, veal and La Valencia specialties of the day. On the other hand, you might choose to have lunch or dinner at the Whaling Bar (done in New England nautical), one of the most popular watering holes in town, or at the Cafe La Rue. Both have the same menu of seafood selections, pasta, specialties of the day, and a goodly assortment of sandwich plates (my favorite is the Brooklyn steak sandwich) and salads.

I must make a separate statement about the extraordinary wine list. Whether you happen to be an oenophile or not, do look down the list of almost 600 individual choices of imported and domestic wines, including a 1961 Chateau Lafite Rothschild (Premier Grand Cru) and a 1961 Chateau Latour (Premier Grand Cru). To paraphrase a much-used quote, if you must ask the price of either of these 1961 gems you can't afford them, but it is nice to look, and there are other fine choices that will accommodate just about every budget.

For evening's relaxation, the La Sala Lounge has a pianist who entertains nightly.

Depending on location (from overlooking the village, viewing the garden or patio, to a partial or full ocean view), rates for singles and doubles are $150 to $275; suites with a partial or full ocean view are $275 to $425.

Sea Lodge, 8110 Camino del Oro (at the foot of Avenida de la Playa), La Jolla, CA 92037 (tel. 619/459-8271). Beginning at the arched stucco registration desk adorned with ceramic tiles, this terra-cotta-roofed resort is Spanish through and through. Overlooking the Pacific on a mile-long beach, the beauty of the property is enhanced by fountains, fine landscaping, open-air walkways, much tilework, graceful archways, and Mexican antiques. There's a large courtyard, the setting for a centrally situated pool, sundeck, and umbrella tables for poolside luncheons. Other facilities here include tennis courts, a sauna, and complimentary underground parking.

The Sea Lodge's dining room, the Shores, is exceptionally lovely, with Old-World arched windows. All tables afford a panoramic view of the beach from beneath the peaked, beamed, barnwood ceiling. Breakfast, lunch, and dinner are served here daily, and the bar is open till 1 a.m.

As for the rooms, they're spacious, equipped with carved wooden beds, large dressing rooms, refrigerators, ceramic tile baths, balconies or lanais, and all the modern amenities (but no air conditioning other than the fresh ocean breeze). The rooms feature an ocean motif and are equipped with refrigerators, coffee makers, color TV, phones, and other amenities. All rooms have balconies or lanais, and some have kitchens.

Rates are seasonal: July through mid-September, singles cost $125 to $200; doubles, $135 to $210; oceanfront deluxe and suites, $249 to $325. Rates are lower the balance of the year.

15. San Diego

The oldest city in California and the second largest on the Pacific Coast, San Diego has a Spanish/Mexican heritage. Interstate 5 connects San Diego with Los Angeles, 137 miles to the north, and San Diego is about 18 miles north of the U.S.–Mexican border at Tijuana.

A couple of years ago San Diego was only the third-largest city on the West Coast. But the numbers who came to look and decided to stay have increased by the day. Now San Diegans are beginning to wonder about the virtues of beauty.

San Diego is probably the best all-around vacation spot in the country, and blessed with the best climate. It's now the eighth-largest city in the U.S., though if you stood at its busiest corner you'd never know it. San Diego's secrets are sunshine (most of the time), mild weather, soft winds, one of the most famous natural harbors in the world, and a very informal lifestyle. This adds up to sailing on Mission Bay or the Pacific; fishing, snorkeling, scuba-diving, and surfing (what else do you do with 70 miles of country waterfront?); lots of golf (there are over 60 courses) and tennis, biking, jogging, sunbathing, even hang-gliding into an unending supply of air currents. Or you can just go fly a kite any day.

Mission Bay Park alone has 4,600 acres for boating and beachcombing. However, to save San Diego from being totally overrun by visitors, the ocean here is cooled to a chilly average of 62°—not exactly bathtub temperature for swimming, but not bad for surfers who wear wet suits—and who cares if you're fishing? Then there's the surrounding territory—within reasonable driving time you can be in the desert, the mountains, or even another country.

About 6,000 pleasure boats are moored in the bay, and that's where the U.S. Navy berths the Pacific submarine fleet, along with an impressive collection of over 100 warships.

Many of San Diego's most popular attractions are discussed below; however, listings of current entertainment happenings are best found in the Sunday edition of the *San Diego Union,* in the *La Jolla Light,* a weekly newspaper appearing every Thursday, and in the *Reader* (a free tabloid), also appearing on Thursday.

The excellent **San Diego Convention and Visitors Bureau and International Visitors Information Center,** 11 Horton Plaza, at 1st Avenue and F Street (tel. 619/236-1212), is open daily from 8:30 a.m. to 5 p.m.; closed major holidays. They offer visitors to San Diego a one-stop service center for information on hotels, entertainment and sightseeing, fishing licenses, boating permits, and even sports events, bullfights, other Tijuana attractions, not to mention Mexican auto insurance. For a recorded message about all sorts of local events, call 619/239-9696.

A similar service is run by the **Visitor Information Center,** 2688 E. Mission Bay Dr. (tel. 619/276-8200), off I-5 at the end of the Claremont-East Mission Bay Drive off-ramp. They're open from

9 a.m. to 6 p.m. (sometimes 5:30 p.m.) Monday through Saturday, to 4:30 p.m. on Sunday.

WHAT TO SEE AND DO

Cabrillo National Monument

Cabrillo National Monument, on Point Loma (tel. 619/557-5450), 10 miles from downtown San Diego (at the southern end of Calif. 209), commemorates the discovery of the California coast by Juan Rodriguez Cabrillo in 1542. From the restored Old Point Loma Lighthouse, you can view in one sweeping glance the ocean, bays, islands, mountains, valleys, and plains that comprise the area. And mid-December through February you can view the migration of the California gray whale. Admission is $3 per private vehicle (if you have a senior 62 or over there's no charge) or $1 per person in commercial vehicles; open daily from 9 a.m. to 5:15 p.m. (9 a.m. to sunset in summer). Perhaps you should go here first to get acquainted with the area before seeking a specific destination.

Cruises

You can watch the glistening skyline of San Diego fade in the distance if you take one of the **San Diego Harbor Excursions** boats (tel. 619/234-4111). One- and/or two-hour cruises depart daily from 1050 North Harbor Drive at the foot of Broadway. One-hour trips ($8.50) leave at 10 a.m., 11:15, 12:45 p.m., and 4:15 p.m.; there is only one 2-hour cruise ($12) at 2 p.m. The two-hour, 25-mile cruise takes you past Harbor and Shelter islands, under an orthotropic bridge, past naval installations on North Island, and out into the Pacific. The one-hour, 12-mile cruise covers part of the same area. The longer excursion departs once daily in winter and spring, three times daily in the summer. Harbor Excursions also has a romantic dinner/dance harbor trip ($42) on Friday and Saturday aboard the sternwheeler Monterey from 7 to 9:30 p.m.

The one-hour cruise leaves the pier approximately every 45 minutes in summer and four times daily in winter and spring. (San Diego Harbor Excursions also runs whale-watch cruises from mid-December to mid-February.)

Fishing

As long as I'm on the topic of water, sport fishing in the ocean is among the finest on the Pacific coast. **H & M Landing,** 2803 Emerson St., Point Loma (tel. 619/222-1144), offers the largest variety of fishing and whale-watching excursions (they've been in business since 1935). Their local fishing trips range from a half-day at the Point Loma kelp beds to full-day fishing around the Coronado Islands. Summer and fall they go out for albacore/tuna, winter and spring it's for rock cod. The really exciting trips are on the 88-foot *Spirit of Adventure* (sleeps 30) for two- to 10-day fishing trips. H & M also has been watching gray whales since 1955 (Pacific Sea Fari

Tours). These trips also afford the opportunity to see sea lions, sea birds, and ocean life of all sorts.

Charter fishing boats also leave from **Islandia Sportfishing,** 1551 W. Mission Bay Dr. (tel. 619/222-1164), in Mission Bay. January to March Islandia also goes whale watching.

You can also fish (for no charge and with no license) off the **Ocean Beach Pier** (tel. 619/224-3359) at the foot of Niagara Street in Ocean Beach, and from the many city lakes (a daily recreation permit is required). For information on lake fishing, contact the **Lakes Recreation Section** of the San Diego Water Utilities Department (tel. 619/465-3474).

Mission Bay Park

Mission Bay Park, just north of downtown San Diego and a bit west of Interstate 5 (tel. 619/276-8200 for information), is a massive aquatic park made up of 4,600 acres of land and water, and 27 miles of beach, ideal for recreation for the whole family. Within the park are resort hotels, sightseeing and deep-sea fishing vessels, golf courses, picnic areas, campgrounds, restaurants, nightclubs, and facilities for all water sports.

But the biggest attraction in the park is **Sea World** 1720 South Shores Rd., (tel. 619/222-6363), a 135-acre marine zoological park featuring killer whales, dolphins, otters, sea lions, even a performing walrus, plus seals, and penguins. At the Penguin Encounter you can visit with some 400 penguins, murres, and the cutest puffins you've ever seen. There also are four major aquariums, including the Shark Exhibit—home to some of the largest sharks living apart from the deep.

Six shows are presented continuously throughout the day including a new killer whale show featuring the calf Baby Shamu, born in September 1988. Shamu made its first theatrical aquarium appearance in March, 1989. The show also highlights adult whales Shamu and Nanu. Shamu, the 7,000-pound killer whale, does high jumps and back flips in the 5-million gallon aquarium at Shamu Stadium; sea lions and otters star in the "Pirates of Pinniped"; high-flying dolphins and two species of small whales perform in "New Friends"; circus acrobats, singers, dancers, world-class skateboarders, and BMX bike riders do their thing in "City Streets."

Cap'n Kids World, a nautical theme playground, is (you guessed it) for kids. Other exhibits range from a whale and dolphin petting pool (adults can participate) to one of the largest collections of waterfowl in the world. Rounding out the bill are shops, band performances, costumed characters (most are part of the Sea World show), rides, and a wide choice of eateries.

One price ($22 for adults, $18 for seniors, $16.50 for children 3 to 11, free for under-3s) admits you to all shows and exhibits. Sea World is open daily from 9 a.m. to dusk, with extended hours during summer and holiday periods when there may be special entertainment, musical groups, or even a spectacular fireworks and laser display. Allow a full day (about eight hours) to see all the shows and exhibits; you'll enjoy it. Parking is free.

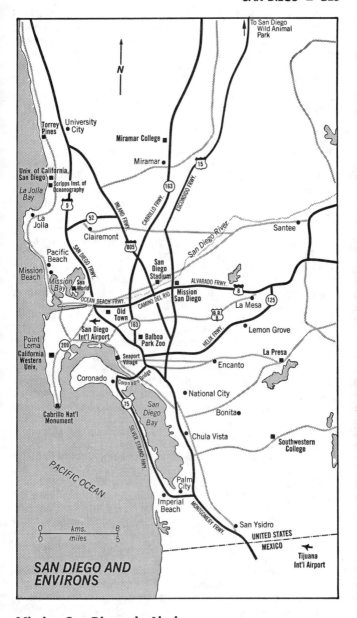

SAN DIEGO AND ENVIRONS

Mission San Diego de Alcala

Mission San Diego de Alcala, 10818 San Diego Mission Rd., Mission Valley (tel. 619/281-8449), is the first in the chain of 21 missions started by Father Junípero Serra in the 18th century. Open daily from 9 a.m. to 5 p.m., the mission has a museum containing original records dating from 1769, the year of its founding, as well as liturgical robes, books, and other relics. A $1 donation is requested. It's still an active parish, and masses are conducted on Sunday.

Balboa Park

Its 1,400 acres of cultural attractions, semitropical gardens, and towering palms and eucalyptus trees make Balboa Park one of the biggest attractions in the city. Just 1¼ miles north of downtown, it can easily be reached in minutes by car or bus. The landmark of the park—and symbol of the city itself—is the **California Tower,** an elaborately decorated carillon tower atop the California Building. The 100-bell carillon chimes each quarter hour and plays a short recital every day at noon.

It's handy to know that admission to all the museums in Balboa Park is free the first Tuesday of each month; however, you won't be the only one looking for small economies, so go early. Museums have limited capacities; you may not be able to get in at a later hour.

Inside the California Building is the **Museum of Man,** 1350 El Prado (tel. 619/239-2001; admission: $3 for adults, $1 for those 13 to 18, 25¢ for children 6 to 12), containing exhibits telling the story of people through the ages, with emphasis on the Indian cultures of the Americas. Open daily from 10 a.m. to 4:30 p.m.

The **International Aerospace Hall of Fame and San Diego Aerospace Museum,** 2001 Pan American Plaza (tel. 619/232-8322), is the home of the history of the great achievers of aviation and aerospace, and of a superb collection of historical aircraft and aviation and aerospace artifacts including art, models, military accoutrements, dioramas, and filmstrip displays. Heroes honored range from the early experimenters to the astronauts, and the planes range from the early gliders to spacecraft. Admission is $4 for adults and $1 for children 6 to 17. Open daily from 10 a.m. to 4 p.m.

The **San Diego Natural History Museum,** 1788 El Prado, at the east end, P.O. Box 1390, San Diego, CA 92112 (tel. 619/232-3821), has a number of fascinating exhibits on the desert and shore ecology, endangered species, gems, dinosaurs, and a Discovery Lab where you can even touch a snake (while it's held by a museum worker). You can learn about desert ecology from the lifelike exhibits. A video screen displays pictures of animals and provides information on those that interest you. As part of the endangered species exhibit, the museum has wildlife products and skins seized by authorities (you can even touch a tiger skin), along with exhibits that show wildlife endangered by commercial exploitation.

On permanent display are whale and dinosaur skeletons, including the only dinosaur ever excavated in San Diego County. (It may be that the climate was less receptive to animal life then.) And if you find earthquakes exciting, the museum also has a working, moving, seismograph. The Sefton Hall of Shore Ecology displays an amazing collection of shells and a videodisc replica of the shore.

There is a gem and mineral exhibit including multicolored tourmaline mined in San Diego County, blue topaz, and orange garnets unearthed locally.

Admission is $4.50 for adults and $1 for those 6 to 18; it's free for kids 5 and under. The museum is open daily from 10 a.m. to 4:30 p.m.

The **San Diego Museum of Art,** 1450 El Prado (tel. 619/232-7931), houses an outstanding collection of painting and sculpture, old masters, and a variety of exciting traveling exhibitions. Admission is $5 for adults, $4 for seniors, military and students with ID, $2 for children 6 to 12; under 6 it's free. Admission is free the first Tuesday of each month. Open Tuesday to Sunday from 10 a.m. to 4:30 p.m. Outside the gallery is a cafe and an interesting sculpture garden including, among others, work by Henry Moore. Free docent tours are conducted at 10 and 11 a.m. Tuesday through Thursday; 1 and 2 p.m. Tuesday through Sunday.

The **Timken Gallery,** 1500 El Prado (tel. 619/239-5548), is right next to the San Diego Museum of Art, along the north side of El Prado. The Timken is a private gallery that does not charge admission. It houses a permanent collection of paintings by old masters plus an impressive array of Russian icons and French tapestries, as well as 19th-century American paintings. Admission is free. Hours are Tuesday to Saturday from 10 a.m. to 4:30 p.m., on Sunday from 1:30 to 4:30 p.m. Closed during September.

Finally, there's the **Hall of Champions,** 1649 El Prado, in the Casa de Balboa (tel. 619/234-2544), honoring San Diego-born athletes who have achieved fame—among them Bill Walton and Maureen Connolly. The theater runs sports films throughout the day. Admission is $3 for adults; $2 for seniors, students, and military with ID; 50¢ for those 6 to 17 years (under 6, free). Open Monday to Saturday from 10 a.m. to 4:30 p.m., on Sunday from noon to 5 p.m. Open daily.

San Diego Zoo

With more than 3,200 animals, this world-famous zoo contains one of the most exotic collections of wildlife anywhere, yet it's right in Balboa Park, just minutes from downtown San Diego. You can wander through the 100 acres, which are also lavishly landscaped as a botanical garden (some of the plants provide food for the animal residents), and admire koalas and baby orangutans in the finest collection of primates ever assembled, and tropical birds with plumage of every imaginable color.

For a bird's-eye view of the animals, you can take the **Skyfari Aerial Tramway** across the treetops of the zoo (included in your admission). There's also a great bus tour in which driver-guides point out some of the more exotic creatures living along the path of the three-mile tour ($3 for adults, $2.50 for children). Admission to the zoo is $11 for adults, $4 for children. There's also a **Children's Zoo** with a petting section and a nursery where baby animals are raised.

From July to Labor Day the zoo is open daily from 9 a.m. to 5 p.m. Between Labor Day and the end of June it closes at 4 p.m. For additional information, call 619/234-3153 or 231-1515.

The Reuben H. Fleet Space Theater and Science Center

Learning by doing and experiencing is the theme of this science complex on the Plaza de Balboa in San Diego's Balboa Park. Named for the pioneer in aeronautics—one of the world's first aerial mail pilots—this super-theater/planetarium allows visitors to experience a trip to outer space (or under water) without leaving the confines of the comfortable 350-seat auditorium. The simulated trip attains a reality never before possible because of the elaborate system of devices used, including a water-cooled Omnimax projector; 70-mm film, the largest available; a fisheye lens; a Star Ball projector that can project 10,000 stars from any point in the universe at any time in history; zoom projectors; and a 76-foot projection hemisphere screen. It's thrilling—more fun than the old 3-D movies.

Featured films have included *To The Limit;* and at the Laserium, *Laserock* and *Lites Out Laserium.* (Children under 5 are not permitted at the Laser shows.) One historic film shown here was *Hail Columbia!,* which traced the trip of the space shuttle *Columbia* from hangar to launch, through space, and back to earth at Edwards Air Force Base in California. Astronauts Young and Crippen are shown in training sequences and answering questions of the press, but some of the most exciting footage was provided by NASA. It includes shots of the cargo bay doors opening in space to show the loss of some of the all-important tiles that were a matter of some concern during the flight, as well as shots of earth from space, and astronauts working in zero gravity. The launch coverage is spectacular as the camera is able to follow the craft farther into space than anyone else can see, even those who watched the launch in person.

Adjoining the theatre is the 8,000-square-foot Science Center, with more than 50 exhibits that beep, blink, float, whisper, and reveal, to make science come alive for visitors of all ages. This is no "hands-off" museum. Here you can match wits with a computerized teaching machine, create designs with sand pendulums, or examine the iris and pupil of your own eye.

Admission to the Science Center is $2 for adults, $1 for juniors ages 5 to 15. Admission to the Space Theater/Laserium is $6.50 for adults and $3.50 for juniors. And, again, children under 5 are not admitted to the laser shows. The building is open daily from 9:30 a.m. to 9:30 p.m. For recorded information on the shows and times, call 619/238-1168; for further information, call 619/238-1233.

The Maritime Museum

The Maritime Museum, 1492 N. Harbor Dr., (tel. 619/234-9153), is a nautical museum on display in its natural habitat—on the water. Moored at the dock near the fish markets, the museum consists of three restored historic vessels, including the *Berkeley,* the first successful propeller-driven ferry on the Pacific coast, launched in 1898 (it participated in the evacuation of San Francisco following the great earthquake and fire of 1906); and the *Medea,* a steam yacht built in Scotland in 1904 (it fought in both world wars). The biggest attraction, however, remains the *Star of India,* the oldest square-rigged tall ship still afloat and sailing. Since its launching in 1863 off the Isle of Man, the British-built ship has been around the world 21 times. Despite the ravages of time and neglect, it has been restored to its original splendor, and now houses museum displays of the old sailing days. You can purchase a boarding pass admitting you to all three ships. It's $6 for adults, $5 for juniors 13 to 17 and seniors, $1.50 for children 6 to 12. The vessels of the Maritime Museum and a gift shop are open daily from 9 a.m. to 8 p.m.

Seaport Village

One of San Diego's centers for shopping and dining is Seaport Village, 849 W. Harbor Dr., at Kettner Blvd. (tel. 619/235-4014). It is easily reached by following Harbor Drive south from the Maritime Museum. Seaport Village is connected to the new San Diego Convention Center by a waterfront boardwalk.

The 22-acre complex, including an 8-acre public park, is beautifully landscaped and has more than 50 shops (and restaurants) including galleries and boutiques selling handcrafted gifts, collectibles, and many imported items. Shops are open daily from 10 a.m. to 9 p.m. Two of my favorite shops are **Hug-A-Bear** (tel. 619/230-1362), with a selection of plush bears and woodland animals, and the **Seaport Kite Shop** (619/232-2268), with kites from around the world. I also enjoy the **Upstart Crow & Co.** (619/232-4855), a delightful combination bookstore and coffeehouse.

A 10-acre expansion is planned to open in 1992 and will include even more retail shops as well as a dozen new restaurant/bars for dining and late-night entertainment. An amphitheater will feature special water events as well as other entertainment.

The restaurants in and near Seaport Village run the gamut from take-out stands to a Mexican bakery and more conventional facilities. The **Harbor House**, at 831 W. Harbor Dr. (tel. 619/232-1141), offers good seafood with a pleasant view.

Adding to the charm of the area are the three plazas that recreate an eastern seaport village, Victorian San Francisco, and a traditional Mexican village.

Old Town

The spirit of the "Birthplace of California," the site of the first European settlement on the West Coast, is captured in the six-block area northwest of downtown San Diego. Although the Old Town was abandoned more than a century ago for a more convenient business center near the bay, it has again become a center of interest—this time as a State Historic Park. Some of its buildings have been restored, and the combination of historic sights, art galleries, antique and curio shops, restaurants, and handcraft centers make this an interesting and memorable outing.

The park is bounded by Congress, Twiggs, Juan, and Wallace Streets. There's a map of Old Town's layout at the intersection of Twiggs and San Diego Streets to help you find your way around.

Many of the historic buildings here have been restored or reconstructed. They include the magnificent **Casa de Estudillo,** the **Machado/Stewart Adobe,** the **San Diego Union's newspaper office,** the old one-room **Mason Street schoolhouse,** and the **stables** from which Alfred Seeley ran his San Diego-Los Angeles stagecoach line. (The latter now houses a collection of horsedrawn carriages.)

Just outside the boundary of the park are two other historic buildings—the "haunted" two-story **Whaley House,** once the center of high society, now fully restored and completely furnished in period antiques.

Old Town is easily reached from Interstates 8 or 5. Take the Old Town Avenue exit off I-5, or the Taylor Street exit from I-8. Free one-hour guided tours are given daily beginning at 2 p.m. from the Machado/Silvas Adobe on San Diego Avenue between Mason and Wallace Streets (tel. 619/237-6770). Further information is available from the **Old Town Visitor Center,** 4002 Wallace St. (tel. 619/237-6770), open from 10 a.m. to 5 p.m.

Adjacent to Old Town is **Heritage Park,** at Juan and Harney, where old Victorian buildings built between 1850 and 1865 have been moved and restored. Shops, including a Caswell-Massey pharmacy (the original New York branch predates the American Revolution!), have been installed in these old homes.

Shelter Island

On the lee side of Point Loma, Shelter Island is actually a peninsula a mile long and 300 feet wide, studded with palm trees and fringed with the white triangular sails jutting up from its many marinas. A favorite center for all types of water sports, it offers public mooring and launching ramps as well as three of San Diego's private yacht clubs. Offshore and deep-sea vessels are available to the saltwater enthusiast. There's even a public fishing pier open 24 hours a day for those who don't want to leave the shore (no fishing license is required). Several luxury hotels are located here.

Harbor Island

More sophisticated than Shelter Island, its older sister, Harbor Island, is a man-made 1½-mile-long peninsula, minutes from the airport, and just across the bay from the towers of downtown San Diego. Besides its landscaped park areas and beaches, the island also contains several luxurious hotels, some of the best nightlife in San Diego, and a number of restaurants. If you arrive from the sea, you can dock at two of the largest and most fully equipped marinas in San Diego.

Wild Animal Park

A sister institution of the world-famous San Diego Zoo, the San Diego Wild Animal Park (tel. 619/480-0100), located in the San Pasqual Valley, 30 miles north of downtown San Diego via Interstate 15 and then by way of Via Rancho Parkway, is a 1,800-acre wildlife preserve dedicated to the preservation of endangered species. Some 1,500 animals from Africa and Asia roam free here, much as they would in their native habitats. You can watch gorillas at play in the giant Gorilla Grotto, or wander around the two immense aviaries where about 1,000 exotic birds fly freely in a lush African setting.

You can visit the striking **Nairobi Village,** a 17-acre complex of native huts, with a gift shop, waterfowl lagoon, and petting Kraal, where kids (and kids at heart!) can pet and play with sheep, goats, antelope, and other animals. Animal shows take place here throughout the day. While you're in the village, visit Mombasa Cooker, Thorn Tree Terrace, and Samburu Terrace for dining with a spectacular view of the park. But, for the conservation-minded, the most impressive experience must be the five-mile "safari" on the **Wgasa Bush Line monorail,** passing through sweeping savannahs and veldts, past herds of animals and flocks of wild ground birds. The monorail stops several times during the trip so that visitors can view, photograph, and ask questions of the well-informed guides. This is a very special place—a not-to-be-missed attraction.

The Wild Animal Park is open daily in summer from 9 a.m. to 6 p.m.; daily till 4 p.m. the rest of the year. Adults pay $15.50; children 3 to 15, $8.50. Price of admission includes the monorail and all animal shows. Parking is $2.

WHERE TO STAY

The **Westgate,** 1055 2nd Ave., downtown (between Broadway and C Street), San Diego, CA 92101 (tel. 619/238-1818, or toll free 800/221-3802, or 800/522-1564 in California), has rightfully been acclaimed by experts as one of the great luxury hotels of the world. In downtown San Diego, the 20-floor structure seems inspired by such outstanding deluxe French hotels as the Ritz of Paris. Its basic decor is a skillful combination of Louis XV, Louis XVI, Georgian, and the most elegant of the English Regency period. All rooms have two-line speaker phones, remote-control color TV, mini-bars, private dressing areas, bathrobes, hair dryers. The color TV is discreetly hidden in an elegant cabinet.

Le Fontainebleau, its award-winning restaurant, has been called "the most elegant dining room built in this century." It should come as no surprise that the cuisine is continental, whereas the Westgate Dining Room (off the lobby) serves traditional American fare. The Fontainebleau is open weekdays for lunch from 11:45 a.m. to 2 p.m.; dinner from 6:30 to 10 p.m., except on Friday and Saturday when it's open from 6 p.m. The Westgate Dining Room is open nightly for dinner from 6 to 11 p.m. Across from the Westgate Dining Room is the intimate Plaza Lounge, also open daily—a local gathering spot for many of San Diego's most talented performers. More than 200 antiques and art objects have been collected from around the globe to give the hotel its ebullience—a world of glittering crystal, paneled and gilt walls, and tapestries. The tasteful decor overflows into the bedrooms, which are equally distinctive and glamorous.

Rates are $128 to $148 for singles, $138 to $158 for doubles. Suites range from $270 to $595.

Sheraton on Harbor Island (tel. toll free 800/325-3535) is another Sheraton complex of two hotels, the **Sheraton-Harbor Island East,** 1380 Harbor Island Dr., San Diego, CA 92101 (tel. 619/291-2900), and the **Sheraton Grand on Harbor Island,** 1590 Harbor Island Dr., San Diego, CA 92101 (tel. 619/291-6400). The properties boast a total of 1,100 handsomely furnished rooms, complete with color TV, direct-dial phone, individual air conditioning, a king-size or two double beds, and 24-hour room service. All rooms have balconies and most have marine views.

Among the dining choices at Sheraton on Harbor Island are: Sheppard's, at Harbor Island East, a gourmet restaurant; Spencers, at Sheraton Grand on Harbor Island, which serves three meals a day, specializing (at dinner) in Black Angus beef; and the Café del Sol (East), a coffeeshop that features a lavish Sunday brunch. Adjacent to Sheppard's is Reflections (East), an elegant lounge with live entertainment and dancing.

The Sheraton boasts a number of other facilities, including a health club, five pools (two for children), saunas, whirlpools, four night-lit tennis courts at Harbor Island East (available to guests of both hotels), jogging course, boat and bike rental, shops, and laundromat. Guests have full access to all facilities at either establishment.

Rooms at the Sheraton Grand on Harbor Island are $130 to $175 single, $150 to $195 double. At Harbor Island East, singles are $120 to $165; doubles, $140 to $185.

The **Bahia Resort Hotel,** 998 W. Mission Bay Dr., San Diego, CA 92109 (tel. 619/488-0551, or toll free 800/288-0770, 800/233-8172 in Canada), enjoys a lovely situation on a peninsula surrounded by the waters of Mission Bay. It's an extremely pleasant place to stay, offering 322 rooms and good facilities. Every one of the rooms here has a picture window, and most offer views of the bay. Half the rooms have kitchens; all have a bath with dressing area, color TV, direct-dial phone, etc. There's an Olympic-size swimming pool on the premises, as well as tennis courts, game room, and shuffleboard court. There's also a dock where you can tie up your boat, or rent one. And then there's the *Bahia Belle,* a sternwheeler that cruises the bay stopping at two other hotels. At night there's dancing to live music aboard the *Belle.*

Off the cozy fireplace lobby is a coffee shop serving breakfast, lunch, and dinner. Virtually a Mercedes car museum, the Mercedes Dining Room features Mercedes-logo carpeting, Mercedes posters, and drawings of antique models on the walls. Adjacent is the Club Mercedes, which offers live entertainment, and the Comedy Isle with comedy acts Tuesday through Saturday.

If you're vacationing with kids, by the way, they'll adore the Bahia—it's the only hotel I know that has four resident seals in a pond.

Rates for one or two persons during the summer are $105 to $230, single or double. They're a bit less the rest of the year.

The **Catamaran,** 3999 Mission Blvd., San Diego, CA 92109

(tel. 619/488-1081, or toll free 800/288-6770, 800/233-8172 in Canada), is beautifully situated on Mission Bay, just a short scenic walk from the ocean. The hotel has 315 rooms, a new Atoll Restaurant, the Cannibal Lounge with live entertainment, and Moray's —a small piano bar. Rates are $130 to $185, single or double.

The San Diego Princess, A Princess Cruises Resort (formerly Vacation Village), 1404 West Vacation Rd., San Diego, CA 92109 (tel. 619/274-4630, or toll free 800/344-2626), offers 449 modern rooms situated on 43 lushly landscaped tropical acres with freshwater lagoons spanned by graceful bridges. Rooms are done in standard modern decor, and each is equipped with every modern amenity as well as a patio or lanai, dressing area, and in-room coffee maker.

Facilities include five swimming pools; eight tennis courts; a sailboat marina; bicycle rental; three restaurants—the Dockside Broiler (very good for steaks and seafood), the Pacific Princess (seafood specialties), and the Village Café (coffeeshop); a cocktail lounge; and a mile of white sand beach.

Rates are $110 to $295 for singles, $125 to $395 for doubles.

A sternwheeler called the *Bahia Belle* cruises the bay, running hourly in summer (less often in winter) and stopping at the Bahia, the Catamaran, and The San Diego Princess. At night there's dancing to live music and cocktails aboard the *Belle;* fare is $7 per adults, $5 for children under 12 (tel. 619/488-0551).

Humphrey's Half Moon Inn, 2303 Shelter Island Dr., San Diego, CA 92106 (tel. 619/224-3411, or toll free 800/542-7400), is a delightful place. Surrounded by lush subtropical plantings, 183 spacious rooms open onto lovely marina views. On the grounds are heated pools for both adults and children, a Jacuzzi, bicycles, table tennis, and room for lawn games.

Humphrey's, the very lovely restaurant adjacent to the inn, features fresh seafood. It has a garden decor with bamboo furnishings, lots of plants and potted palms, and slowly whirring fans overhead. A blazing fire in a stone fireplace warms the entranceway; another asset is a lovely view of the boat-filled bay. There's a terrace for outdoor dining, and jazz entertainment at the piano bar. From April to October, the hotel helps sponsor great jazz concerts in the park by the bay with top-name performers.

Rooms at Humphrey's Half Moon Inn are pretty and resort-like, with bamboo and rattan furnishings and seashell-motif bedspreads. They are equipped with every modern amenity. There's also free in-room coffee, 24-hour switchboard, complimentary movie channel, and free transportation to the airport or the Amtrak station.

Rates are $95 to $115 single, $115 to $135 double. Children under 16 in a room with their parents are free.

Mission Valley is the most centrally located resort area in San Diego. Around its Hotel Circle are many restaurants, motels, and hotels. It also contains one of the largest shopping complexes in the country, Fashion Valley Center.

Town & Country, 500 Hotel Circle North, San Diego, CA 92108 (tel. 619/291-7131, or toll free 800/854-2608, 800/542-

6082 in California). With over 1,000 rooms (housed in two high-rises and several bungalow-style buildings), this is one of the largest hotels in San Diego. It's something of a "city within a city," offering just about any convenience or facility you might desire. Each attractively appointed room is equipped with color TV, direct-dial phone, and full bath; the newspaper is delivered to your room each weekday morning. A shuttle bus takes guests back and forth between the hotel and airport. On-the-premises facilities include a gift shop, barber and beauty salons, a tour information desk, car rental, etc.—even a gas station.

In addition, the Town & Country has four swimming pools, a therapy pool and sauna. Guests can also use the Atlas Health Club for men and women just across the street for a nominal fee. Club facilities include, among other things, racquetball and tennis courts, weight and aerobics rooms, massage therapy, and outdoor pool and indoor whirlpool spa.

When it comes to good food and drink, the Town & Country offers a world of variety within its four restaurants, plus the Lanai Coffee Shop and Sunshine Deli. The Gourmet Room features mouth-watering prime rib; then there are the zesty Italian dishes of Bonacci's, Kelly's Steak House (guess what they serve), and Cafe Potpourri—all of which make dining a pleasure at Town & Country.

Entertainment ranges from the unbounded energy of Crystal T's Live to the simplicity of the piano bar at Kelly's to the live bands and good-hearted imbibing in the Abilene Country Saloon and Le Pavillon Lounge.

Singles at Town & Country are $77 to $120; doubles and twins are $97 to $145. Suites go for $195 to $385. There's usually a "limited availability" special on singles—be sure to ask.

Mission Valley Inn, 875 Hotel Circle South, San Diego, CA 92108 (tel. 619/298-8281, or toll free 800/854-2608), is a low-rise hotel that provides pleasant accommodations in two-story buildings.

The 210 rooms all have air conditioning, color TV with in-house movies, coffee maker, and direct-dial phone. Many have balconies or patios overlooking lawns and gardens. In addition to three swimming pools, facilities include a putting green, shuffleboard, and a therapy pool. A barbershop and service station round out the list of services. Guests can also use the Atlas Health Club behind the hotel; it has complete exercise facilities as well as a volleyball court, tennis and handball/racquetball courts, and massage rooms. For dining, there's a 24-hour coffeeshop in the hotel as well as the Hacienda Steak House for lunch, dinner, and Sunday brunch.

Rates range in the summer from $65 to $90 for singles or doubles, lower the rest of the year. The more expensive rooms are poolside.

Fabulous Inns of America, 2485 Hotel Circle Pl., San Diego, CA 92108 (tel. 619/291-7700, or toll free 800/824-0950, 800/647-1903 in California), is a four-story modern complex at the extreme western end of Hotel Circle. There are 178 rooms and suites, each with individual balcony, color TV, bath with phone, dressing room, air conditioning, direct-dial phones, and some with refrigerator. There's even a generous-size heated outdoor swimming pool and Jacuzzi on the premises; an 11-hole (you heard me correctly—11 holes) golf course and tennis facilities are across the street.

Singles are $55 to $72, doubles $65 to $85.

Motel 6, 2424 Hotel Circle North, San Diego, CA 92108 (tel. 619/296-1612), is a low coral-and-blue rancho-style motel, with an exterior balcony partially enclosing a swimming pool terrace. Rooms are simply furnished in a contemporary style, with TV, air conditioning, and phone (local calls are free). The rate for one is $34, $6 for each additional adult.

WHERE TO DINE

What had been rated as the best restaurant in San Diego—Gustaf Anders—has left for Santa Ana in Orange County. Nonetheless there remains a large selection of restaurants catering to all sorts of tastes and offering menus to match—gourmet French, ribs, dim sum, a great variety of seafood, more seafood, Mexican style ("gringo" and otherwise), Japanese (with and without sushi), hamburgers, etc.

In the section below are some favorite places chosen from the several hundred restaurants in San Diego.

Lubach's, 2101 N. Harbor Dr., corner of Hawthorn Street on the Embarcadero (tel. 619/232-5129). Some people consider this to be among the better dining establishments in the city. The decor is traditional—tables, red-leather booths and banquettes, brick fireplace—and the food is consistently good. A specialty is poached salmon in hollandaise sauce. Nonseafood entrees include veal chop sautéed with mushrooms and roast duck à l'orange. Dinner entrees cost $15 to $27.50. The luncheon menu features salads and open-faced sandwiches, ranging in price from $8 to $14.

Open weekdays for lunch from 11:30 a.m. to 4 p.m., Monday to Saturday for dinner from 4 p.m. to midnight. Jackets are required for men at dinner. Reservations advised. There's free valet parking.

Anthony's Star of the Sea Room, 1360 Harbor Dr., at the foot of Ash Street (tel. 619/232-7408). The Ghio family welcomes you to a dramatic setting overlooking the panorama of the San Diego harbor. What you get here are delicacies from the sea. These tasty seafaring morsels aren't exactly cheap, but they are good and fresh. Next to the three-masted schooner *Star of India,* the restaurant on the Embarcadero is renowned for its gourmet abalone, grilled swordfish, and clams Genovese. Also good is the broiled seafood brochette. For an appetizer, you'd do well to order the "pick o' the sea" hors d'oeuvres—personally selected by Catherine Ghio. For dessert, try the fresh strawberries (in season).

Open daily except holidays from 5:30 until 10:30 p.m. (for reservations, which are a must, call after 2 p.m.). Coat and tie required for men.

The adjoining **Anthony's Fish Grotto** (tel. 619/232-5103) is less expensive and more informal. It was established in 1946 by the Ghio and Weber families. Reservations are not accepted—you just arrive—it's a bit like waiting for a train during rush hour in Grand

Central (in New York), but don't let that discourage you. Fish and chips, done in a light batter, is a family favorite. The house specialty is shellfish casserole à la Catherine (made with lobster meat, crab legs, shrimp, and scallops). But I suggest that if sand dabs are on the menu that day, order them. Most entrees are priced from $8 to $14. A fine dessert is Anthony's cake zabione zabaglione.

Open daily from 11:30 a.m. to 8:30 p.m.

Across the street is another Ghio enterprise, **Anthony's Harborside** (tel. 619/232-6358), also serving seafood meals. You'd think they'd be competing with themselves, but all three establishments are mobbed nightly.

Tom Ham's Lighthouse, 2150 Harbor Island Dr., Harbor Island (tel. 619/291-9110), is built at the tip of Harbor Island beneath a lighthouse (the official Coast Guard no. 9 beacon). You not only get good meals here, but can enjoy a museum as well. A collection of marine artifacts was gathered from around the world, forming a nostalgic reminder of San Diego in the early 1800s. Featured on the dinner menu are such specialties as seafood Newburg, scampi, scallops tomatillo, and Angel shrimp. Dinner entrees range from $14 to $30. A buffet lunch including an elaborate salad bar and three hot entrees is offered in addition to sandwiches, salads, and hot specialties ($7 to $14). Be sure to save room for dessert; the apple pie is scrumptious.

Tom Ham's Lighthouse is open for lunch weekdays from 11:15 a.m. to 3:30 p.m.; a Sunday buffet brunch ($10) is served from 10 a.m. to 2 p.m.

The **Sandtrap Restaurant and Lounge,** 2702 N. Mission Bay Dr. (tel. 619/274-3314), at Mission Bay Golf Course, south of Grand Street (turn right, and right again, just before the freeway entrance south). Or to put it another way—it's one mile north of the tourist information center on Mission Bay Drive. When you think you've exhausted all possibilities for having a really great breakfast at 7 a.m. without resorting to fast food, head for one of San Diego's best-kept secrets—the Sandtrap Restaurant. It's a happy restaurant. It has a small counter and a large publike dining room that overlooks a duck pond with its waterfall and the golf course's putting green.

The prices are right, the food's terrific, and the service is cheerful—especially hard to find at 7 a.m. The three-egg omelets are delicious in whatever form you choose. For a real heart-warmer, there's a memorable ortega chile-and-cheese omelet you'll probably write home about. And that's just the beginning! There's always a big breakfast special, usually accompanied by cottage fries or fresh fruit, for a modest $4.50.

For breakfast, lunch, or dinner, the quantities served require a hearty appetite—even the salads are a full meal. For lunch, try one of the delicious daily specials, or the sea legs supreme salad ($5 to $6.25). Two of the most popular lunchtime sandwiches at the Sandtrap are the six-ounce sirloin steak at $5.75 and the half-pound hamburger, done exactly as ordered, for $4.25, both with fries and cole slaw or fruit. Homemade soups are a specialty of the house and a bargain at $2.75 with rolls. Dinners range from $7.25 to $13 (the highest price is for the peppersteak or prime rib). There's also fresh fish daily for lunch and dinner. With your entree there's a choice of soup or salad.

The dinner special changes daily. Monday through Thursday it may be barbecued short ribs, carne asada, corned beef and cabbage, or old-fashioned pot roast (all $8.25). Weekends it's prime rib for $10.25. The dinner specials are $1 less for early birds who dine between 4 and 6 p.m.

It's hard to beat the quality, price, and service at the Sandtrap. There's a full bar, and color TV to boot, and entertainment Friday and Saturday nights.

The restaurant is open from 7 a.m. to 9 p.m. Sunday to Thursday, to 10 p.m. on Friday and Saturday. If you want to try the Mission Bay 18-hole Executive Golf Course after breakfast or lunch, bring your clubs (or you can rent them in the pro shop).

---

16. On to Tijuana

If you'd like a short trip south of the border but want to be back in San Diego by nightfall, you can take one of the many tours offered by various companies (see below). They are available from most San Diego hotels and cover just about every Tijuana attraction.

GETTING THERE

One of the easiest ways to get to the border is the **Tijuana (San Diego) Trolley** (tel. 619/233-3004). Big red trolleys (actual electric streetcars imported from Germany) depart from the corner of Kettner Boulevard and C Street, just across the street from the Amtrak station, every 15 minutes from 5 a.m. to 7 p.m., and every 30 minutes thereafter, with the last trolley returning from the border at 1 a.m. Be sure to take the trolley that says San Ysidro. The one-way trip to or from the border takes 45 minutes and costs $1.50 per person one way from Kettner Blvd. (have exact change, in coins). There are 18 stops on the line, since it doubles as commuter transportation, but it's a comfortable, interesting, and inexpensive way to reach the border. Once at the border you'll need a taxi to get into town.

Mexicoach (tel. 619/232-5049) has daily round-trip express buses to downtown Tijuana and Tijuana Airport, the jai alai games, and the bullfights for $11 round trip, $5.75 one way. They depart from the Amtrak terminal, 1050 Kettner Blvd., at Broadway, every hour on the hour from 9 a.m. to noon, then at 2, 4, and 6 p.m. The trip takes about 35 minutes going, 45 minutes to an hour returning (to pass through Immigration). The last bus returns at 6:45 p.m. weekdays, 9 p.m. weekends.

And, of course, **Gray Line San Diego,** 1670 Kettner Blvd. (tel. 619/231-9922), has a full range of exciting San Diego and Tijuana tours from $22 to $46 for adults, $13 to $29 for children.

If you'd like to do it yourself, stop by the **San Diego Convention and Visitors Bureau's International Visitor Information**

Center, 11 Horton Plaza downtown, at 1st Avenue and F Street (tel. 619/236-1212); they have information about Tijuana attractions. There's also a tourist information center at the border crossing.

If you drive, you might want to consider leaving your car on the U.S. side of the border and taking a bus or taxi the three-quarters of a mile into town; traffic tends to pile up returning to the U.S. *Note:* If you do drive in, be aware that *no U.S. insurance is valid in Mexico.* If you should be involved in an accident across the border, this can be troublesome at best. But you can buy special coverage near the border for a few dollars a day, or from AAA if you're a member. Whatever you do, *don't* drive into Mexico without it.

By the way, U.S. citizens don't need a passport within 72 miles of the border for visits of less than 72 hours (although foreigners should carry theirs) to go to Tijuana, and you can shop with U.S. dollars. However, it's wise to have identification (for instance, a driver's license) with you.

WHAT TO SEE AND DO

Thoroughbred racing is held at Agua Caliente every Saturday and Sunday; **greyhound races** take place Wednesday to Monday nights. **Jai alai** games take place nightly except Thursday at 8 p.m. at the Fronton Palacio (tel. 706/685-2524), Avenida Revolución at Calle 7. Admission is $2.50 to $5. From May to September you can see bullfights on Sunday at 4 p.m. You can visit the **Tijuana Cultural Center,** located less than a mile from the border and across from the Plaza Rio Shopping Center. It was designed to celebrate Mexico's heritage, and contains an Omnimax Space Theater, an anthropological museum, a book store and arts and crafts center, and a performing arts center. Finally, you'll want to do some **shopping** at the duty-free stores along Tijuana's main street, Avenida Revolución.

WHERE TO EAT

The best restaurant choices in Tijuana are **Pedrin's,** 1115 Avenida Revolución at Calle 7 (tel. 706/685-4052), and **La Costa,** at Calle 7A 150 off Avenida Revolución (tel. 706/685-8494). They're owned by the same family and have similar menus; Pedrin's has more style, La Costa lower prices. They're both seafood places, and the food is so good it's worth making the trip just to dine at one of them.

INDEX

GENERAL INFORMATION

SIGHTS AND ATTRACTIONS

Los Angeles Area

Anaheim & Environs

Coastal Towns

Desert & Palm Springs

ACCOMMODATIONS

Los Angeles Area

Anaheim & Environs

KEY TO ABBREVIATIONS: *B* = Budget; *E* = Expensive; *FC* = First Class; *M* = Moderately priced

Coastal Towns

Desert & Palm Springs

NOW, SAVE MONEY ON ALL
YOUR TRAVELS!
Join Frommer's™ Dollarwise® Travel Club

Saving money while traveling is never a simple matter, which is why the **Dollarwise Travel Club** was formed 31 years ago. Developed in response to requests from Frommer's Travel Guide readers, the Club provides cost-cutting travel strategies, up-to-date travel information, and a sense of community for value-conscious travelers from all over the world.

In keeping with the money-saving concept, the annual membership fee is low—$18 for U.S. residents or $20 for residents of Canada, Mexico, and other countries—and is immediately exceeded by the value of your benefits, which include:

1. Any TWO books listed on the following pages.
2. Plus any ONE Frommer's City Guide.
3. A subscription to our quarterly newspaper, *The Dollarwise Traveler*.
4. A membership card that entitles you to purchase through the Club all Frommer's publications for 33% to 50% off their retail price.

The eight-page **Dollarwise Traveler** tells you about the latest developments in good-value travel worldwide and includes the following columns: **Hospitality Exchange** (for those offering and seeking hospitality in cities all over the world); **Share-a-Trip** (for those looking for travel companions to share costs); and **Readers Ask . . . Readers Reply** (for those with travel questions that other members can answer).

Aside from the Frommer's Guides and the Gault Millau Guides, you can also choose from our Special Editions. These include such titles as **California with Kids** (a compendium of the best of California's accommodations, restaurants, and sightseeing attractions appropriate for those traveling with toddlers through teens); **Candy Apple: New York with Kids** (a spirited guide to the Big Apple by a savvy New York grandmother that's perfect for both visitors and residents); **Caribbean Hideaways** (the 100 most romantic places to stay in the Islands, all rated on ambience, food, sports opportunities, and price); **Honeymoon Destinations** (a guide to planning and choosing just the right destination from hundreds of possibilities in the U.S., Mexico, and the Caribbean); **Marilyn Wood's Wonderful Weekends** (a selection of the best mini-vacations within a 200-mile radius of New York City, including descriptions of country inns and other accommodations, restaurants, picnic spots, sights, and activities); and **Paris Rendez-Vous** (a delightful guide to the best places to meet in Paris whether for power breakfasts or dancing till dawn).

To join this Club, simply send the appropriate membership fee with your name and address to: Frommer's Dollarwise Travel Club, 15 Columbus Circle, New York, NY 10023. Remember to specify which single city guide and which two other guides you wish to receive in your initial package of member's benefits. Or tear out the next page, check off your choices, and send the page to us with your membership fee.